Los Cabos &
Baja California Sur

Great Destinations Mexico

FIRST EDITION

Los Cabos &
Baja California Sur

Great Destinations Mexico

Kevin Delgado

The Countryman Press
Woodstock, Vermont

ISBN 978-1-58157-042-7

Cover photo © Kerrick James Photography
Frontispiece photo by Jason MacBeth
Interior photos by the author unless otherwise specified
Book design Bodenweber Design
Page composition by Chelsea Cloeter
Maps by Mapping Specialists, Ltd., Madison, WI, © The Countryman Press

Published by The Countryman Press, P.O. Box 748, Woodstock, VT 05091

Distributed by W. W. Norton & Company, Inc., 500 Fifth Ave., New York, NY 10110

Printed in the United States of America

10 9 8 7 6 5 4 3 2 1

Recommended by *National Geographic Traveler* and *Travel + Leisure* magazines.

[A] CRISP AND CRITICAL APPROACH, FOR TRAVELERS WHO WANT TO LIVE LIKE LOCALS.
— *USA Today*

Great Destinations™ guidebooks are known for their comprehensive, critical coverage of regions of extraordinary cultural interest and natural beauty. The authors in this series are professional travel writers who have lived for many years in the regions they describe. Each title in this series is continuously updated with each printing to ensure accurate and timely information. All the books contain more than one hundred photographs and maps.

Current titles available:

THE ADIRONDACK BOOK

ATLANTA

AUSTIN, SAN ANTONIO & THE TEXAS HILL COUNTRY

THE BERKSHIRE BOOK

BIG SUR, MONTEREY BAY & GOLD COAST WINE COUNTRY

CAPE CANAVERAL, COCOA BEACH & FLORIDA'S SPACE COAST

THE CHARLESTON, SAVANNAH & COASTAL ISLANDS BOOK

THE CHESAPEAKE BAY BOOK

THE COAST OF MAINE BOOK

COLORADO'S CLASSIC MOUNTAIN TOWNS

THE FINGER LAKES BOOK

GALVESTON, SOUTH PADRE ISLAND & THE TEXAS GULF COAST

THE HAMPTONS BOOK

HONOLULU & OAHU: GREAT DESTINATIONS HAWAII

THE HUDSON VALLEY BOOK

LOS CABOS & BAJA CALIFORNIA SUR: GREAT DESTINATIONS MEXICO

THE NANTUCKET BOOK

THE NAPA & SONOMA BOOK

PALM BEACH, MIAMI & THE FLORIDA KEYS

PHOENIX, SCOTTSDALE, SEDONA & CENTRAL ARIZONA

PLAYA DEL CARMEN, TULUM & THE RIVIERA MAYA: GREAT DESTINATIONS MEXICO

SALT LAKE CITY, PARK CITY, PROVO & UTAH'S HIGH COUNTRY RESORTS

SAN DIEGO & TIJUANA

SAN JUAN, VIEQUES & CULEBRA: GREAT DESTINATIONS PUERTO RICO

THE SANTA FE & TAOS BOOK

THE SARASOTA, SANIBEL ISLAND & NAPLES BOOK

THE SEATTLE & VANCOUVER BOOK: INCLUDES THE OLYMPIC PENINSULA, VICTORIA & MORE

THE SHENANDOAH VALLEY BOOK

TOURING EAST COAST WINE COUNTRY

If you are traveling to, moving to, residing in, or just interested in any (or all!) of these enchanting regions, a Great Destinations guidebook is a superior companion. Honest and painstakingly critical, full of information only a local can provide, Great Destinations guidebooks give you all the practical knowledge you need to enjoy the best of each region. Why not own them all?

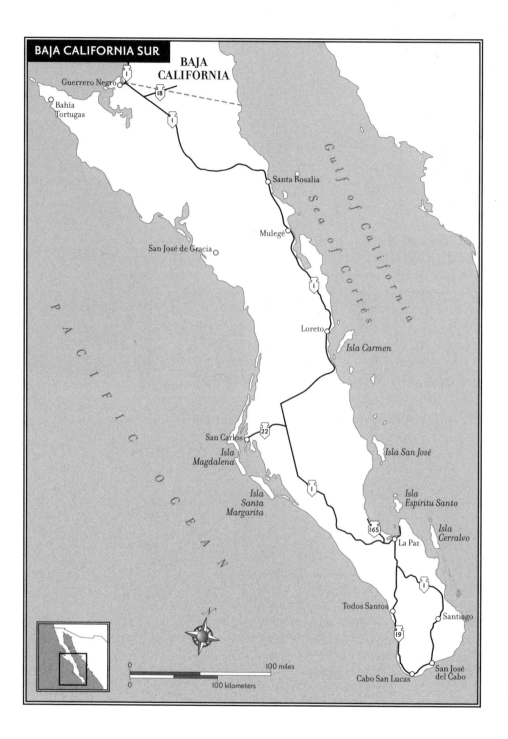

BAJA CALIFORNIA SUR

BAJA CALIFORNIA

Guerrero Negro
Bahía Tortugas
Santa Rosalia
Mulegé
San José de Gracia
Loreto
Isla Carmen
San Carlos
Isla Magdalena
Isla Santa Margarita
Isla San José
Isla Espíritu Santo
Isla Cerralvo
La Paz
Todos Santos
Santiago
Cabo San Lucas
San José del Cabo

Gulf of California
Sea of Cortés
PACIFIC OCEAN

100 miles
100 kilometers

CONTENTS

Acknowledgments

I arrived in San Diego, California, as a 17-year-old country boy who had spent his entire life within a few miles of a small Wyoming town. Despite the fact that I was just one generation removed from my Mexican roots, my provincial life experiences had made that fact all but irrelevant, and at the time, even San Diego seemed an exotic and frightening otherworldly place. When several months later, while waiting tables in a restaurant, a co-worker invited me to go with her and her friends across the border for a night of dancing, I reluctantly agreed to go only because I had been looking for some way to get to know her better. Though trips to Tijuana's Avenida Revolución have long been a rite of passage for underage San Diegans, to me it seemed like utter madness. This was my introduction to Baja California in the early '90s: a bar-lined street, packed with hucksters and rowdy American teenagers. That evening, after several beers and a couple tequila shooters, I was willing to say anything to impress that co-worker of mine. I told her that I had actually been thinking about taking a trip farther down into Baja or maybe even living in Mexico for a while. You can imagine my surprise when her reaction was, "Take me with you!" As it turned out, we lived together in Mexico for a time, thanks to her persistence. And together we fell in love with the whole country, from Oaxaca to Mexico City to La Paz. Even when life took us to New York City, it was hard to forget the allure of Mexico. Writing this now, I realize that it was that co-worker who busted open my provincial shell and showed me the world. Thank you so much, Mary.

I am forever in the debt of the cast of characters whose stories and insights have contributed to this book. Thanks especially to Mike Brady for all the rides to and from the border and the travel and photography advice. Thanks to John Harten, Greg Zsulgit, and the other Yampounding Sherpas for your wisdom and for dragging me along on all those adventures. Thanks to Jason MacBeth and Andrew MacBeth for your generosity and fishing expertise.

I am thankful for the kindness, support, and assistance of the hoteliers, restaurant owners, tour operators, and others whom I visited during my research. Thank you to Betty and Monica as well as to Penny and Todd for keeping an eye on the kids, and to Daniel, Summer, Riley, and Isabel for your patience; to my parents for always giving me a chance; to my brothers and sisters (Mickey, DJ, Lori, Barbie, Davie, Teddy, Brian, Penny, Darren, Ryan, and Sean) for making me who I am; to my old buddy, Brian Schwartzkopf; to Mona Klausing just for being there; and, notably, thank you Simon Lozano and Craig Sodaro for teaching me to write. Without you, I would likely still be a poor excuse for a waiter.

INTRODUCTION

On the surface, the southern region of the Baja Peninsula is almost a world unto itself. The capital city of La Paz has a population of fewer than 200,000 people and is separated from the principal regional city of Tijuana by 946 miles of rocky desert. The Sea of Cortés separates the region from the Mexican mainland with a thousand miles of open water. This state is so isolated that many people from the interior of Mexico wonder what language is spoken here or if they need a passport to visit. In fact, most visitors come from California, so it's quite easy to get by with English.

Early inhabitants of this region were simple nomadic fishermen who lived in harmony with their natural surroundings. During the colonial period, the conquistador Hernán Cortés sent five expeditions to the region in search of a passage that would link the Atlantic and Pacific Oceans. On the fifth expedition, Cortés established the settlement of Santa Cruz at the present day site of La Paz. However, the Spaniards found living conditions difficult in this arid region, and the native inhabitants refused to submit to their rule. The colony of Santa Cruz was abandoned after only two years.

The area remained largely forgotten for more than a century. Then in 1695 Jesuit missionaries established the Misión Nuestra Senora de Loreto. From here, the Jesuits began establishing missions from Cabo San Lucas north to present-day San Diego, San Luis Obispo, and San Francisco. Also, as Spain established trade routes between the Philippines and Acapulco, sailors began to dock in the calm waters of the Sea of Cortés. The Spanish influence continued to grow on the peninsula and by the 19th century, most of the present-day communities had been established. In 1888 the Mexican government divided the territory of Baja California into northern and southern parts. While Loreto and La Paz had once been the administrative and economic centers of the region, the pull of the United States began to draw people northward. Today the northern region of the peninsula has a population of almost 3 million people while the southern region is home to fewer than 500,000.

Though it recently fast become famous as one of Mexico's best tourist destinations, the region remained in obscurity until the 1970s. In fact, before the country's 1,060-mile-long Federal Highway 1, or Carretera Transpeninsular (Transpeninsular Highway), opened in 1973, Baja California Sur (southern Baja California) was one of the least traveled regions in the world. Even after the highway opened, development came slowly. The two-lane road had no shoulders and rapidly became rutted and washed out by winter rains. Serious development did not begin until the 1990s, and even then it was uneven, concentrating mainly in the area of Los Cabos and some spots on the gulf side. As a result, travelers can still find long stretches of secluded beaches relatively close to areas rife with amenities. Furthermore, southern Baja's rich environment offers a wide variety of unique experiences such as whale watching in the Sea of Cortés, horseback riding in the Guerrero Negro Desert, and swimming in a resort hotel pool.

The area around Los Cabos at the tip of the Baja Peninsula is certainly the region's most famous tourist destination. The twin towns of Cabo San Lucas and San José del Cabo are an adult playground famous for golf, deep-sea fishing, and health spas. The towns have very different personalities, showcasing the magnificence of the area in divergent ways. Cabo San Lucas offers an upper-class resort atmosphere and lively nightlife while San José del

Cabo is a more traditional Mexican town lined with modern beach resorts and elegant shops.

Take an easy 135-mile drive up the gulf coast and you will find La Paz, a tranquil city famous for sport fishing and scuba diving. It is the second-largest city on the Baja Peninsula but retains the feel of a small colonial Mexican town. A number of beautiful gulf islands are located nearby in calm, blue waters.

Farther north you will discover Loreto, one of Baja's best-kept secrets. Like towns to the south, Loreto has plenty of beaches, natural beauty, and opportunities for adventure such as sea kayaking, hiking, and sport fishing. Matched with its rich history and the fact that it is not surging with tourists, Loreto is an extraordinary destination.

Take an hour's drive into the inland desert, and you will come to the town of Mulegé, literally an oasis in the desert. The Río Mulegé, which flows through town, is the only freshwater river on the peninsula. Nearby in the high, red mountains, Baja's long history is demonstrated by ancient petroglyphs on the walls of canyons. The origins of these paintings trace back to before Baja's first-known inhabitants.

Southern Baja exists as a natural masterpiece. Enjoy all it has to offer, and it will beckon you back again.

Practical Information

Customs and Immigration

Technically speaking, customs and immigration can be a real pain. For those departing from border states, you can mitigate some of this inconvenience by either driving in or crossing the border and flying out of Tijuana or some other Mexican airport. Crossing the U.S.-Mexico border on foot or by car is much less of a hassle than making your way through airport security because of lighter luggage checks although the wait at the border can be much longer. Furthermore, airport entry requirements may be different than border entry requirements.

Recently, reentry requirements for U.S. travelers to Mexico have been a complete mess. On January 23. 2007 new rules took effect requiring U.S. citizens to show a passport when reentering the United States from Mexico, Canada, and the Caribbean by air. This caused such a large backlog on passport applications that on June 8, the rules were amended until at least September 2007 to allow American travelers to Mexico to reenter the U.S. by simply showing that they had applied for a passport. As early as Summer 2008, passports will be required for reentering the U.S. by land and sea, though that deadline too may be pushed back.

Despite the confusion, what is certain is that you need to find out what the rules will be at your time of travel and work towards getting a passport as soon as possible. Many travelers have already had delay their travel plans or scrap them altogether because of passport delays. The State Department has a website where you can check the status of your passport application (https://passportstatus.state.gov/opss/OPSS_Status_i.asp) but the information provided here is optimistic at best and getting through with a direct call can be nearly impossible. The bottom line is that it is best to get a passport before you need it. Getting one via a rush application can be expensive. Also, be sure to make a copy of your birth certificate before you mail it away with your passport application. Therefore, if your passport doesn't show up because of the backlog (which is predicted to be major), you will still be able to enter Mexico. Furthermore, if land-entry rules still haven't changed, you can fly to Tijuana and cross by land then complete your journey home from San Diego. This is hardly ideal, but it's better than canceling your trip altogether.

To enter Mexico, you currently need a photo ID and a birth certificate in order to obtain a tourist card. This is an official Mexican document declaring that you have stated that the purpose of your visit to Mexico is tourism and that your visit will last no more than 180 days. This document costs $20 and anyone staying in Mexico for more than 72 hours and traveling beyond the border zone (about 70 miles south) needs to have a tourist card. If you are driving into Mexico, you can get this document at the immigration station just across the border. If you are flying out of a Mexican airport, such as Tijuana, you will get this document as you pass into the boarding area of the airport. And if you are flying into Mexico from another country, the cost of this document is included in the price of your air fair and you will receive

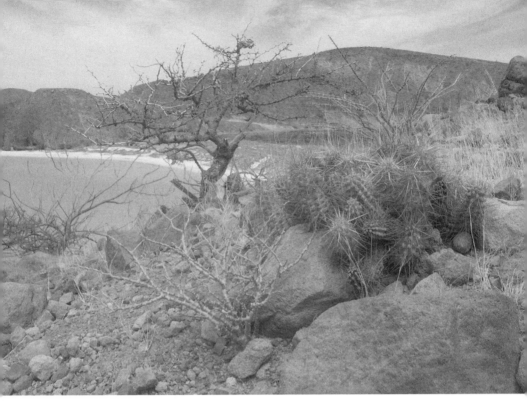

Baja California is a unique blend of desert landscapes and beautiful beaches.

it, along with instructions on filling it out, while on the plane. Once you disembark, customs and immigration will stamp it, indicating that you are in the country legally.

DRIVING IN BAJA

Just a few decades ago, a description of driving to the southern regions of the Baja Peninsula would include rugged 4WD vehicles rumbling down rutted dirt roads and passing through dusty towns offering few accommodations or provisions to arrive at deserted stretches of white sand with no tourists for miles. That Baja certainly had its allure, but it is fading into history, greatly due to the paved and relatively well-kept Mexico 1 that has made the southern regions of the Baja Peninsula accessible to minivans, SUVs, and hatchback sedans alike.

While Baja offers a variety of options for getting around, the spread-out nature of the region does not lend itself to public transportation. And though walking can be a great way to experience the cities such as Cabo San Lucas, La Paz, and Loreto, so much of what makes these places worth visiting is located outside the confines of the city that it really does make sense to have your own transportation. Rental cars are readily available at all of these locations (see the specific destinations for details), and for a little bit extra, you can even pick up the car in one city and drop it off in another. Furthermore, the beautiful destinations of southern Baja are located close enough to the United States that driving to them is a definite option for many travelers.

Driving in larger Mexican cities can be an intimidating undertaking, with other drivers prying their way into the smallest opening in traffic and putting the onus on you to avoid a collision—as well as treating stop signs and traffic lights as mere suggestions instead of requirements. With regard to driving in Baja California, these circumstances cease as soon as you get past Tijuana and get onto the open highway. Along Mexico 1, the greatest danger is quite the opposite of intimidating traffic: complacency. The Carretera Transpeninsular runs along the graceful Pacific Ocean and skirts the calm waters of the Sea of Cortés. The dazzling, enchanting vistas are sure to make you forget your troubles—and also make it easy to forget that, despite its beautiful views and relative convenience, this road is also fraught with hazards. One of the most common is the livestock that commonly wander onto the road. This is generally not a problem if you are minding your speed. However, you do *not* want to come careening through a mountain pass to find a herd of cattle sitting on the road ahead of you. Another problem is the lack of guardrails on the road, even where it winds along steep cliffs. As you drive through areas such as these, it will become abundantly clear that the road was not engineered with the kind of safety standards that are common north of the border. Add to this the frequent potholes and steep or even nonexistant shoulder, and you quickly come to a bit of advice that should be self-evident: Drive slowly!

There may be times when you will have the urge to throw this bit of advice out the window—say, you have found yourself trailing a slow-moving vehicle for miles before you have the opportunity to pass, and you feel the need to make up some lost time. Resist this temptation. I have seen some pretty horrible accidents involving tourists along the treacherous stretch of mountain highway just south of Loreto and north of La Paz.

Another piece of advice: Do not drive at night. The dangers presented by narrow roads, wandering animals, and unprotected cliffs are exacerbated at night. This especially true of animals, which congregate at the edge of the roadway where the grass grows greenest. One Baja traveler told me that he has successfully navigated Mexico 1 at night by sidling up behind trucks as a way of protection against loitering livestock. However, that seems like a lot of trust to put in the hands of the trucker in front of you. The best advice is to find a place to get some rest, and get going again in the morning when it's safe.

Interestingly, Baja drivers have developed signals to communicate safety to one another. For example, an extended forefinger and pinky (similar to the "Hook 'em Horns" sign common at University of Texas football games) means that there are cattle on the road ahead. Another signal of danger ahead is flashing headlights. If you get this warning sign, slow down and proceed with caution. Except for a few brief stretches, Mexico 1 is a narrow two-lane highway that requires you to drive into the oncoming lane to pass slower-moving vehicles. Yet another indicator is a left-turn signal from a slower-moving vehicle in front of you, which indicates that it's safe to pass. Often the vehicle will move to the right slightly to make their intention even clearer. Be careful not to mistake this signal with a regular left-turn signal, which would generally be accompanied by brake lights. Also, keep in mind that regardless of what the driver in the vehicle ahead of you is signaling, what happens during the process of passing them is ultimately your responsibility. Do not pass along stretches with unbroken center lines (despite what you see locals doing), and make sure you have a good view of the road ahead as you proceed.

Speed limits are posted in kilometers. This can be a bit confusing if your speedometer does not include kilometers. However, since 60 miles per hour is roughly equal to 100 kilometers per hour, multiplying the posted speed limit by 6 and dropping the last decimal will give you a rough estimation of the allowed speed in miles per hour.

Tijuana has earned a reputation for being a place where tourists are singled out for traffic offenses, though the problem is not nearly as bad as it used to be. Cabo San Lucas is another place where tourists run the risk of being singled out if they drive expensive-looking rentals and act rowdy. It is true that in the past, some Mexican law enforcement officers supplemented their low incomes through *mordidas,* or bribes, though this happens less and less as Mexico has enforced anticorruption laws. The chances of this happening to you are slim, particularly if you drive safely and obey the traffic laws. After all, Baja California's economy depends on tourism, and it would not be in their interest to shake down every foreigner who passed through. If it does happen to you, you can either pay the officer and move on with your day, or accept the ticket. If you are ticketed, you have the right to ask to pay the ticket by mail. The most common practice, though, is to have you follow the officer to the nearest police station, where you will pay the fine. There have been incidents where tourists have refused to go, and the officer has removed the license plates from the vehicle, obliging that person to go to the station, anyway, to pay the fine to get the plates back. Bottom line: Drive safely, and don't set yourself apart.

In Case of Arrest
If you do get into trouble and are arrested, contact your nearest consulate immediately. Also, the State Tourist Assistance Office located in La Paz (612-122-5939) will assist you with legal help or if you wish to register a complaint during normal business hours.

Insurance
Under Mexican law, motorists are required to have sufficient currency to cover damages or insurance from a Mexican company in the event of an accident. Non-Mexican insurance does not fulfill this responsibility. If you are involved in an automobile accident, you are basically considered guilty until proven innocent. You will be detained until the local authorities determine who is at fault, and you will be required to demonstrate "financial responsibility," which is defined as being in possession of an inexpensive Mexican insurance policy or $5,000 and $10,000 in cash. Therefore, it is not a good idea to drive in Mexico without Mexican liability insurance. If you are renting a car, you will pay for this insurance through the rental company. However, if you are driving your own vehicle into Mexico, you'll need to purchase insurance on your own. This insurance is relatively inexpensive, and it comes with peace of mind. Plenty of companies offer this insurance at all major U.S.–Mexico border crossings and on the Internet. Here are a few just in case:

Adventure Mexican Insurance
1-800-485-4075 (U.S.)
www.mexadventure.com
P.O. Box 1469, Soquel, CA 95073

Baja Bound Insurance Services
888-552-2252
www.bajabound.com

Instant Mexico Auto Insurance
1-800-345-4701; fax 610-690-6533
www.instant-mex-auto-insur.com
223 Via de San Ysidro, San Ysidro, CA 92173

Military Stops

If you travel by road in Mexico, you will soon encounter a military checkpoint. Along Baja California Sur, the main checkpoint is located northbound on the Transpeninsular Highway several miles north of Loreto.

For the average American who is not used to such things, this can be a jarring experience. After all, you just came down here to have a good time, right? Just keep in mind that everybody goes through this, and it isn't really a big deal. Despite what you may have heard about corrupt cops shaking down every tourist who comes along for payola, as long as you've done nothing wrong, you have nothing to worry about.

These stops are actually largely the result of Mexico attempting to satisfy their allies from north of the border that they are doing everything in their power to stop the flow of drugs northward. Keep in mind that these young soldiers are just doing their job. Many of them come from the poorer parts of Mexico, and they are occasionally even illiterate—meaning that your political opinions about unwarranted searches could hardly have less significance to them. Therefore, it's best just to cooperate so you can be on your way.

Generally, you will be stopped for only a few minutes. The soldiers will likely ask to see your identification and to look in your trunk. It is always a nice gesture to offer them a cold soda on a hot day. Assuming that you are not carrying any drugs, guns, or other illegal paraphernalia, you will soon be on your way.

CAUTION: Guns are illegal in Mexico. There have been cases of Americans unwittingly crossing the border into Mexico while in possession of firearms that are perfectly legal in the United States only to find themselves locked up for months or even years in a Mexican prison. *Do not take firearms into Mexico with you under any circumstances.*

Stopping for Gas

Petroleos Mexicanos—or PEMEX—is Mexico's state-owned nationalized petroleum company. Its midgrade gasoline, Magna Sin, is rated at 87 octane and should be fine for cars that run on unleaded regular in the United States. Mexican Premium is rated at 92 octane.

Though PEMEX stations are not as abundant as gas stations north of the border, you will find them in all major stops on your itinerary. They are generally open 24 hours a day, and they do not take credit cards; pesos or dollars only here. The upside to this is that PEMEX stations make a great place to break large bills since the attendants carry a lot of cash. Speaking of the attendants, they will pump your gas and clean your windshield if you need it. It is customary to tip them about 10 pesos, or $1USD.

MONEY AND MONEY EXCHANGE

American dollars are widely accepted and in some places even preferred in Mexico. However, your money will go further if you use pesos. For both convenience and the fact that you don't have much choice, prices are usually rounded off to equal 10 pesos to the dollar. This means that since the official exchange rate is currently fluctuating at more than 10.9 pesos for every dollar, you will generally be overpaying about 9 cents for every dollar you spend.

Mexican currency notes come in denominations of 20, 50, 100, 200, 500, and 1,000. Breaking larger bills is a persistant problem in Mexico, particularly at smaller independent establishments. I once had to wait half an hour after finishing a meal while the restaurant owner ran around to nearby shops trying to make change for a 500-peso note. The best strategy to avoid such a situation is to pay with larger bills when spending money at larger

Road Signs

The first time you come upon some road signs in Mexico, it can be confusing and even disconcerting if you think you're missing something that you should be aware of. If you don't speak Spanish, you should try to acquaint yourself with these signs as much as possible before driving since many of them have to do with safety.

Accesso a Playa	Beach Access
Alto	Stop
Ceda El Paso	Yield
Circulación	Direction of Traffic
Concida Cambio de Luces	Dim Your Lights
Conserve Su Derecha	Keep to the Right
Curva Peligrosa	Dangerous Curve
Despacio	Slow Down
Desviación	Detour
Doble Circulación	Two-Way Street
Inspección	Military Inspection Ahead
Maxima	Speed Limit (posted in kilometers per hour)
No Hay Paso	Road Closed
No Rebase	No Passing
No Tire Basura	No Littering
Peligro	Danger
Pendiente Peligrosa	Dangerous Downgrade
Precaución	Caution
Solo Izq.	Left Turn Only
Vado	Dip
Zona de Derrumbes	Falling Rock Zone

businesses and save your smaller bills and *monedas* (coins) for small establishments and street vendors.

The quickest and easiest way to get Mexican currency is simply to go to a Mexican ATM and withdraw pesos. These machines generally offer cash at the wholesale bank rate instead of the less-favorable tourist rate, making ATMs not only convenient but also offering the best value. Once you withdraw currency in Mexican denominations, your bank will convert it back to the dollar amount and charge you that way. Additional transaction fees do apply. ATMs are usually accessible 24 hours a day. As in many banks north of the border, ATMs are located in an entrance area between the outer and inner doors to the bank. After normal business hours—as is the case in the U.S.—insert your card into the slot next to the outer door, and you will be buzzed inside to do your withdrawal.

It's probably not such a good idea to rely solely on ATMs as your source for money. In towns such as Loreto and Todos Santos where ATMs are rare (or in Mulegé, where there is no ATM at all), have a little extra cash on you in case of an emergency. Banks or *casas de cambio* (exchange houses) offer respectable exchange rates. Hotels offer the worst exchange rates. It's always a good idea to exchange at least $50 or $75 into pesos before leaving the U.S. so that you'll arrive in Mexico with pesos for your cab ride or a meal. If you are driving to Baja California Sur, some of the best exchange rates you will find are located near the

Mexican money

border such as along San Ysidro Boulevard east of the 5 and 805 Freeways. A high concentration of *casas de cambio* means there is competition to offer favorable exchange rates. Traveler's checks are another good option. Although it can be time consuming to convert them into cash, banks don't charge extra fees for cashing traveler's checks. The rate of exchange will generally be less favorable than for cash, however.

Credit cards are widely accepted in Los Cabos and La Paz. However, outside of those areas, an acceptance of credit cards is less common. The benefit of using a credit card is that you will receive the more favorable wholesale rate. The drawback is that if you're spending money in a place that accepts credit cards, chances are that it's an establishment that is geared toward serving tourists—and thus you get less bang for your buck than at places that cater to locals.

MAKING HOTEL RESERVATIONS

Making reservations at hotels in Baja can be a tricky experience. Larger resorts accept hotel reservations over the Internet with the use of a credit card, but many smaller hotels—particularly ones owned by American expatriates—require a process that's a little less organized. Most will accept the initial hotel reservation via their Web site or by e-mail. However, to confirm the reservation, many require that you send a deposit check to a specified address, often inside the United States. In areas where the tourism industry is less developed, such as Loreto and Mulegé, many hotels require payment by cash only. You may find this to be an inconvenience. Still, the unique ambiance offered at these smaller, independent hotels makes the extra effort well worth it.

Note that when calling to make reservations, the direct-dial prefix for Mexico from the United States is 011-52.

CALLING HOME

It isn't a good idea to dial direct long-distance or international calls from your hotel room. Hotels often add their own surcharges, even to local calls. This also applies to bringing and using your cell phones while in Mexico. It may seem extremely convenient to take your phone out of your pocket and dial away, but you'll likely wish you hadn't at the end of the month when you get a phone bill packed with hefty international roaming charges. Even receiving calls on your cell can result in exessive charges.

Public phones in the larger towns are provided by a company called Ladatel, which offers long-distance calls with a *tarjeta de teléfono* (phone card) issued through TelMex, the national phone company of Mexico. You can buy prepaid Ladatel phone cards in pharmacies, convenience stores, and supermarkets. Another option is to obtain a calling card though your own phone company back home.

INTERNET ACCESS

If you are bringing a laptop computer, many hotels offer wireless Internet access as part of their amenities. However, there is always added risk to traveling with a laptop. Several cybercafes throughout Baja California Sur offer travelers access to the Internet for a nominal fee. If you do use these machines, it's always a good idea to click on "Internet Options" and clear the cache before logging off. You don't want any of your personal information sitting on the computer after you have left. However, your best bet is to log into personal accounts sparingly on public computers since unscrupulous hackers have been known to bug computers in cybercafes and even hotels with software designed to gain access to personal information—especially banking and e-trade accounts.

ELECTRICITY

Mexico's electrical system is the same as in the United States and Canada: 110 volts AC. The outlets are compatible with any electrical appliance, recharger, or extension cords you may bring. However, the outlets in older or smaller hotels may not have polarized plugs (in which one prong is slightly larger than the other). Pick up an adapter at any hardware or discount store.

LANGUAGE

Spanish is the primary language spoken in Baja California. But tourism being what it is here, you will get along quite well speaking English in areas where there are lots of

Cybercafés

CABO SAN LUCAS
DR. Z'A INTERNET CAFÉ AND BAR
624-143-5390
Lázaro Cárdenas
Open daily 9 AM to 8 PM

CAFÉ ON-LINE
624-143-7283
Cabo San Lucas Avenue, one block from
Plaza Las Glorias
Open Monday–Saturday 9 AM to 8 PM;
closed Sunday

SAN JOSÉ DEL CABO
CLUB INTERNET
Avendia Zaragoza in front of the medical clinic
Open daily 9 AM to 10 PM

TODOS SANTOS
PANCHO BANANO
612-145-0885
Hidalgo #11 e/ Benito Juárez and Colegio Militar
Colonia Centro
Open daily 7 AM to 9 PM

LA PAZ
BAJA NET
612-125-9380
Madero 430
Open Monday through Saturday 8 AM to 9 PM

travelers. Particularly in Los Cabos, it is quite common for gringos to drop in for a week and go home without ever having spoken a word of Spanish. You will find that waiters, taxi drivers, tour guides, rental-agency clerks, and anyone else who deals with tourists for a living is quite adept at speaking English.

As you move away from tourist areas, you should not expect to get by on English alone. It is worth your while to make an attempt to learn at least the most basic Spanish phrases. Not only will this help you communicate better, it will also go a long way toward ingratiating you with your Mexican hosts. And that's never a bad thing.

FOOD AND WATER

Getting used to the food in Baja can sometimes take a period of adjustment, particularly if you are accustomed to the spices. A little common sense will go a long way toward making sure you don't get sick while you're enjoying yourself with sun and fun. Spend the first few days of your trip taking it easy. Many people go on vacation, suddenly find themselves free of the workaday hours and the social mores of home—and sometimes tend to cut loose and overdo it. Resist this urge—at least for a little bit. Give yourself time to adjust to jet lag, new cuisine, and the other strains traveling to a new place puts on your body.

Many larger resorts have purified water systems, and smaller hotels generally offer complimentary bottled water. Try to carry bottled water wherever you go so that you have it on hand to keep yourself hydrated. Be sure to brush your teeth with bottled water if you're staying at a hotel without a purified system. Restaurants serve ice made of purified water, so it's fine to have ice in your Coke. You may see street vendors selling flavored *aguas frescas* (fresh waters) with flavors such as *sandía* (watermelon), *limón* (lemonade), *melón* (can-

Helpful Phrases

When it comes to conversation, Mexicans tend to appreciate formalities more than their neighbors to the north. When approaching someone for information, don't forget to greet them with the time-appropriate salutation (*buenos días, buenas tardes, buenas noches*), even if it's the only Spanish you can think of at the moment. Try not to say simply "*Hola,*" which comes across as abrupt.

Good morning. – *Buenos días.*	Key – *Llave*
Good afternoon. – *Buenas tardes.*	Order – *Orden*
Good evening (after 8 PM). – *Buenas noches.*	Fork – *Tenedor*
Goodbye. – *Adios.*	Spoon – *Cuchara*
Please. – *Por favor.*	Knife – *Cuchillo*
Thank you very much. – *Muchas gracias.*	Napkin – *Servilleta*
You're welcome. – *De nada.*	Food – *Comida*
Do you speak English? – *¿Habla usted ingles?*	Coffee – *Café*
I don't understand. – *No intiendo.*	Tea – *Té*
How do you say . . . in Spanish? –	Beer – *Cerveza*
¿Como se llama . . . en español?	Wine – *Vino*
My name is . . . – *Me llamo . . .*	Milk – *Leche*
Where is . . . ? – *¿Dónde está . . . ?*	Juice – *Jugo*
To the right. – *A la derecha*	Money – *Dinero*
To the left. – *A la izquierda.*	Expensive – *Caro*
Straight ahead. – *Derecho.*	Cheap – *Barato*
What is the rate? – *¿A cuanto es?*	Post office – *Correo*
Shower – *Ducha*	Driver's license – *Licencia de manejar*
Towels – *Toallas*	Gas station – *Gasolinera*
Soap – *Jabón*	Border – *Frontera*
Toilet paper – *Papel higiénico*	Passport – *Pasaporte*

taloupe), and *fresa* (strawberry). These are delicious and can be quite refreshing—but there is no guarantee that they are made with purified water. It's a good idea to ask just to be sure, though the answer is likely to be yes either way. The bottom line is that by consuming these refreshments, you are taking a calculated risk, and you need to be aware of that.

In fact, any time you consume peeled, raw fruits and vegetables, or eat from a small "locals" restaurant or street vendor, you are taking a risk of getting sick. You can help to prepare your body for these risks by eating plenty of yogurt for several weeks prior to your trip. Scientific studies have shown that the live active cultures in yogurt have properties that protect the intestinal tract from gastrointestinal infection.

WHAT TO BRING

Obviously, if you are traveling to Baja California, you are going to want to bring a camera, a bathing suit, and some flip-flops. However, just because it's Mexico doesn't mean that you can buy certain items cheaper than you would in the United States. For example, if you plan on going snorkeling, it's a good idea to pick up a mask and snorkel before leaving for Mex-

It's customary to tip your tour guides.

ico because you'll often find a much larger selection—and better prices—at your local sporting goods store or on the Internet than at the beach, where they know they can charge you exorbitant prices because you need the equipment.

Another item that you'll need if you plan on leaving the tourist zone for any length of time is a roll of toilet paper. Some off-the-beaten-path restrooms will charge you a few pesos and give you a couple of squares, but some places there just *isn't* any. Better to come prepared than find yourself in a situation where you have to improvise. Additionally, you'll want to have a tube or bottle of disinfectant hand lotion or disinfectant wipes to freshen up with. This comes in handy in a variety of situations.

One saying seems to have gotten truer in recent years: There are two types of luggage; carry-on luggage and lost luggage. We all know people who have taken trips and ended up spending days waiting for their luggage to arrive at their destination. It's best to pack light and carry all of your belongings aboard with you as you make your way south. But this is not always a possibility. A good trick is to make arrangements with your hotel and ship your belongings ahead. This costs extra, of course, but the peace of mind that it buys is really priceless.

TIPPING

Being a former waiter, I am all too familiar with the frustration of foreign tourists skipping out without tipping just because they aren't familiar with the local customs. That's just a bad excuse to be cheap. Many large all-inclusive resorts uphold a no-tipping policy; in such cases where an exception has expressly been made, it's OK not to tip. Otherwise, be polite, and plan on tipping service personnel the customary amount.

Bellboys should be tipped based on the pieces of luggage they carry to your room. Restaurant servers are customarily tipped around 15 percent of the total bill; however, if you're dining with a large group, a service charge may be automatically added to the bill. The tipping of chambermaids is optional though highly appreciated. You should tip the gas station attendant about $0.50USD and/or let them keep the change when it equals less than a peso.

If you take a tour, it's standard to tip the guide about 10 percent the cost of the trip. This is particularly important if you have a guide who goes out of his way to make sure that you are well informed and have a good time. Taxi drivers are generally not tipped in Mexico, except if they give special service or provide you with good advice. Even then, it is at your discretion since many taxi drivers will bend over backward to give you advice even if you're not looking for it.

HEADING TO THE BEACH

Baja has some of the most pristine and undeveloped beaches you will find anywhere. The drawback to this is that you will not have the security of a lifeguard. Even at hotel pools and crowded beaches like Medano Beach in Cabo San Lucas, there are no lifeguards to pull you out of the water if you get into trouble. This should be of particular concern to anyone traveling with children. Even the calm water of Nopoló Beach presents a dangerous environment for unattended kids. The crashing oceanic waters on the Pacific side of the peninsula are far more hazardous, though even the seaside beaches in San José del Cabo can have dangerous breakers and riptides. If you are unfortunate enough to get caught in an undertow (a strong current under the surface of the water that can pull you away from the beach), swim parallel to the beach until you get out of it instead of swimming against it directly toward the beach.

Another amenity that is lacking from Baja beaches is easy access to convenience stores. Be sure to pack plenty of water and sunblock before you set out for the beach. You can also save yourself a few dollars by buying sunblock before your arrival in Baja. It's an absolute necessity and one that's generally sold at inflated prices in hotel gift shops.

BEACH ETIQUETTE

All the beaches in Baja California—in fact, all the beaches throughout Mexico—are federal property. Therefore, no hotel or homeowner can restrict access to a beach from the water or make their own guidelines as to what you can do on the beach. However, hotels can restrict you from crossing their property to get to the beach, and they often set up private areas with palapas and tables for their guests. That being said, many people have no problem waltzing through the lobby of a beachfront resort as if they were a guest to get to a choice spot on the beach. Whether you choose to do so is entirely dependent on what you feel comfortable with.

Another aspect of Baja beaches is the amount of clothing that you're required to wear (or not wear) when playing along this beautiful coast. Mexico as a whole is a pretty conservative and traditional place, and decency laws prohibit going nude or even topless in public. Still, there are a few places in Baja where going topless is readily acceptable, such as the beach in front of the Whales Inn near Loreto. Also, keep in mind that Baja California Sur is a relatively empty place with miles and miles of vacant beaches, offshore islands, and hidden desert arroyos. While it's not recommended that you violate decency laws, there is nothing

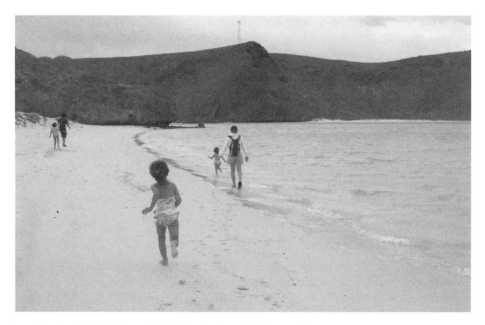

Traveling with kids in Baja can be both challenging and quite rewarding.

to stop you from going around in the buff if you suddenly find yourself on a deserted beach with no one around for miles. Just be sure to keep your clothes within a reasonable distance in case someone should wander by.

If you do find yourself on a deserted beach, resist the temptation to drive your vehicle along the shoreline. It is illegal to drive on beaches in Mexico, and doing so can result in stiff fines.

TRAVELING WITH KIDS

Baja California is an ideal setting to take a break from the kids. On the other hand, you will probably find yourself constantly thinking it would have been great to bring the kids. This is especially true at beaches such as Balandra in La Paz or Nopoló in Loreto, where the water is calm, shallow, and crystal clear, and the fish scurry at your feet. If you do decide to take the kids along, there are extra hoops you will have to jump though. First, new passport requirements for U.S. citizens returning from abroad also apply to children. Getting a passport for a child under the age of 14 requires filling out additional documents as well as having both parents' consent. That said, it is no longer necessary for single parents or unaccompanied minors traveling in Mexico to have notorized documentation authorizing travel as long as each child has a valid passport and tourist card. Once that's taken care of, just remember to apply plenty of sunscreen.

BAJA CALIFORNIA FOR GAYS AND LESBIANS

Generally speaking, Mexico is a fairly conservative and widely Catholic country. Particularly among the smaller towns in the lower Baja Peninsula, much of the population is traditional and provincial in their views. Still, while southern Baja in general—and Los Cabos in particular—has not developed the reputation for being an attractive destination for gay travelers that, say, Puerto Vallarta has, this region has plenty to offer gay and lesbian vacationers. There are many wonderful gay-friendly and even gay-owned businesses throughout Baja California Sur as well as tour groups that offer custom gay-friendly cruises, kayak adventures, and other excursions. The Rainbow Bar (624-143-1455) on Boulevard Marina in Cabo San Lucas is the only true gay bar in town, though most Los Cabos establishments are friendly and tolerant to all of their guests. Among the gay- and lesbian-friendly accommodations that exist here are:

CABO SAN LUCAS
THE BUNGALOWS BREAKFAST INN
624-143-5035 or 1-888-424-CABO (U.S.)
www.cabobungalows.com
Boulevard Miguel Angel Herrera

TODOS SANTOS
TODOS SANTOS INN
612-145-0040
www.todossantosinn.com
Calle Legaspi #33

LA PAZ
HOTEL MEDITERRANE
612-125-1195
www.hotelmed.com
Allende 36

LA CASA MEXICANA INN
612-125-2748
www.casamex.com
Calle Bravo 106

LORETO
BAJA OUTPOST
613-1351134 or 1-888-649-5951 (U.S.)
www.bajaoutpost.com
Boulevard Adolfo Lopez Mateos

SUKASA BUNGALOWS
613-135-0490
www.loreto.com/sukasa
Boulevard Lopez Mateo y Calle Fernando Jordan

TRAVELING WITH PETS

Bringing pets to Baja California is a common practice for those driving across the border. If you are flying in, airlines have their own rules about this, so you should check ahead. Mexico allows dogs and cats into the country as long as the owner has a notorized letter from a veterinarian stating that the animal is in good health and has the proper vaccinations. However, if you're driving, it's unlikely that this will be an issue.

Keep in mind, though, that there are certain risks to be considered before bringing an animal down to Baja. Very few hotels allow pets, and those that do generally charge extra. (Be sure to check ahead when making reservations.) Hot weather can also become an issue with some animals. However, the biggest danger with regard to pets is that Mexican towns—from giant Mexico City to the tiny town of Loreto—have a problem with stray animals. There is always the outside chance that these animals carry diseases or that your animal will eat one of the poison-laced treats that are occasionally left out to thin the numbers of stray dogs. Unless you are prepared to constantly look after your pets, it might be a better idea just to leave them at home.

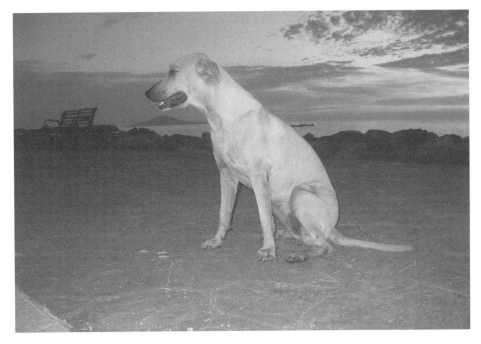

Stray dogs are a problem throughout Mexico—just one good reason to leave yours at home.

GETTING MARRIED IN MEXICO

As "destination weddings" have become a more common practice, Baja California has become an increasingly popular destination to hold such an affair. Not only is Baja relatively close and stunningly beautiful, but it also makes for a great honeymoon. And if you're going to ask your guests to do some traveling anyway, why not bring them to a place that resembles paradise?

As with any wedding—outside of Las Vegas!—getting married in Mexico requires planning, coordination, and the completion of documents. One solution to make the process easier is to complete the legal paperwork in the United States and simply perform the ceremony in Mexico. However, if you want your ceremony to be more than symbolic, you'll need to fulfill several requirements at the location in Mexico where you'll be married.

Keep in mind that religious weddings are not officially recognized in Mexico and thus do not change your legal marriage status. Therefore, to have your wedding legally recognized in Mexico and back home, you'll need a civil ceremony performed by a Spanish-speaking judge who resides in the city where you're getting married. You can also arrange to have this ceremony performed at an outside site for an additional fee. In Los Cabos, the civil ceremony can be performed in the judge's chambers any weekday except for Tuesday at noon or 1 PM.

In addition to the judge, you'll need at least two witnesses who are 18 or older and fulfill several other legal requirements that you'll have to get out of the way for your marriage to be legally binding. Completing these requirements will necessitate arriving in Mexico several days before the ceremony. You'll need certified copies of your birth certificates as well as passports and copies of your tourist cards. If you have been married previously, you'll need papers indicating that you have been legally divorced for at least a year. There is also med-

MEXICAN HOLIDAYS

January 1: New Year's Day*

January 6: Three Kings Day

February 2: *Día de la Candelaria* (commemorates Baby Jesus being presented at Jerusalem temple)

February 5: Constitution Day *

February 24: Flag Day

Sunday before Ash Wednesday: Carnival

March 19: Saint Joseph's Day

March 21: Benito Juarez's Birthday*

Palm Sunday to Easter: Holy Week

April 30: *Día de los Niños* (Children's Day)

May 1: Labor Day*

May 3: Holy Cross Day

May 5: Battle of Puebla

May 10: Mother's Day

June 24: Saint John the Baptist Day

June 29: Saint Peter and Saint Paul's Day

September 1: President's State of the Union Address

September 16: Independence Day*

October 12: *Dia de Raza* (Discovery of America)

October 14: Saint Francis Day

November 1, 2: *Dia de Todos Santos* and *Dia de Muertes* (All Saints and All Souls Day)

November 20: Revolution Day (Revolution of 1910)*

December 8: Immaculate Conception

December 12: Virgin of Guadelupe Day

December 24: Christmas Eve

December 25: Christmas*

December 31: New Year's Eve

Legal Holiday– banks and government offices closed

ical lab work that needs to be performed in Baja California Sur.

With all of these ancillary details, it's probably a really good idea to hire a wedding coordinator to help you out, especially if you don't speak Spanish. Several wedding planners work out of Los Cabos, and many of the hotels in San José and the Tourist Corridor offer their own wedding planners. Check the hotel Web sites for more details.

The following are some wedding planners that you might want to check out:

Baja Weddings
624-105-3230 or 949-226-8320 (U.S.);
fax 624-104-3230 or 949-315-3191 (U.S.)
www.bajawedding.com
Plaza del Rey #3, km 6 Mexico 1,
Los Cabos

Bella Brides
624-105-1605 or 972-346-6427 (U.S.);
fax 624-105-1606
www.bellabridescabo.com
Casa Bella Hotel, Hidalgo 10, Colonia Centro.
Cabo San Lucas

Perfect Weddings by Sergio
624-144-5998 or 1-800-576-2520 (U.S.);
fax 775-254-9640
www.perfectweddingsbysergio.com
511 East San Ysidro Boulevard J-131
San Ysidro, CA

Sunset Weddings
624-143-5016 or 858-427-0658 (U.S.);
fax 624-143-5017
www.asunsetwedding.com
Boulevard Lázaro Cárdenas,
Edificio Posada Local #7
Cabo San Lucas

Cabo San Lucas town square

1

CABO SAN LUCAS

At the tip of the thousand-mile Baja Peninsula along sun-drenched rocky cliffs and white sand beaches sits Cabo San Lucas, a once-tiny fishing village now transformed into a booming resort town. With its convenient location near the West Coast of the United States and its increasing reputation as a golf destination—not to mention its well-established reputation as a sport-fishing and party town—Cabo San Lucas has probably only begun to be a hotspot.

Located at the point where the Pacific Ocean meets the Sea of Cortés, Cabo is centered on a three-hundred-slip marina that's usually filled with everything from small boats to luxury yachts. The boardwalk that runs along this marina is where you'll find the town's accumulation of tourist restaurants, disco bars, and shops pushing everything from hokey T-shirts to fine jewelry. While there are plenty of bargains to be had here, the vendors who line the streets harassing passersby can be rather annoying. At night this district comes alive with partying Americans taking advantage of the numerous drink specials offered up. It's not the height of Mexican culture, but you can have a good time here. Most visitors to Cabo confine themselves to their resort hotels and the waterfront; however, up in the hills is a surprisingly vibrant Mexican town where you can find good family-owned restaurants and cozy inns that cater to a slightly different crowd than you'll find at the all-inclusive resorts.

Because Cabo is a tourist destination in the midst of a development boom, you will also find plenty of swindlers waiting to rip you off. Carrying your wallet in your front pocket or a money belt is never a bad idea, and be wary of anybody claiming that they can make you a special deal. If you are looking for a particular service—for instance, a car rental—and they offer you anything other than what you asked for, either insist on getting exactly what you want, or go somewhere else. This is particularly true when it comes to timeshare hucksters. If someone offers you a gift in exchange for "looking at a new hotel," be aware that what they are really offering is several hours in hard-sell hell. This is probably something that you want to avoid—especially since you came to Cabo to relax and enjoy yourself.

HISTORY

In 1520s the Aztec conqueror Hernán Cortés (whom generations of American schoolkids were taught to call "Hernando Cortez") was so moved by rumors of an offshore island to the northwest that he sent a letter to the king of Spain in which he related reports of a land "rich in pearls and gold" that was inhabited by warrior women. These reports were likely inspired by a 1504 novel by Garci Rodriguez de Montalvo that stated: "Know that on the

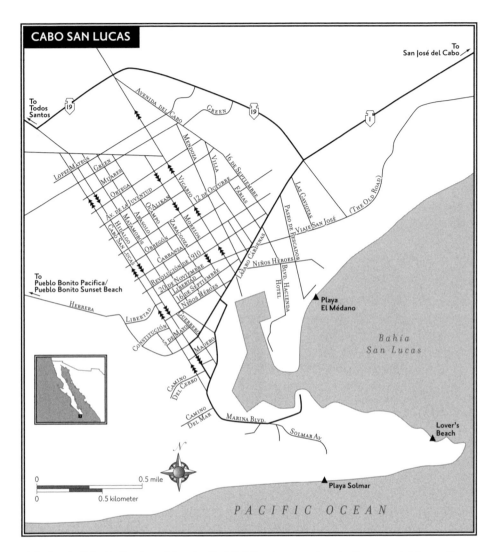

right hand of the Indies is an island called California, very close to the terrestrial paradise and is inhabited by women, without any man among them." Over the next two decades, Cortés commissioned several expeditions to the Baja Peninsula but never discovered his tribe of Amazon women. His navigator, Francisco de Ulloa, circumvented the peninsula, yet despite his findings, the belief that Baja was an island persisted for decades.

In 1565 a small ship called the *San Lucas,* captained by Andrés de Uraneta, sailed east from the Philippines to the California coast and established a Spanish trade route from Asia. Over the next several centuries, Spanish galleons carrying the richest treasures ever to be transported on the high seas left the Philippines en route to Acapulco and ultimately made their way back to Spain. Ships would sail this route only a couple of times a year at most. Though the trip from Acapulco to Manila was a relatively easy one, the trip back was considered one of the longest and most dangerous voyages one could make, often taking upward of seven months to make. A great number of crewmen would die of malnutrition

GENERAL INFORMATION

Police
624-143-3977
Boulevard Marina at Plaza Bonita Mall (on the boardwalk), Cabo San Lucas

American Consulate
624-143-3566
Boulevard Marina, Local C-4, Plaza Naútica, Cabo San Lucas

Canadian Consulate
624-142-4333
#9 Plaza Jose Green, Boulevard Mijares, San José del Cabo

Medical Service
624-143-3434
López Mateos between Leona Vicario and Morelos Colonia Ejidal, Cabo San Lucas

Fire Department
624-143-3577
Camino Real and Boulevard Marina behind McDonald's, Cabo San Lucas

American Express Office
624-142-1349
Plaza Misión and Boulevard Mijares, San José del Cabo

Courier Service
DHL Worldwide Express
624-143-1430
Plaza Copán on Lázaro Cárdenas, Cabo San Lucas
Mail Boxes Etc.
624-143-3032
Plaza Bonita Mall, Cabo San Lucas

Cellular Phone Rental
Cabo Cell
624-143-5950
Lázaro Cárdenas,, Edificio Pioneros, Local 2, Cabo San Lucas
www.cabocell.com.mx

and disease during this trip, and on at least one such crossing, not one person was left alive onboard. However, the European demand for Asian silks, spices, gold, and other goods was so high that the lucrative profits from these voyages justified the danger.

Landfall from these return voyages was often made around Cabo San Lucas, which eventually made the cape, along with the bay of La Paz, a popular spot for British and Dutch pirates to wait for these vulnerable, treasure-laden galleons. In November 1587 the British pirate Sir Thomas Cavendish captured the Spanish galleon *Great Saint Anne,* prompting King Phillip II of Spain to order the establishment of a small fort at Cabo San Lucas to rid the area of pirates. This fort helped to open the Baja Peninsula to exploration. Pearls were discovered in the Sea of Cortés, and settlements started to spring up all along the coast. In 1730 Jesuit missionaries established the Mission of San Jose 20 miles to the northeast. Together, the two settlements became known as Los Cabos, or "the capes." However, due to a lack of a steady water supply, they remained largely undeveloped for nearly 250 years.

In 1917 an American fishing company moved into the area and built a floating platform to catch tuna. This more or less established Cabo San Lucas as a fishing village. Cabo San Lucas had a population of about 400 by the 1930s, when sport fishermen began to discover the area, but it would remain largely inaccessible to most people for another 40 years. Still, word continued to get out about the abundance of fish to be had off the coast of Baja, and in 1948 several American celebrities, including Bing Crosby, Desi Arnaz, and John Wayne, invested in a small hotel on the East Cape called Las Cruces. This kicked off a minor development boom of hotels from La Paz to Cabo San Lucas. But the area remained accessible only to long-range yachts, small planes, and off-road vehicles. It wasn't until the Carretera Transpeninsular—the Transpeninsular Highway—opened in the 1970s that development really got under way in Cabo.

By the mid-70s the population of Cabo San Lucas had grown only to about 900 when FONATUR began to pour money and resources into the region. Development included a freshwater pipeline, a 300-slip marina in Cabo San Lucas, and an international airport in San José del Cabo. Initially, clientele were mainly sportfishermen attracted to Cabo's many fishing tournaments. In recent years, though, Cabo has attracted an extremely broad range of visitors, from golfers and beach lovers to families and eco-tourists. Today Cabo San Lucas has a permanent population of around 40,000, many of whom are expatriate Americans. This growth has brought a stable infrastructure and development of services that ensures a good standard of living for both visitors and residents.

GETTING THERE

The best way to get to Los Cabos is to fly into the international airport, located 13 miles north of San José del Cabo and 29 miles northeast of Cabo San Lucas. With an average of more than 200 flights a week, the airport is the busiest in Baja California Sur. Its two terminals service several major airlines, including Aeromexico, Alaskan Airlines, American Airlines, America West, Continental, Delta, and Frontier.

All ground transportation away from the airport is found outside the doors from the baggage-claim areas. The best option is one of the bright yellow minivans. They are reliable and charge a government-controlled rate of around $20, sparing you the annoying task of bartering down the $60 rate that is charged by the regular taxi companies. A much cheaper but inconvenient bus service begins with a short $5 taxi ride and ends with a 20-minute walk.

The bus trip from Tijuana is about a thousand miles and can take anywhere from 24 to 30 hours. Though it is a long and arduous ride, Mexican buses are generally comfortable and clean and usually play American movies with Spanish subtitles. The primary bus company operating in Baja California is Autotransportes de Baja California (ABC). Contact them at 664-683-5681; www.abc.com.mx. If you prefer to drive to Los Cabos yourself, Mexico 1, the Carretera Transpeninsular (Transpeninsular Highway), is the only thoroughfare to get you there. You should not drive on this road at night since some areas are pocked with potholes, cattle often wander across the road, and there are stretches that are rather treacherous to begin with, even in daylight.

If you're coming from mainland Mexico, you can catch a ferry to La Paz from Mazatlan or Topolobambo. Reservations are recommended. For more information, go to www.bajaferries.com, and click on the American flag on the top right for English.

GETTING AROUND

Downtown Cabo San Lucas is dense enough for walking. Even many of the outlying hotels are less than a 20-minute stroll from the action. This option is made even more attractive by the fact that parking can be a problem here, particularly during spring break when the streets become clogged with vehicles. Taxis are generally easy to get, though they do charge prices typical of tourist centers. Rides within the center of town usually cost around $5, while drives out to the Tourist Corridor will run you $20 and up. There are several car rental kiosks along Lázaro Cárdenas, but beware of their "specials." Some of them will try to bait-and-switch you with timeshare seminars in exchange for a "free" rental that turns out not to be free at all. Los Cabos does have a municipal bus system that runs within and between the two cities. You will see shaded bus stops, but you can flag down a bus from just about anywhere by waving your arms. When asked, most drivers have no problem letting you off at specific beaches and hotels. The buses run approximately every 20 minutes along the main highway, and the fare is around $1.50 or less, depending on how far you're going.

CAR RENTAL COMPANIES

Alamo
LÁZARO CÁRDENAS
624-143-6060
between Cicario and Mendoza
open Monday through Saturday 7 AM to 8 PM,
Sunday 7 AM to 7 PM

Dollar
LÁZARO CÁRDENAS
624-143-1250 or fax 624-143-1255
at the corner of Narciso Mendoze

PLAZA LAS GLORIAS
624-143-1600 or fax 624-142-1098
at Boulevard Marina
open Monday through Friday 7 AM to 8 PM,
Saturday and Sunday 7 AM to 7 PM

Hertz
LÁZARO CÁRDENAS #6
624-105-1428 or fax 624-414-7650
open Monday through Friday 8 AM to 8 PM,
Saturday 8 AM to 7 PM, Sunday 8 AM to 6 PM

National
LÁZARO CÁRDENAS
624-143-1414 or fax 624-142-1099
Posada Cabo San Lucas
open daily 7 AM to 8 PM

HOTEL RIU
624-146-7160
open daily 8 AM to 6PM

Thrifty
BOULEVARD MARNIA LOCAL K-3
624- 143-1666
open daily 7 AM to 9 PM

WEATHER

Cabo San Lucas certainly has a unique location that gives it one of the most pleasant climates you'll find anywhere. It's located below the Tropic of Cancer and at the meeting point of the cool Pacific Ocean and warm Sea of Cortés, factors that act to moderate the weather. Consequently, Cabo San Lucas is slightly cooler than La Paz or even San José del Cabo. During the summer, the heat can be a bit uncomfortable, with highs reaching into the mid-90s in August and September. These months are also the height of the hurricane season. Landfall for hurricanes is relatively uncommon in Los Cabos, though Hurricane John, a Category 3 storm, did cause havoc when it made landfall near San José del Cabo in early September 2006. Usually, though, these occasional storms only manage to cause heavy rains. The average annual rainfall is around 10 to 12 inches, and September is the wettest month, during which Cabo usually sees three or four days with rain that adds up to about 4 inches. Rain is uncommon from February through July, during which period temperatures range from the 70s to the upper 80s. At night temperatures can drop to the low 60s during the winter but will remain in the upper 70s during summer months. However, in Los Cabos, the juncture of the Pacific Ocean and the Sea of Cortés has quite a different effect on their surroundings, with the Pacific side of Los Cabos generally about 10 degrees cooler than the eastern side that borders the Sea of Cortés.

ACCOMMODATIONS

Cabo San Lucas is a tourist town, and as such, it has no shortage of hotel options. Médano Beach is lined with resort hotels, and Solmar Beach has a good stretch of resorts, as well. For the most part, these resorts are designed to allow guests to fly into Cabo, never leave the hotel grounds during their stay, and fly out. They are glorious in scale and luxurious in atmosphere. However, the pampered experience provided at these large resorts can be not only expensive but also overwhelming. For travelers looking for a more down-to-earth vacation, Cabo San Lucas also has several boutique hotels where you can surround yourself with a more traditional sort of elegance. These hotels are generally on the smaller side and feature rooms with unique decors; they are also usually within walking distance to the many bars and restaurants that line Lázaro Cárdenas and Boulevard Marina. Whatever you choose, Cabo San Lucas has the facilities and service to meet your desires.

Budget Options

CABO INN HOTEL

Managers: Stanley and Maria Patenaude
624-143-0819 or 619-819-2727 (U.S.)
www.caboinnhotel.com
20 de Noviembre and Mendoza
Credit Cards: MC, V (with reservations; walk-ins cash only)

This charming budget hotel has 19 air-conditioned rooms constructed around a shaded courtyard that is perfect for getting to know fellow travelers. The entire hotel is decorated with colorful Mexican decorations, with *saltillo* tile floors, handmade furniture, and palapa roofs. The rooms are airy and clean, and the staff is friendly and knowledgeable about Cabo San Lucas. The hotel has a community kitchen, first-floor rooms have refrigerators, and a small pool is on the premises. However, the hotel's best feature may be its convenient location just a few blocks from downtown. Rates: $58 to $70 for a standard room double occupancy and $90 to $120 for palapas.

CASA PABLITO BED & BREAKFAST HOTEL

Proprietors; Ed and Pat Giddings
624-143-1971
www.casapablitoloscabos.com
Miguel Hidalgo and Felix Ortega
Credit Cards: MC, V

This 15-suite bed-and-breakfast hotel located right in downtown Cabo San Lucas is built around an attractive central courtyard. In the center of this courtyard is a Jacuzzi palapa-roofed canteen that borders a deep-blue pool. The hotel's interior and exterior are decorated in a Mexican hacienda style, featuring salmon-colored stucco walls with blue and red accents, giving this hotel an authentic Mexican feel. Rooms are equipped with a queen or two twin beds as well as kitchenettes that include a small stove and refrigerator. Breakfast is served daily from 8 AM to 11 AM (9 AM to noon on Sundays) in a colorful canteen area. Rates: $90 to $110 from October 16 to April 30; $70 to $80 from May 1 to October 15.

HOTEL MAR DE CORTEZ

Manager: Simon Yee Sanchez
624-143-0032 or 1-800-347-8821 (U.S.); fax 624-143-0232
www.mardecortez.com
Lázaro Cárdenas and Guerrero
Credit Cards: MC, V

Constructed in the late 1960s, this rather large hotel is located toward the south side of town near the marina. Built well before the tourist boom, the Colonial-style hotel has a garden pool, private parking, and a restaurant on the premises. The 90 air-conditioned rooms come in a variety of options. First-level standard rooms are fairly good sized and offer a combination of queen-, double-, and twin-sized beds or a single king. Second-level terrace rooms come with a queen and a twin as well as a terrace overlooking the courtyard. Garden-view rooms have two double beds and an extra-large shower and bathing area as well as a private patio or a balcony overlooking the pool. Whichever you settle on, the rates are surprisingly reasonable: They start at $50 for standard room double occupancy.

HOTEL QUINTA DEL SOL

Manager: Luis Alvarez
624-144-4500; fax 624-144-4542
http://quintadelsol.com
Lázaro Cárdenas and El Bordo
Credit Cards: MC, V

This hotel, located in a small complex slightly east of the main drag, is affiliated with the Best Western hotel franchise. Many Americans will find it very familiar because it's built like an American budget hotel: long two-story buildings, with exterior corridors leading to the parking lot. The 72 air-conditioned rooms are clean and comfortable and decorated like any other American budget hotel with two double beds and kitchenettes. A small swimming pool is on the premises as well as a small convenience store and a 24-hour security guard who checks cars in and out. Rooms come with a continental breakfast. The hotel's biggest drawback is its location, which is a bit out of the way. Rates: $84 to $93 for a standard room double occupancy.

HOTEL SANTA FÉ

Manager: Angel Guzman
624-143-4401 or 1-877-845-5247
www.hotelsantafeloscabos.com
Ignacio Zaragoza and Álvaro Obregón
Credit Cards: MC, V, AE

This 46-room budget hotel is about a five-minute walk from downtown Cabo San Lucas. Rooms are equipped with a queen-sized bed and a sofa bed as well as a small, fully furnished kitchenette. A laundry room is on the premises, though the hotel also offers a laundry and dry-cleaning service. Other amenities include an outdoor pool, a well-lit parking area, a small restaurant, and a gift shop. The hotel also provides guests with satellite TV as well as a currency exchange service. Rates: average $75.

LAS MARGARITAS INN

Manager: Jorge Edgar Cota Castro
624-143-6770; fax: 624-143-0450
Lázaro Cárdenas and Zaragosa
Credit Cards: MC, V, AE

Located in the heart of downtown Cabo San Lucas, this hotel provides a convenient location and roomy accommodations. The 16 one- and two-bedroom air-conditioned units are decorated in basic-budget hotel whites, blues, and pastels. The bedrooms have king- or queen-sized beds, and the living rooms are equipped with sleeper sofas and fully furnished kitchenettes. Provisions won't be a problem since the hotel is located across the street from a large grocery store and a bakery. There is also plenty of on-site parking, which can be a big plus during the busy season when the streets fill up with tourists. Rates: $70 to $90 for a standard room double occupancy.

LOS MILAGROS

Owners: Sandra Scandiber and Ricardo Rode
624-143-4566; fax 624-143-5004
www.losmilagros.com.mx
Matamoros 116
Credit Cards: None

Los Milagros means "the miracles," and though it is no miracle what makes this little hotel so tranquil, it is certainly a surprising find in the heart of bustling downtown Cabo San Lucas. The two-level white adobe-style building with a private roof terrace and a small pool in a shaded courtyard is less than two blocks from the famous Cabo Wabo restaurant. Double rooms are furnished with two full-sized beds while single rooms have a queen-sized bed, and each has a large bathroom. Rooms

are tastefully decorated in a classical Mexican style with *saltillo* tile floors, thick wooden dressers, and wrought-iron headboards. Suites also have kitchenettes. The hotel provides cable TV and high-speed Internet hookups in every room as well as laundry service for a nominal fee. Rates: $70 to $85 for a standard room double occupancy.

MARINA CABO PLAZA

Manager: Lourdes Valadez Diaz.
624-143-1833 or 619-954-8000 (U.S.); fax 624-143-2077
www.marinacaboplaza.com
Boulevard Marina 39
Credit Cards: None

This condominium hotel is located right on the marina and near Médano Beach. The rental units come equipped with wet bars, air-conditioning, and kitchenettes. They also have private patios or balconies that overlook the marina. A security guard is on duty at all times, and guests will have no problem finding plenty of dining choices and other services within short walking distance. Rates: average $100.

SEVEN CROWN HOTEL

Manager: Griselda Torres
624-143-7787
www.sevencrownhotels.com
Lázaro Cárdenas and 16 de Septiembre
Credit Cards: MC, V, AE

This hotel offers 40 air-conditioned rooms furnished with either one king-sized bed or two double beds. Rooms are all equipped with cable TV and a minifridge, and an outdoor pool in the courtyard is perfect for touching up your tan before heading to the beach. The rooms are somewhat blandly decorated, but they are clean, and the location is close to bars and restaurants as well as the marina. Rates: $75 to $85 for a standard room double occupancy.

SIESTA SUITES HOTEL

Manager: Juan Bautista
624-143-2773 or 1-866-271-0952 (U.S.)
www.cabosiestasuites.com
Zapata between Guerrero and Hidalgo
Credit Cards: MC, V

A great option for travelers who are looking for a hotel that is centrally located but has the comforts of home. They offer 20 air-conditioned units equipped with separate bedrooms, cable TV, and good-sized, fully furnished kitchens. One-bedroom suites are furnished with a double bed and a sofa and dinette in the living room. They also have a few hotel-style rooms that are furnished with two queen-sized beds and a sofa. A pool is on the premises. Rates: start at $59 for a standard room double occupancy and $69 for a penthouse suite. Weekly and monthly rates are also available.

VILLA LA PALOMA

Manager: Brenda Alvarez de Nasser
624-143-3461; fax 624-143-1159
www.hotelvillalapaloma.com
Lázaro Cárdenas and El Bordo
Credit Cards: MC, V, AE
Special Features: Concierge service

This 32-suite condominium hotel is located within a gated community of four-story buildings set around a swimming pool and palapa bar and restaurant. The concierge at the front desk will arrange golf, sportfishing, or any other activities or tours that are on your itinerary. Each air-conditioned unit has a furnished living room, with cable TV and wireless Internet, as well as a full kitchen. Bedrooms are furnished with queen-sized beds with wooden headboards and vanity tables. Rates: average $80.

Midrange Hotels

BAHÍA CONDO HOTEL

Manager: John Esquivel
624-143-1888 or 1-800-932-5599
(U.S./Canada); fax 624-143-1891
www.grupobahia.com
Playa El Mèdano
Credit Cards: MC, V
Special Features: Concierge desk, swim-up bar, near the beach

Overlooking the harbor and located just a block away from Mèdano Beach, this 76-unit condominium hotel has a great location. A large patio pool has a Jacuzzi and a swim-up palapa bar. The on-site Médano Restaurant (143-2479) has a full bar and offers room service. This restaurant specializes in seafood, Mexican dishes, and big breakfasts and has a happy-hour special. However, with this location, you will surely be tempted to do a little exploring off the hotel grounds. Unlike some condominium rentals, this hotel offers daily maid service, and the elevators are even run by a doorman. Rooms are air conditioned and furnished with queen-sized beds. Some units also have sofa beds. All of the studio condominiums are equipped with satellite TV, full kitchens, and private balconies overlooking either the pool or the Sea of Cortés. Rates: $95 to $105 from April 22 to December 15 and $129 to $139 from December 16 to April 21.

THE BUNGALOWS BED & BREAKFAST

Manager: Sra. Estella Alonso
624-143-0585 or 1-888-424-2226 (U.S.)
www.cabobungalows.com
Boulevard Miguel A. Herrera
Credit Cards: MC, V, AE
Special Features: Gourmet breakfast, heated pool

This charming hotel lies off the beaten path in the hills above Cabo San Lucas. While it may not be the best hotel for young partiers in town for spring break, it is perfect for couples and other travelers looking for a tranquil place to rest after a long day at the beach. The staff is friendly and accommodating and more than happy to help you plan excursions. The hotel's 16 air-condi-

The Bungalows Breakfast Inn

tioned rooms face an inner courtyard dominated by a heated pool and a lushly shaded
garden. Gourmet chocolates and freshly cut
flowers welcome you to your room, which is
decorated in a rustic Mexican style with
thick wooden furniture and colorful fabrics.
The grounds of the hotel are lush and
meticulously manicured, and a trickling
garden fountain sets a mood of quiet and
privacy. Guests are invited to choose from
the video library in the main house, where
every morning a delicious gourmet breakfast is prepared. This meal is usually vegetarian, though special meals are available
upon request. Breakfast is served on a
palapa-roofed breakfast nook overlooking
the pool, the perfect setting to plan
an(other) adventurous day in Cabo. Rates:
$135 to $155 for standard rooms ($115 to
$135 during August and September). Hon-
eymoon suites and bungalows are slightly
more expensive.

CASA RAFAEL'S
Manager: Rafael Arraut
624-143-0739; fax 624-143-1697
Calle Médano
Credit Cards: MC, V
Special Features: Fine-dining restaurant,
cigar room, wireless Internet

This boutique hotel is located just a hundred yards from Médano Beach and a short
walk from the marina. The tall aqua-blue
house is surrounded by desert landscaping
and has a sun deck, swimming pool, and 10
large guest bedrooms that are uniquely decorated. Internet service, a fax machine,
concierge service, plus a plain ol' translation service are all available at the front
desk. The hotel also offers a fine-dining
experience in their restaurant, which is
complete with tropical birds and a piano
bar. Here you will find an extensive wine
list with more than 120 selections from

around the world. Room service from this excellent restaurant is also available to guests. Rates: $75 to $100 for double occupancy; $25 per extra person.

CASTILLO BLARNEY INN
Managers: Shonna and Juan Corral
624-143-2160
www.blarneycastleinn.com
Calle Libertad, Col. Lienzo Charro
Credit Cards: MC, V
Special Features: Private accommodations, Internet access, Jacuzzi pool

This Irish-themed boutique hotel is located on a hill overlooking Cabo San Lucas and caters to travelers looking for something different than prepackaged all-inclusive resorts. It features nine private air-conditioned suites, each with a view of the Sea of Cortés below. These suites vary in size and can accommodate anywhere from 3 to 10 people. Large, clean, and decorated in a modern style, each unit features a full kitchen—complete with cookware, dishes, and utensils—a private deck, and satellite TV as well as daily maid service. The property also has a swimming pool, Jacuzzi, and a communal barbecue grill. Set off a bit from the action in town, this hotel offers a great escape yet is only a five-minute drive from downtown. Rates average $185.

TESORO LOS CABOS
Manager: Alfredo Casas
624-143-1220; fax 624-143-1235
www.tesororesorts.com
Boulevard Marina, Lot 9
Credit Cards: MC, V, AE

This large 286-room hotel is located on the marina and is walking distance to the restaurants and bars of Cabo San Lucas. The property has a large pool, where activities are planned daily, as well as an on-site spa that offers everything from manicures to body treatments. Standard rooms come furnished with two twin-sized beds or a single king. They also have sofas, satellite TV, and a terrace or balcony facing either the city or the marina. The minifridge is stocked with beer and soda, but you will thank yourself later and save some money by purchasing refreshments elsewhere. If you're hungry, the on-site La Vista Restaurant (143-1220) serves up a buffet breakfast with a view of the marina. For lighter fare, check out Café Canela Bistro & Bar (143-3435) located on the marina. Another fun option is the Caborey Dinner Cruiser (143-8260), a 144-foot catamaran that departs from Tesoro Los Cabos. Rates: $132 to $187 for a standard room double occupancy from January through April 15 and $99 to $110 from April 16 through December.

VIVA CABO HOTEL
Manager: Javier de Uranga
624-143-5810; fax 624-143-2242
Plaza de la Danza, Boulevard Marina
Credit Cards: MC, V, AE
Special Features: Restaurant/bar, satellite TV, laundry facilities.

This quiet and quaint hotel may be small on the outside, but it has plenty to offer. It features eight large air-conditioned studio suites that are furnished with either a king-sized bed or two twins. Rooms are decorated in whites and pastels that seem to evoke old Americana and come equipped with kitchenettes and satellite TV. Guests of the hotel have access to the pool and fitness center next door at the Plaza Nautica. This hotel also enjoys a great location: walking distance from the bars and restaurants of Cabo San Lucas. Rates average $95.

Luxury Hotels

CABO VILLAS RESORT
Manager: Alejandro Vergara
624-143-9199 or 1-877-382-2932 (U.S.)
www.cabovillasbeachresort.com
Callejon del Pescador s/n Colonia El Médano

Credit Cards: MC, V
Special Features: Rooftop restaurant, two pools, on-site spa, beachfront bar

This resort hotel is located on the northeast side of Médano Beach. The large property skirts the beach and has one small pool and a second enormous one. Suites are equipped with two TVs, a full kitchen, and wireless Internet access for a small fee. Located atop the main building is a Mexican seafood restaurant called the Sunset Grill (143-9199 ext. 2026), where you can enjoy a gourmet meal with a fantastic view of the Sea of Cortés. It also features live music on Monday and Friday nights. If you want to get closer to the action, visit the Baja Cantina (143-9773), a beachfront palapa bar with an all-day happy hour. Or if you'd rather be relaxing, visit the on-site Manos Massage & Treatment center for a rubdown and some aromatherapy. Rates average $288.

CASA BELLA

Manager: Barbara Ungson
624-143-6400 or 425-444-9104 (U.S.); fax 624-143-6401
www.cabo-condo.com
Hidalgo #10, Colonia Centro
Credit Cards: MC, V
Special Features: Fitness center, satellite TV, catering chef available

This Colonial-style condominium with a lush garden courtyard features a beautiful patio pool. The terrace patio overlooks the Sea of Cortés and is a great place to relax in the evening. The house is spacious and gorgeously appointed, with handmade terracotta tile and original art throughout. Its three bedrooms can accommodate up to eight people. The master bedroom has a king-sized bed plus a spacious bathroom with a Jacuzzi tub. The first guest bedroom is furnished with a queen-sized bed, while the second guest bedroom has two twin beds. The entire house is equipped with wireless Internet access and satellite TV,

and a daily continental breakfast is included in the price of your stay. Rates: $350 to $425 for a one-bedroom condominium.

HOTEL FINISTERRA

Manager: José Garcia Castro
624-143-3333 or 1-800-347-2252 (U.S.); fax 624-143-0590
www.finisterra.com
Boulevard Marina
Credit Cards: MC, V, AE
Special Features: Beachfront location, three pools, two Jacuzzis, two restaurants.

Right on Solmar Beach, south of the marina, is this resort hotel. Its location on the wide Pacific beach gives the Finisterra the sense of being isolated while still being a short walk from the action in town. This hotel offers 287 terraced suites overlooking either the Pacific Ocean or the Sea of Cortés. Each room is furnished with two double beds or one king. The hotel is built into a cliff above the beach and faces a large area surrounded by palm trees that includes three swimming pools and two Jacuzzis. The hotel has an on-site fine-dining restaurant called The Blue Marlin (143-3333) that's open for breakfast and dinner. For more casual fare, check out La Palapa at Finisterra (143-3333 ext. 1948), a poolside palapa restaurant serving up Mexican and American comfort food. Rates: $140 to $229 for city-view rooms and $171 to $270 for ocean-view rooms. Palapa suites are more expensive.

HOTEL RIU PALACE CABO SAN LUCAS

Manager: José Luis Garcia
624-146-7160 or 1-888-666-8816 (U.S.); fax 624-146-7161
www.riu.com/palacecabosanlucas
Camino Viejo a San Josè
Credit Cards: MC, V, AE
Special Features: All-inclusive lavish vacationing

One of the newest hotels in Los Cabos, this all-inclusive resort—which resembles a giant southern Spanish palace built right on Médano Beach—puts an emphasis on lavish living. The hotel has 642 units of varying accommodations, including some with their own Jacuzzis. Rooms are spacious and nicely appointed and feature a fully stocked minibar. Because of the all-inclusive rate, domestic and imported alcoholic beverages as well as juices, sodas, bottled water, and anything else you want is complimentary everywhere on the premises. The hotel features two separate pool areas—equipped with two swim-up bars—that open onto the beach as well as a beauty salon and a fitness center. Rates average $430.

HOTEL SOLMAR SUITES
Manager: Lupita Ceceña Chong
624-146-7700 or 1-800-344-3349 (U.S.);
fax 624-143-0410
www.solmar.com
Avenida Solmar #1 Colonia Centro
Credit Cards: MC, V, AE
Special Features: Saturday-night fiesta, on-site activity center.

This hotel located on Solmar Beach is sheltered from the city by granite cliffs. However, despite its secluded location, the main strip of Cabo San Lucas is only a 10-minute walk away. With 190 units, the hotel offers guests a variety of accommodations. Each room is furnished with either a king-sized bed or two double beds and a living-room area that varies depending on your room choice. All rooms are also equipped with satellite TV and a minibar. The property features two heated pools, a Jacuzzi, and tennis courts, and an activity center offers everything from scuba diving and snorkeling to horseback riding and ATVs. After working up an appetite, visit the Fiesta Mexicana Restaurant (146-7700 ext. 5360) for oceanfront Mexican cuisine. On Saturday nights, catch live mariachi music and an all-you-can-eat buffet. Rates: $145 to $170 for Gardenview suites with double occu-

pancy; $25 for each additional person. Junior, Studio, and Deluxe suites are more expensive.

MARINA FIESTA RESORT & HOTEL
Manager: Manuel Delcallejo
624-143-1220 or 1-877-243-4880 (U.S.);
fax 624-145-6021
www.marinafiestaresort.com
Marina Cabo Lote 37 and 38
Credit Cards: MC, V, AE
Special Features: Two swimming pools, swim-up bar, two restaurants, massage room, gym

This large resort hotel features 155 suites built around a large swimming pool area that opens right onto the marina. Its location puts the resort within walking distance of the city's bars and restaurants, but with all the featured amenities, you don't even have to leave the hotel grounds if you so choose. The hotel offers a variety of accommodation options ranging from a relatively cramped junior suite on up to the 1,800-square-foot Presidential Suite or the 2,000-square-foot penthouse. All rooms are furnished with either double- or queen-sized beds. The on-site spa offers guests the opportunity to pamper themselves with a massage or a facial, and the hotel has two restaurants for those who just want to hunker down and enjoy the surroundings. Rates: $260 to $360 double occupancy.

MELIÁ SAN LUCAS
Manager: Raul Petraglia
624-145-7800 or 1-800-336-3542 (U.S.);
fax 624-143-0420
http://mecabo.travel
Médano Beach
Credit Cards: MC, V, AE
Special Features: Fitness center, concierge service, baby-sitting service.

Located on Médano Beach, this resort offers guests a fashionable retreat. The 150 units are done up in a modern decor, including numerous paintings and sculptures by renowned Mexican artist Yuri Zatarain. Rooms face a gorgeous pool area centered by a swim-up palapa bar. Just beyond is the beach. When you get hungry, you can check out Nikki Beach (145-7800, ext.789) a stylish fusion restaurant. A hotel for many types of travelers, its amenities include 24-hour room service, a children's pool, and a tennis court. Rates: $275 to $700 per night plus 12 percent tax and 10 percent service charge.

PLAYA GRANDE RESORT

Manager: Ricardo Rojas
624-145-7575 or 1-800-344-3349; fax 624-143-6655
www.playagranderesort.com
Avenida Playa Grande #1
Credit Cards: MC, V, AE
Special Features: Multiple pools, fitness center, on-site sport fishing and diving, tennis courts.

Located on an isolated stretch of Solmar Beach south of Cabo San Lucas, this elegant hotel is built around an enormous beachfront pool area boasting waterfalls, children's areas, two swim-up bars, and a Jacuzzi overlooking the ocean. The 259 units all have balconies facing the Pacific plus satellite TV, king-sized beds, and full-sized baths. The hotel also features the Brigantine Restaurant (145-7575, ext. 3305), a fine-dining Mexican restaurant. For a more relaxed atmosphere, check out the Calima Restaurant (145-7575), a poolside Mexican restaurant with a party atmosphere. Rates: $273 to $310 for a junior suite double occupancy.

PUEBLO BONITO LOS CABOS

Owner: Ernesto Coppel
624-142-9797 or 1-800-990-8250; fax 624-143-1995
www.pueblobonito-loscabos.com
Médano Beach

Credit Cards: MC, V, AE
Special Features: Concierge service, gym, dry cleaning/laundry, child-care facilities

This resort is right on Médano Beach and offers 148 suites, all with private balconies that open to a view of Land's End. Junior suites—which are quite large and can accommodate up to four people—are equipped with a living room area, two double beds, and a kitchenette. Not that you will be doing much cooking with two restaurants and a casual dining pool bar on site. Cilantro's (142-9797, ext. 642) is a fine-dining seafood restaurant with an ocean view. Las Palomas (142-9797) is the hotel's Mexican restaurant where you can dine in an air-conditioned dining hall or on a large terrace. The hotel is decorated in the style of a Mediterranean villa, with white stucco and blue trim. The hotel towers over a large palm-tree-lined pool area that opens onto the beach. Rates start at $215.

PUEBLO BONITO ROSÉ

Owner: Ernesto Coppel
624-142-9898 or 1-800-990-8250 (U.S.); fax 624-143-5972
www.pueblobonito-rose.com
Médano Beach
Credit Cards: MC, V, AE
Special Features: On-site spa and workout facilities, laundry/dry cleaning, baby-sitting

This massive 260-suite resort located on Médano Beach is the sister hotel of the Pueblo Bonito Los Cabos. Like that hotel, this one has a Mediterranean theme, with long white-stucco buildings built around a central square dominated by an expansive pool area and palm gardens. Large junior suites are furnished with two double beds in a bedroom separated from a living room that has a sofa, chairs, and a kitchenette. All units have a private terrace or balcony. An on-site spa has a gym and treatment facilities where you can get a massage or a facial.

The resort also has two fine-dining restaurants. Mare Nostrum (142-9898, ext. 8310) is a seafood restaurant with international specialties. L'Orangerie (142-9898, ext. 8300) is a French restaurant with oceanfront dining. For more casual dining, lounge at the pool bar with some chips and guacamole. Rates: $207 to $343 for a junior suite double occupancy.

VILLA DEL PALMAR RESORT & SPA
Manager: Luis Aguilar
624-145-7200 or 1-877-845-5247 (U.S.); fax 624-143-2664
www.villadelpalmarloscabos.com
Camino Viejo at San José
Credit Cards: MC, V, AE
Special Features: Fitness center, on-site medical clinic, cyber café, kids' play room.

This enormous 459-unit resort is located on Médano Beach. Guests arrive to a stunning vaulted lobby area that leads to the back of the property, where one finds a hotel built around a graduated patio—with two pools—that opens up to the beach with Land's End visible in the distance. Attendants roam the property catering to lounging guests. Find a variety of room options here, from junior suites to three bedroom suites. All are spacious and have balconies with a view of the sea. For dinner, try the Bella California Restaurant (145-7000, ext. 512) for fine Italian and Californian cuisine. Rates: start at $176.

RV Parks

EL ARCO TRAILER PARK
624-143-1686
Carretera Transpeninsular (Mexico 1)

This RV park is located just over 3 miles east of Cabo San Lucas on the north side of Mexico 1. It features 40 RV spaces and 24 campsites. Facilities have hot showers, flush toilets, and a laundry room. The property is also equipped with a pool and a restaurant/bar. Rates: around $15 per night for RVs with full hookups and $8 for tents. Reservations are accepted.
El Faro Viejo Trailer Park
624-143-0561; fax 624-143-4211

ANTONIO MIJARES AT MATAMOROS
Located 12 blocks north of downtown Cabo San Lucas—two blocks off a paved road—this facility features 28 large spaces with full hookups. There is also a restaurant/bar and a gift shop on the property. Rates: $15 per night for two people plus $3 for each additional person.

VAGABUNDOS DEL MAR RV PARK
624-143-0209; fax 624-143-0551
Carretera Transpeninsular (Mexico 1)

This RV park is situated on a 3-acre site a couple of miles out of town on the south side of Mexico 1. It features 85 spaces with full hookups, flush toilets, coin laundry, and hot showers. The property also has a large heated pool, restaurant/bar, boat-washing facilities, and a 24-hour security guard. Rates: $18 per night.

DINING

Cabo San Lucas has plenty of great places to eat. That's all you need to know. You will not have a tough time finding somewhere to eat in this town. In fact, some restaurants along the main strip of Lázaro Cárdenas and Boulevard Marina will come looking for you, encouraging you to come in and enjoy their specials. This can get annoying. Farther away from this area, the atmosphere becomes more relaxed, and you can find some real gems off the beaten path.

Mexican

FELIX RESTAURANT
624-143-4290
Hidalgo between Madero and Zapata

Price: Inexpensive to Moderate
Serving: D
Wheelchair Accessible: Yes

This restaurant, located a block and a half from the marina, offers very traditional Mexican dishes such as *pazole* (a soup with meat and hominy) as well as interesting dishes that are not so traditional, like *puerco con piña* (pork with pineapple). Open daily from 4 PM to 10 PM.

HACIENDA DEL CUERVO
624-105-1615
Plaza Naútica at Boulevard Marina
Price: Moderate to Expensive
Serving: B, L, D
Wheelchair Accessible: Yes

Located in a plaza near the marina, this restaurant offers traditional Mexican cuisine as well as several dishes with a modern twist. Dine on an open patio with a fountain in the center, and be entertained by strolling mariachis. The chef, who hails from Mexico City, prepares mainland favorites, such as chicken mole, with sheer authenticity and also offers coastal specialties like fresh fish served Veracruz style. Or try a Mexican innovation like lobster in vanilla sauce and coconut rice. Open daily 8 AM to midnight.

JUSTO AL GUSTO
624-143-6966
On the marina next to the lighthouse
Price: Moderate to Expensive
Serving: B, L, D
Wheelchair Accessible: Yes

This establishment is located on the marina behind the Hotel Tesoro and offers fine Mexican seafood in a relaxed atmosphere. The extensive menu has many delicious choices. The marina location is romantic and friendly and is a perfect place to catch the sunset while enjoying a wonderful meal. Open daily from 7 AM to 11 PM.

LA CASA DEL DORADO
624-143-2017
Narciso Mendoza and Álvaro Obregón
Price: Expensive
Serving: B, L, D
Wheelchair Accessible: Yes

Located four blocks north of Lázaro Cárdenas, this seafood restaurant has a relaxed, family atmosphere. The menu includes many traditional Mexican seafood dishes. Meals are attractively prepared and served on an open-air patio. Open Monday through Saturday 8 AM to 10 PM.

LA FONDA RESTAURANT
624-143-6926
Avenida Hidalgo and 12 de Octubre
Price: Moderate
Serving: L, D
Wheelchair Accessible: Yes

Though this restaurant is a fair distance off the beaten track, the authentic Mexican flavors found here make it worth the trip. The dining room is done in Colonial decor, and the servers are attired in traditional garb. The attentive, friendly service and elegant atmosphere stand in contrast to the gaudy, over-the-top experience offered by many of the restaurants on the main strip. Open daily 1 PM to 10 PM.

LOS AJOS
624-143-7706
Lázaro Cárdenas between Vicario and Mendoza
Price: Inexpensive
Serving: B, L, D
Wheelchair Accessible: Yes

This all-you-can-eat buffet-style Mexican restaurant is located on Cabo's main strip near the Puerto Paraiso Mall. The buffet features more than 20 different dishes. This place is very popular among locals. Open daily from 8 AM to 9 PM.

Diners enjoy mariachi music with their Mexican food.

MI CASA

624-143-1933
Avenida Cabo San Lucas
Price: Moderate
Serving: L, D
Wheelchair Accessible: Yes

Mi Casa is located on the west side of the town square, a couple of blocks north of Boulevard Marina. Besides being painted in bright pastel colors, this restaurant looks like an old Mexican cantina. There is no doubt that the food here is authentic with dishes like *chiles en nogada* and *mole poblano*. Open daily noon to 10:30 PM.

THE OFFICE RESTAURANT

624-143-3464
Médano Beach at Paseo del Pescador
Price: Moderate to Expensive
Serving: B, L, D
Wheelchair Accessible: Yes

This beachside restaurant provides a surprisingly elegant atmosphere. The extensive menu is packed with seafood and steaks prepared with Mexican flair. They put on a fiesta every Thursday night at 6:30, with piñatas and candy for the kiddies and tequila shooters and dancing for the older "kids."

PANCHO'S RESTAURANT AND TEQUILA BAR

624-143-0973
Hidalgo and Zapata
Price: Moderate
Serving: B, L, D
Wheelchair Accessible: Yes

With an atmosphere that is nothing if not festive, Pancho's offers an extensive menu of Mexican favorites and a long list of tequilas. Located one block off Boulevard Marina, the restaurant is open daily from 7 AM to 11 PM.

Steak and Seafood

ALEXANDER RESTAURANT
624-143-2092
On the marina at Plaza Bonita
Price: Expensive
Serving: L, D
Wheelchair Accessible: Yes

This marina fine-dining restaurant is located among the many hotspots of Plaza Bonita. The diverse menu mixes the influence from the owner's Swiss origin with Mediterranean and tropical flavors, and seafood lovers in particular will have plenty to choose from. The chef specializes in fondue, with cheese, beef, and seafood fondue on the menu. Several interesting seafood, steak, and chicken dishes are offered, as well. Open Monday though Saturday 8 AM to 11 PM and Sunday 5 PM to 11 PM.

BAJA CANTINA DOCKSIDE
624-143-1591
Marina at Tesoro Los Cabos Hotel
Price: Moderate to Expensive
Serving: B, L, D
Wheelchair Accessible: Yes

This casual-dining restaurant has a relaxed atmosphere quite different from the pushy experience offered at some of the tourist restaurants along the main strip. They offer a few traditional Mexican specialties and plenty of good ol' American favorites. They also offer an extensive breakfast menu. For families looking for a fun place to have a meal, there are a few kids' meals on the menu, as well. Baja Cantina Dockside is located in a waterfront palapa-roofed building at Tesoro Los Cabos at the marina. Open daily from 7 AM to 1 AM. A second location, Baja Cantina Beach at Cabo Villas Resort, Médano Beach, offers beachside dining daily from 8 AM to midnight.

BRASIL STEAK HOUSE
624-143-8343
Zapata between Guerrero and Hidalgo
Price: Expensive
Serving: D
Wheelchair Accessible: Yes

Located a block off Lázaro Cárdenas, this traditional Brazilian steak house will make you thank heaven that you're not a vegetarian. There are no menus here. Instead, *garzons* come to your table periodically, starting you off with an array of appetizers, then moving to a variety of pasta and vegetable salads, and finally a selection of 12 cuts of meat that are sliced directly onto your plate. These cuts include New York steak, rib eye, lamb, ribs, chicken, and turkey. Open daily from 5 PM to 11 PM.

CASABLANCA
624-143-0447
Médano Beach
Price: Moderate
Serving: L, D
Wheelchair Accessible: Yes

One of the nicer restaurants located on Médano Beach, it offers a wide variety of seafood specialties as well as several steak and chicken dishes. Sit down to a nice meal with a great view of the beach, and enjoy everything from a chicken quesadilla to filet mignon. Or relax and enjoy shrimp cooked in a variety of ways. Open daily from 10 AM to 10 PM, this restaurant also offers fresh sushi served daily from 1 PM to 10 PM.

EDITH'S
624-143-7580
Médano Beach
Price: Moderate to Expensive
Serving: D
Wheelchair Accessible: Yes

An elegant dining experience right on the main beach of Cabo San Lucas, this beachside steak-and-seafood restaurant is a stylish outdoor restaurant featuring palapa-roofed dining areas. Edith's offers the best of Baja cuisine, with prime cuts of beef and freshly caught lobsters as well as classic Caesar salads (a Baja innovation in itself) to fresh sea bass and rack of lamb. Reservations are recommended, particularly for groups. Open daily from 5 PM to 11 PM.

THE FISH HOUSE
624-144-4501
Plaza de la Danza on Boulevard Marina
Price: Expensive
Serving: L, D
Wheelchair Accessible: No

Although the extensive menu includes several steak, chicken, and pasta dishes, the emphasis here—unsurprisingly—is seafood. Lobster lovers can choose their own live lobster from the tank or order a lobster tail combo. A nice wine list offers more than 100 selections from around the world. Dine on the glassed-in outdoor patio that overlooks Cabo's main strip. Open daily from noon to 10 PM.

LA CASA DEL POZO
624-143-6569
Avenida el Pescador and Niños Héroes
Price: Expensive
Serving: L, D
Wheelchair Accessible: Yes

This steak-and-seafood restaurant features an extensive menu that includes several traditional Mexican dishes such as chiles rellenos (cheese-stuffed chiles), which accompany all steak meals. Handmade tortillas and homemade breads are also featured. Meals are served on an open-air patio. Open Monday through Saturday 1 PM to 9:30 PM.

LA GOLONDRINA TRADING POST
624-143-0542
Paseo del Pescador
Price: Expensive
Serving: D
Wheelchair Accessible: Yes

This restaurant has an extensive menu with all sorts of steak and seafood as well as tradi- tional Mexican specialties. Dinners are large and served on a beautiful open-air patio shaded by a huge golondrina tree laden with lanterns. Open daily 5 PM to 10:30 PM.

LA PARRILLADA
MEXICAN STEAK & BBQ
624-143-7424
Hidalgo near Boulevard Marina
Price: Moderate to Expensive
Serving: L, D
Wheelchair Accessible: Yes

Here at this Mexican steakhouse—located a block off Boulevard Marina—you will enjoy baby back ribs as well as chicken and seafood with a baked potato and steamed vegetables. And plenty of free chips and salsa. This is a fun restaurant with a casual atmosphere, including live music every evening. Reservations are recommended during the busy tourist season. Hours vary, depending on the season.

OLÉ-OLÉ TAPAS RESTAURANT & BAR
624-143-0633
Plaza Bonita
Price: Expensive
Serving: B, L, D
Wheelchair Accessible: Yes

Located in Plaza Bonita on the marina, this Spanish restaurant has a surprisingly diverse menu with plenty of steak and seafood dishes to choose from as well as items like barbecue ribs and several Mexican dishes. The menu also offers some nice dessert choices plus espresso drinks for after dinner. Open daily from 7 AM to 11 PM.

SANCHO PANZA WIND BISTRO
624-143-3212
At Tesoro Los Cabos Hotel
Price: Expensive
Serving: D
Wheelchair Accessible: Yes

This elegant restaurant located on the marina has many specialties that primarily feature seafood. Also featured is an extensive wine list with choices from around the world. Plus they have some of the best live music in Cabo, with Latin jazz, blues, and dance music. The kitchen is open from 4 PM to 11 PM. The music starts around 7:30 PM and continues well into the night.

Asian

ARTS & SUSHI

624-144-4554
Plaza Bonita
Price: Moderate
Serving: L, D
Wheelchair Accessible: Yes

This unique restaurant, located behind Olé Olé on the east side of Plaza Bonita, features a combination of sushi and Japanese food with a gallery of Latin American art. The restaurant offers patio seating for those who want to enjoy Cabo's prime people watching, or enjoy people watching of a different kind by sitting inside at the sushi bar, where the chefs put on a show of acrobatic cutlery. For refreshments, enjoy a Japanese beer or one of a variety of sakes offered here. Open daily from 11 AM to 11 PM.

LAN'S CABO

624-143-8828
Plaza Bonita
Price: Moderate
Serving: L, D
Wheelchair Accessible: No

This Chinese restaurant is located in the Plaza Bonita mall, the heart of the action in Cabo San Lucas. If you are in the mood for Chinese, Lan's does it up right with plenty of great selections, including soups and specialty dishes that will make your mouth water. Open daily from 1 PM to 10 PM.

NICKSAN JAPANESE RESTAURANT

624-143-4484
Plaza del la Danza on Boulevard Marina
Price: Expensive
Serving: L, D
Wheelchair Accessible: Yes

With a very extensive menu, this Japanese restaurant and sushi bar offers a fine-dining experience not to be forgotten. The restaurant also features a full bar with many types of sake. Open daily from 11:30 PM to 10:30 PM.

Italian

CAPO SAN GIOVANNI

624-143-0593
Vincente Guerrero near Cabo Wabo
Price: Moderate
Serving: D
Wheelchair Accessible: Yes

This Italian restaurant, located right in the middle of the action in Cabo San Lucas, has a friendly atmosphere and plenty of good food. The dining room is cozy to the point of being slightly cramped, but the patio is comfortable and romantically lit. In any case, the crowds are an indication of how good the food is here. Chef Gianfranco Zappala likes to mingle with his guests to make sure that they are enjoying themselves. His menu is filled with southern Italian specialties that feature plenty of seafood and pasta. Open Tuesday through Sunday 5 PM to 11 PM.

LA DOLCE ITALIAN RESTAURANT

624-143-4122
Hidalgo and Zapata
Price: Moderate
Serving: D
Wheelchair Accessible: Yes

Located a block off Boulevard Marina, this casual-dining establishment offers tradional Italian dishes with plenty of pasta choices and antipasti as well as some great wood-fired pizza. Open daily from 6 PM to 11 PM.

LA TRATTORIA RISTORANTE
624-143-0068
Plaza Bonita
Price: Moderate
Serving: B, L, D
Wheelchair Accessible: Yes

This Italian restaurant is centrally located at the Plaza Bonita mall. The friendly staff serves up all of your favorite Italian dishes, including lasagna, seafood fettuccini, antipasti, and pizza baked in a wood-fired oven. Open daily from 11 AM to midnight.

Party Restaurants

BILLYGAN'S ISLAND RESTAURANT
624-143-4830
Médano Beach and Paseo del Pescador
Price: Moderate
Serving: B, L, D
Wheelchair Accessible: Yes

There's nothing quite like having breakfast in your bathing suit just steps away from the sand. At this Médano Beach restaurant, you can enjoy that experience and come back for lunch or dinner to find that the party is still going strong. That party atmosphere includes daily bikini contests, two-for-one drink specials beginning at 8 AM, and spicy couples dance contests that would barely be legal in some states. Oh, yeah, and they have food, too, featuring seafood as well as burgers and sandwiches. Needless to say, this restaurant attracts a younger crowd, but it's a great place for people-watching. Open daily from 8 AM to 10 PM.

CABO WABO CANTINA
624-143-1188
Vincente Guerrero at Lázaro Cárdenas
Price: Moderate to Expensive
Serving: L, D
Wheelchair Accessible: No

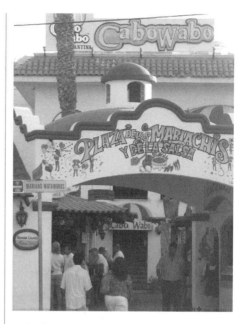

World-famous Cabo Wabo Cantina epitomizes Cabo's nightlife.

Inspired by the 1988 Van Halen song of the same name, this cantina is probably the most famous restaurant in town. Located right in the heart of Cabo's main strip, this bar/restaurant serves up a variety of steak and seafood dishes at reasonable prices. Dine on their open-air patio, and then stick around for the party as live music is played at the Cabo Wabo nightclub every night during the winter. Occasionally, the Red Rocker himself, owner Sammy Hagar, shows up to perform. The restaurant is open from 11 AM to 11 PM, and the club goes from 7 PM to 2 AM.

EL CORAL
624-143-0150
Boulevard Marina and Hidalgo
Price: Inexpensive
Serving: L, D
Wheelchair Accessible: Yes

The sign out front says it all: tequila shots free!! (after dinner only) all you can drink 6 PM to 10 PM. OK, so maybe this isn't five-star dining, but you can get a steak and seafood dinner here for about what you'd pay for a hamburger in the United States. Located right on the main strip, this restaurant has an open-air dining area dominated by a large bar. The tables are handmade and hand painted, sporting colorful Mexican tablecloths, and faded portraits of Pancho Villa adorn the wall. Open daily from 10 AM to 11 PM.

THE CRAZY LOBSTER

624-143-6535
Hidalgo and Zapata
Price: Inexpensive to Moderate
Serving: B, L, D
Wheelchair Accessible: Yes

With happy hour running from 10 AM to 6 PM, there is no doubt that the objective at the Crazy Lobster is to party. This is the Cabo that many travelers come looking for: lobster, beer, and fun. In fact, you can go surf and turf with lobster and a New York steak (the most expensive item on the menu) for well under $20, or pace yourself with fish tacos for less than $2. Open daily from 8 AM to 10 PM.

GIGGLING MARLIN BAR & GRILL

624-143-1182
Boulevard Marina and Matamoros
Price: Inexpensive to Moderate
Serving: B, L, D
Wheelchair Accessible:

The specialty at this restaurant/bar located right at the center of Cabo's main strip is the laid-back atmosphere, where travelers can meet up with old friends and make new ones. Any place that offers stiff drinks and more than 15 appetizers is somewhere to kick back and enjoy yourself. However, if you're looking for a full meal instead, you can get anything from hamburgers to filet mignon. At night, the party picks up with people taking body shots and upside-down tequila shooters, and a live show includes audience members. This restaurant also televises all major sporting events. Open from 8 AM to 1 AM.

MANGO DECK BAR & GRILL

624-143-0901
Médano Beach and Paseo Pescadores
Price: Moderate to Expensive
Serving: B, L, D
Wheelchair Accessible: Yes

Located right on Médano Beach, this place attracts a younger crowd with an extensive menu and a two-for-one happy hour that runs from 8 AM to 6 PM. The fajitas here are very good, but the menu also features steaks, lobster, and even fettuccini. Open daily from 8 AM to 11 PM.

MARGARITAVILLA

624-143-3630
Plaza Bonita on the marina
Price: Expensive
Serving: B, L, D
Wheelchair Accessible: Yes

Hard to miss since it's on the corner of Plaza Bonita, right on the marina, this two-story restaurant has two bars and terrace seating overlooking the marina yachts. The menu is extensive, offering many kinds of fare from salads to steaks and seafood to pasta and Mexican dishes. They also show all major sporting events on TVs mounted throughout the restaurant. Open daily from 8 AM to 11 PM.

BARS AND NIGHTLIFE

Partying is serious business in Cabo, and people come here to party morning, noon, and night. By day, most of the action is found at Médano Beach. At night, the restaurants fill up early, while the clubs and discos get going around 11 PM or midnight, and many continue until 3 or 4 AM. In Baja California, not even Tijuana's Avenida Revolución can match Cabo's propensity for drinking, dancing, and letting it all hang out.

AGAIN & AGAIN

624-143-6323
Lázaro Cárdenas across from the Puerto
Paraiso Mall

If you're barhopping, you'll probably end up
here at some point. The music at Again &
Again varies from disco to Spanish rock to
Norteño. They often have theme nights with
contests. Open daily from noon to 4 AM.

BAROMETRO

624-143-1466
Marina Boardwalk next to Puerto Paraiso Mall

This lounge, conveniently located in the
center of Cabo's nightlife, is a great place to
kick back with a martini and enjoy some
live music. They also offer a menu with Italian specialties and wood-fired pizza. Open
daily from 11 AM to 2 AM.

CALIENTE RACE, SPORTS, & BOOK

624-143-2866
Boulevard Marina at Plaza Náutica

This Mexican mainstay is a great place to
check out your favorite sporting event and
maybe place a bet or two. Plenty of drinks,
good food, and off-track betting are offered
at this bar. They show all major sporting
events, and with TVs tattooing almost every
inch of wall space, you won't miss a moment
of the action. Open 10 AM to midnight during the week and 9 AM to midnight Saturday
and Sunday.

CASINO REAL SPORTS BAR

624-143-1934
Boulevard Marina at Plaza Náutica

This bar offers a full menu and every sporting event imaginable on more than 40 TVs.
There is also a game room with pool tables,
video games, and dartboards. Open 10 AM to
midnight during the week and 9 AM to midnight Saturday and Sunday.

EL AGAVE BAR

624-143-5460
Lázaro Cárdenas near Squid Roe

This tequila bar, conveniently located near
all the action, offers more than 150 kinds of
tequila. They also have some nice appetizers
to keep your energy up while you people
watch. Open daily 10 AM to 11 PM.

EL SQUID ROE BAR & GRILL

624-143-0655
Boulevard Marina near Plaza Bonita

This club is located in a building that somewhat resembles a giant chicken coop from
the outside. Inside, three levels of pure pul-
sating partying make it one of the most
famous and popular clubs on the Cabo
scene. Open daily noon to 3 AM.

JUNGLE BAR

624-143-7401
Plaza de los Mariachis, Boulevard Marina

This bar located between Cabo Wabo and
the Giggling Marlin offers food, drinks,
and dancing. Don't forget to add your
signature to the thousands that cover the
walls and furniture. Nightly specials.
Open 10 AM to 4 AM.

LOVE SHACK

624-144-3253
Morelos and Niños Héroes

This sports bar has a small pub atmosphere
combined with loud music. It's located just
north of Lázaro Cárdenas and offers pool,
burgers, and drinks until 3 AM.

THE NOWHERE BAR

624-143-4493
Plaza Bonita on the Marina

Located right on the marina at Plaza Bonita,
this bar has the perfect location to sit back
with a drink and enjoy the view. It opens at
10 AM—happy hour runs from 5 PM to 9 PM—

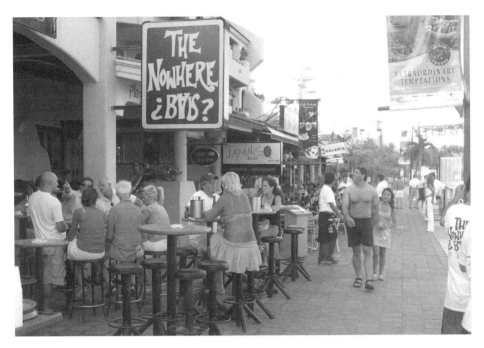

Lunchtime along the boardwalk in Cabo San Lucas

and the party continues until 3 AM. It features dancing with a DJ and ladies' night on Tuesday.

ONIX

624-143-8999
Zaragoza and Niños Héroes

Located just north of Lázaro Cárdenas, this restaurant/bar offers a small menu but specializes in unique mixed drinks.

VOS

624-143-6700
Lázaro Cárdenas and Boulevard Marina

This upstairs lounge in the middle of Cabo's nightlife scene offers a small menu of interesting tapas and plenty of mixed drinks and cocktails. It also has a great view of the downtown area. Wednesday through Monday 6 PM to 2 AM. Closed Tuesday.

ZOO BAR

624-143-5500
Boulevard Marina across from Plaza Bonita

Don't be afraid to party like an animal at this centrally located dance club. Local and guest DJs mix rock, hip-hop, and techno music. Every Thursday is ladies' night. Open daily 9 PM to 4 AM.

BEACHES

Despite the fact that Cabo San Lucas is located right on the water, the choice of beaches within the town is a bit spare. Médano Beach, though clean and great for a swim, can get crowded and is not always the best place to relax if you're traveling with children. Lover's Beach is a must, but the area that is appropriate for swimming can get crowded, and access to this beach is limited. Solmar Beach is gorgeous but not appropriate for swimming. If you are looking for more tranquil beaches for snorkeling or just playing in the water, your best bet is to take a trip out to the Tourist Corridor in the morning, before the crowds show up.

Lover's Beach (Playa del Amor)

No trip to Cabo San Lucas is complete without a jaunt over to Lover's Beach. Located adjacent to the famous arch, this beautiful white-sand beach is a wonderful place to play in the water. The most common way to reach this beach is by water taxi or glass-bottom boat. This 10-minute trip comes complete with a tour of the arch as well as Land's End, a rock sticking out of the water that represents the very tip of the Baja Peninsula. Before depositing you on Lover's Beach, tour guides will also take you around to the beach's treacherously choppy Pacific side, commonly referred to as Divorce Beach. When you disembark, keep in mind that the men who run up offering to help you off the boat and carry your cooler onto the beach are not doing it out of the kindness of their hearts. They will expect a tip for this service. Shoo them away if you don't want to pay them. Being the attraction that it is, Lover's Beach can be a bit crowded, but generally there's plenty of room to wade out and play in the waves that lap onto the shore. It's probably a good idea to stay out of the water on Divorce Beach since the waves strike hard against the shore, and the rip currents are strong. Be sure to bring plenty of good sunscreen since shade is scarce here, and the Cabo sun is strong. There are also no bathrooms on this beach, and the only service is provided by a few vendors walking around selling bottles of water at a significantly inflated price. Tours to the beach begin running around 9 AM. You make arrangements with your guide when you want to be picked up, but the last boat departs from the beach at around 3 PM.

Taking a panga ride is the easiest way to get to Lover's Beach.

Las Playitas

Las Playitas is actually a series of small beaches that lie along the inner harbor from the cannery out to Lover's Beach. Often underwater during high tide, these beaches are often overlooked by tourists. However, when the tide goes out, they become a favorite picnic spot for locals and a great place for snorkeling

Médano Beach

Médano Beach is the main beach in Cabo San Lucas. Located east of Lázaro Cárdenas and the Puerto Paraiso Mall, this is where you will find all the beachfront action. You can get to the beach through any of the hotels along it, or take a water taxi from the marina for about $3 per person. The beach lies along several miles of arc-shaped bay and is lined with resorts and restaurants. The sand is clean and combed, and the water is calm and safe for swimming.

In the morning you should have no problem finding a palapa or umbrella to sit under, but the beach fills up as the afternoon wears on. The beachside restaurants allow you to use their shaded chairs as well as their restrooms as long as you continue to order drinks and snacks. This is not a bad tradeoff for a shady place to people watch and escape the hot sun.

Médano is also filled with vendors selling goods ranging from jewelry and beach coverups to linens and home decorations. Feel free to bargain if you find something you like. Many times you can get a good deal over a nice margarita. If you are not interested, a simple "No gracias" will let them know, and they will be on their way.

For entertainment you can parasail, banana boat, kayak, or rent Jet Skis at this beach. Jet Skis usually run around $50 for a half hour, but here, too, you can bargain down for a cheaper price or extended time. If you're in the mood to stay on the beach, there's always a party going on, with all-day happy hours and various beach contests. Médano is by no means a tranquil beach, but you can have a good time here.

Solmar Beach

Solmar Beach, located on the Pacific Ocean south of Cabo San Lucas, is kind of the polar opposite of Médano. This wide, peaceful beach is free of vendors and great for long walks but not safe for swimming or playing in the water. The beach runs from south of the marina east to the rocks of Land's End. At the east end of the beach, you'll often find guides who will lead you over the rocks to Lover's Beach for a nominal fee. This climb requires minimal footwear, such as a pair of Teva sandals, and is a bit strenuous. As with most of the area beaches along the Pacific side, Solmar has dangerous rip currents and undertows. The sound of the ocean crashing against the sand may make for an appealing atmosphere, but you're much better playing in the lapping waters of the Sea of Cortés. Get to this beach through the resorts that are facing it, located on Avenida Solmar at the south end of Boulevard Marina.

RECREATION

Cabo San Lucas is a playground, and numerous types of diversions are available just minutes away from wherever you're staying. Almost any hotel can sell you tickets or make arrangements for these activities, but you might consider making your own to ensure that you go with a company you're comfortable with. This is particularly true if you're staying in a larger, less personal hotel and are going on more expensive excursions like fishing or div-

The beaches of Las Playitas are popular with locals.

ing trips. For outings like these, you definitely want to make sure that you're going with a quality company.

Information booths are set up all around Cabo San Lucas where tourists gather and where you can ask about activities going on around town. This is a place where you can do many things in a day that you don't otherwise have the opportunity to do *ever*. For example, in a single afternoon, you can swim with dolphins at **Cabo Dolphins** (173-9500) then head down to Médano Beach where several tour companies offer parasailing, in which you rise hundreds of feet in the air while being pulled behind a motorboat. Or you can spend an afternoon in paradise riding horseback along a deserted beach. You will also have no trouble finding tour companies that offer Jet Ski tours of the cape or relaxation on a sailboat that takes you out into the deep blue waters of the Sea of Cortés. Don't forget your Dramamine.

Diving/Snorkeling

Cabo San Lucas's unique location at the convergence of two major bodies of water makes it a prime spot for diving and snorkeling. In fact, famed French oceanographer Jacques Cousteau called the Sea of Cortés the world's richest sea. Two major ocean currents meet in the waters off Cabo San Lucas: the California Current, which moves south along the West Coast of the United States, and the Northern Equatorial Counter Current, which brings warm tropical water north up the coast of Mexico. This convergence mixes nutrient-rich water, creating eddies and gyres that concentrate baitfish in this area, resulting in the waters off Cabo having some of the most diverse marine life found anywhere on the planet.

Jet skis head toward Médano Beach.

The best dive sites in Cabo San Lucas are found around the sea side of El Arco and Lover's Beach. Here, divers plunge into a world that contains a myriad of sea life.

LAND'S END This dive site is located at the southernmost rock of Baja that pokes out of the water just south of Lover's Beach and El Arco. Depths begin at around 25 feet and drop to around 70 feet. Because this is where the Sea of Cortés meets the Pacific Ocean, there are typically strong surges and currents, making this a dive best suited for experienced divers. Some sea lions usually hang out here, and there are opportunities to get up close and personal with them. Farther down, you will encounter rock walls covered with anemones and other sea organisms as well as angelfish, parrotfish, tuna, barberfish, lobsters, and giant hawkfish, among other creatures. Lucky divers may even encounter giant whale sharks.

NEPTUNE'S FINGER Located in Cabo Bay between El Arco and Lover's Beach, this dive site is marked by a huge slab of rock that juts out of the ocean. Here you will drop down to a depth of about 25 feet to a pile of huge boulders covered with seafans. This area is rich in other gorgonias, as well, plus sea sponges and plenty of tropical fish.

PELICAN ROCK This is a clam-protected dive site. With depths beginning at about 20 feet and bottoming out at around 60 feet, Pelican Rock is appropriate for all skill levels. Sea fans cover the slopes of this rock along with schools of Mexican goatfish, angelfish, parrotfish, and lobsters. It is also not unusual to spot eels, rays, and whitetip reef sharks hanging out here.

SAND FALLS East of Neptune's Finger and Pelican Rock, away from the rocky cliffs and Lover's Beach, is an underwater canyon that sinks 120 feet into a blue abyss. This site—appropriate for advanced divers only—is where you will find the famous Sand Falls first discovered by Jacques Cousteau—sand formations that resemble huge cascades. These vertical canyon walls are covered with sea fans and other gorgonias, and all around is such sea life as octopuses, sea horses, and frogfish, among others.

Fishing

Within 40 miles of the Cabo marina is some of the best sport fishing to be found anywhere. In fact, Cabo San Lucas is known as the marlin capital of the world, having earned this moniker with year-round opportunities for nabbing the game fish. Striped marlin migrate into the area in late winter and stay plentiful until midsummer. This is a smaller species of marlin, though it is not unheard of to hook 600-pound striped marlin in the cape area. The larger species of blue and black marlin populate the waters in the summer and fall.

But Cabo is not just for marlin. Over fifty thousand sailfish are caught in the waters off Cabo every year. Other fish commonly caught here include dorado, yellowtail, wahoo, and roosterfish. Your experience will depend significantly on the time of year you come and how much you want to spend. The more than 350 charter boats operating out of the marina include everything from 21-foot *pangas* to 100-plus-foot luxury yachts. When making arrangements for your fishing trip, ask plenty of questions, and be sure that you are comfortable with the company you choose. A day of fishing on an average-sized boat with a capacity of four to eight passengers can run $500 to $1,000, so you want everything to be just

Dorado are a common catch along the cape.
Andrew MacBeth

right. Make sure you know exactly what is included and what their refund policy is just in case you get to the dock to find a floating jalopy waiting for you. Most trips come with a lunch, but you should be prepared to bring your own *cerveza*. Also, you will generally have to buy your own baitfish, which runs about $2 a fish down at the docks. Your skipper should arrange for that to be available for you. Keep in mind that only one billfish is allowed per boat, though there is no limit to the number of catch and releases. During the busy season, running from May through October, it's best to book your boat as far in advance as possible. This is particularly true during October, when the fishing tournaments are taking place.

Kayaking

Cabo San Lucas offers exciting excursions for kayakers of all skill levels. The calm waters of Cabo San Lucas Bay are great for testing your skills, whether paddling around Médano Beach or heading out to Lover's Beach and El Arco. (For more advanced kayakers, multiday trips up the coast are also available.) Kayaks also provide an ideal method of ecotourism. Kayaking tour companies offer this service as a way to get up close and personal with gray whales, whale sharks, and other sea creatures as they pass through the Sea of Cortés.

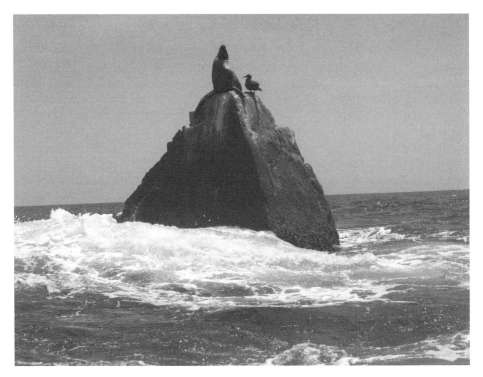

Kayak out to Land's End where perhaps sea lion will share the view.

Off-Roading

Most people come to Cabo San Lucas to jump in the water. However, Cabo's dusty back roads offer plenty of adventure, as well. Several tour companies in town offer dirt bikes, quads, and dune buggies. Some have their own facilities and some offer multiday adventures in the Baja desert, trekking along isolated beaches and dunes or down roads used in the Baja 1000.

Whale Watching

If your trip to Cabo San Lucas takes place between January and March, you will no doubt see whales breaching the water as they complete their 6,000-mile journey from their summer homes in Alaska and Siberia or begin their voyage in the opposite direction. The most common whale is the gray whale, which calve their young in shallow lagoons midway up the Baja Peninsula. (Although these lagoons are hundreds of miles from Cabo San Lucas, they are wonderful settings for viewing these majestic creatures.) Several tour companies in town offer trips right off the coast in small boats or kayaks to get you close up and even eye to eye with the grays and other whales passing through the region. More in-depth trips are also available to Magdelena Bay, the closest calving lagoon to Cabo San Lucas, where you can witness these beautiful creatures frolic with their newborn offspring.

Tour Companies

ADVENTURAS AZUL

624-144-4680 or 602-324-9007 (U.S.);
fax 624-144-4670
www.aventurasazul.com
Marina Cabo Plaza, Local 39-K

This PADI-certified diving operation specializes in guided diving tours. They also offer snorkeling and whale-watching tours.

AEREO CALAFIA ECO-ADVENTURE FLIGHTS

624-143-4302
www.aereocalafia.com.mx
Boulevard Marina, Local A-4, Hotel Plaza Las Glorias

This company operates a fleet of light planes and offers tours throughout Baja California Sur. Check their Web site for flights, fares, and packages.

AMIGOS DEL MAR

624-143-0505 or 513-898-0547 (U.S.); fax 624-143-0887
www.amigosdelmar.com
Boulevard Marina

A PADI, SSI, NAUI, and NASDS certified diving facility, they offer guided tours as well as diving instruction and certification. They also offer natural-history sunset cruises and whale-watching excursions.

ANDROMEDA TOURS

624-143-2765 or 624-147-7136 (cell)
www.scubadivecabo.com
Médano Beach between Paseo del Pescador and Paseo de la Marina

This PADI-certified diving company offers dives from 40 to 120 feet, depending on skill level. They also rent Jet Skis, wave runners, and kayaks and offer parasailing as well as glass-bottom boat trips to Lover's Beach.

Catch a whale-watching cruise from the Cabo San Lucas marina.

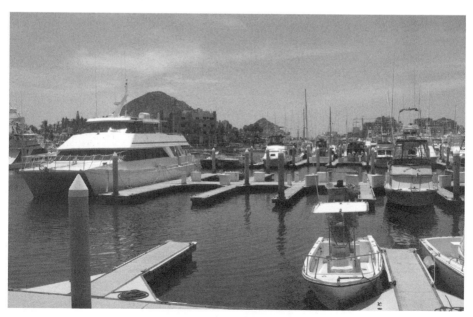

BAJA OUTBACK HUMMER EXPEDITIONS

624-142-9215 or 624-145-2105 (cell)
www.bajaoutback.com
Boulevard Marina

Day tours as well as four-day tours of the cape in H2 Hummers are offered by this company. Day tours last from five to seven hours and can handle groups of up to 45.

BAJA'S ACTIVITIES

624-143-2050
www.bajasactivities.com
Located in front of the Tesoro Hotel

This company arranges a variety of land and water activities. In the Cabo San Lucas area, they offer ATV tours of secluded Pacific beaches as well as Jet Ski tours. On the East Cape, they offer ATV tours of the coast near Punta Gorda as well as horseback riding and snorkeling tours. They also rent scooters for getting around town.

CABO DOLPHINS

624-173-9500 or 888-303-2653 (U.S.)
www.cabodolphins.com
Boulevard Marina, Lote 7

This facility is home to a family of Pacific bottlenose dolphins. For $165 you can swim with the dolphins for an hour. Children must be at least 5 years old and those under 10 must be accompanied by an adult. For $299 you can be "trainer for a day" and swim with the dolphins for more than four hours. Participants must be at least 12 years old and in good physical condition.

CABO EXPEDITIONS

624-143-2700
www.caboexpeditions.com.mx
Plaza Las Glorias Resort, Local C-7

Diving around Neptune's Finger

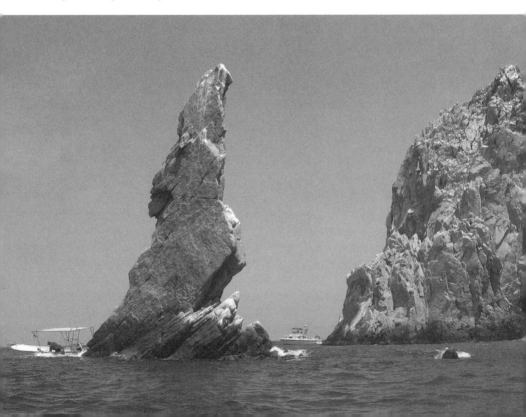

Action-filled excursions on the water are the specialty of this company. These include parasailing ($35 for single and $70 tandem), scuba diving, and snorkeling adventures as well as wave-runner tours and whale-watching adventures.

CABO MAGIC SPORTFISHING
624-105-0403 or 888-475-5337 (U.S./Canada)
www.cabomagic.com
Lázaro Cárdenas

Specializing in sport-fishing expeditions, this company operates a fleet of boats. They have 10 fishing yachts ranging in size from 35 to 78 feet as well as several smaller boats in the 31 to 34 foot range and rent about a half dozen 23-foot *pangas*. They also offer quad ATV tours.

CHARTER LOS CABOS
624-143-4050 or 624-355-3106 (cell)
www.chartercabos.com
Plaza Bonita Mall

This company operates a fleet of eight luxury vessels, including three sailboats and two yachts.

FLY HOOKER SPORTFISHING
624-143-8271 or 624-147-5614
www.flyhooker.com
Lázaro Cárdenas

Fly Hooker offers sportfishing excursions aboard their 31-foot Bertram Flybridge Sportfisher.

JT WATER SPORTS
624-144-4566
www.jtwatersports.com
Médano Beach

JT Watersports offers a variety of water activities including parasailing, wave runners, kayaks, and snorkeling adventures. The also offer sunset cruises and glass-bottom-boat tours.

LAND'S END DIVERS
624-143-2200, 624-157-0582 (cell), or 408-785-6318 (U.S./Canada); fax 624-143-4106
Boulevard Marina

At the Tesoro Los Cabos Cabos Hotel, Land's End Divers operates three customized dive boats that can accommodate six to eight divers per boat. Divers are taken to the popular dive spots in the bay as well as great spots farther afield, such as Cabo Pulmo and Gordo Banks.

OCEANUS
624-143-3929
www.oceanusloscabos.com.mx
Boulevard Marina
Across from the marina

This company takes divers and snorkelers out on a 70-foot, two-deck party boat. Snorkeling trips run $45, and you will be dropped at Cabo's famous arch and nearby spots to enjoy the sea life. For $85 you can also dive in a personal mini sub, an odd-looking air tank that fits around your head like a fishbowl and you ride like a bicycle.

OCEAN RIDERS ADVENTURE TOURS
624-144-4129 or 624-129-8222 (cell)
www.oceanriders.com.mx
Plaza Bonita

Adventurers go out on speedboats for a fun and bumpy tour of Los Cabos. You'll definitely want some Dramamine for this.

PISCES FLEET SPORTFISHING
624-143-1288 or 619-819-7983 (U.S.); fax 624-143-0588 or 619-270-5421 (U.S.)
www.piscessportfishing.com
Cabo Maritime Center Marina 8-6, Suite D-1

This fleet has been operating out of Cabo for more than a quarter of a century. They offer several fishing charter boats of around 30 feet as well as many yacht charters ranging from 32 feet all the way up to a 111-foot deep-sea vessel.

SILVERADOS SPORTFISHING
624-144-4903; fax 624-143-4684
www.silveradosportfishing.com
Hidalgo and Madero, Cabo San Lucas 23410,
Mexico

This company operates a fleet of ten vessels
ranging from 26 feet to 43 feet (most are
around 33 feet).

SUN RIDER ADVENTURE
624-143-2252; fax 624-143-1402
www.sunridertours.com
Marina Dock #4

Boat tours of Los Cabos as well as snorkeling and whale-watching tours are provided
by this company. A restaurant right aboard
the boat can accommodate up to 150 people
with covered and open-air seating.

TIO SPORTS OCEAN & DESERT
624-142-4599 or 624-147-7310 (cell)
www.tiosports.com
Médano Beach in front of Hotel Meliá

This sports-adventure company offers a
variety of excursions, including wave runners, kayaking, ATVs, and scuba diving at
Cabo San Lucas and the East Cape.

TROPICAT
624-143-3739
www.tropicatcabo.com
Camino del Cerro 215 El Pedregal

This company offers sailing tours and private charters aboard a 65-foot-long, 30-

foot-wide Hobie Cat that can accommodate
up to 90 passengers.

UNDERWATER DIVERSIONS
624-143-4004 or 949-226-8987 (U.S.)
www.divecabo.com

This PADI-certified dive center takes guests
to dive sites all around Los Cabos. They can
accommodate up to 16 divers.

URSULA'S SPORTFISHING
624-143-6964 or 624-147-7104 (cell)
www.ursulasfishing.com
Boulevard Marina and Hidalgo

Three sportfishing vessels ranging between
28 and 35 feet are offered by this company.

WIDE OPEN ADVENTURES
624-143-4170 or 949-635-2292 (U.S.); fax
949-635-2298 (U.S.)
www.wideopencabo.com
Plaza Naúdica, Marina Blvd Local B1

This off-roading tour company offers a
four-day adventure that runs from Cabo San
Lucas to La Paz. They also operate a test
track on a 1,500-acre ranch located north of
the city.

YAEL CLASSIC SAILBOAT
624-148-6977
www.cabosail.com
Marina Dock G

This company offers three to five hour
snorkeling tours aboard the *Yael*, a 44-foot
classic sailboat.

Other Diversions
After you've gone swimming with dolphins, ridden horseback on a tropical beach, and
parasailed behind a motorboat, you might be ready for a more mundane afternoon. The
Cinema Paraíso (143-3838) at the Puerto Paraíso mall shows Hollywood's latest releases. Or
you can head over to Caliente (143-2866) or Casino Real (143-1934) at Plaza Náutica and

A glass-bottom boat offers a good view of local sea life.

try your luck with off-track betting or place a bet on your favorite team, and then kick back and enjoy the action. You might also want to check out these two sites:

EL FARO VIEJO   El Faro Viejo, or "The Old Lighthouse," is located 500 feet above a sand dune beach along the Pacific Ocean known as Playa El Faro Viejo. The lighthouse was built in 1890 but has since been replaced by a more modern one. Ruins are all that's left of the lighthouse, which requires a vigorous climb to reach, but the view is spectacular. Several tour companies in town also offer ATV or horseback tours of the site. To get here from Cabo San Lucas, take a left at Kilometer 2 off Highway 19 on the way to Cabo Falso.

IGLESIA DE SAN LUCAS   Iglesia de San Lucas, or the Church of San Lucas, is located on Calle Cabo San Lucas off the main plaza. Known as the most widely attended church in Los Cabos, it was built in 1730 and is a rather unadorned structure compared to many colonial churches in Mexico. However, unlike most things in Cabo San Lucas, it has managed to retain much of its original ambience. Services are Saturdays at 7 PM and Sundays at noon and 8 PM. Bilingual services are held on Sunday at noon. Phone 624-143-2666.

SHOPPING

Although San José del Cabo and nearby Todos Santos are known for shopping much more than Cabo San Lucas, Baja's party-central town is also well equipped with shops offering everything from marginally offensive T-shirts to Mexican handcrafts and fine jewelry. A walk down Cabo's main strip in the middle of the afternoon will repeatedly be met with the calls of merchants soliciting your business, so you don't have to look too hard to find these shops. The stores listed here represent a sampling of what's available.

Arts and Crafts

Artesanias Diana II (624-143-6989; Boulevard Marina and Hidalgo) This shop offers Talavera (artistic pottery) as well as Taxco silver jewelry and arts and crafts from around Mexico. Open daily from 9 AM to 9 PM.

Casa María (624-143-8861; Lázaro Cárdenas and Matamoros) Find a nice selection of arts and crafts, including hand-blown glass, Mexican pottery, and metalwork here. Open Monday through Saturday 9 AM to 9 PM and Sunday 9 AM to 2 PM.

Lombok (624-105-0142; Plaza del Sol, Boulevard Marina #3) This shop offers interesting beachwear, handmade furniture, plus a wide variety of Mexican *artesenía* and handmade jewelry. Open daily from 10 AM to 7 PM.

Mexican Pottery (624-105-0046; Madero between Hidalgo and Guerrero) This store sells Puebla Talavera of all sorts. Open Monday through Friday 10 AM to 9 PM and Saturday 10 AM to 4 PM.

Clothing and Swimwear

Cabostyle (624-143-8595; Plaza Bonita) Here you'll find a wide range of beachwear and beach accessories for the whole family. Open daily from 9 AM to 10 PM.

Chicas Sin Limites (624-143-1500; Hidalgo at Plaza Amelia Wilkes) Beachwear, evening wear, and lingerie can be found at this boutique. Open Monday through Saturday from 9 AM to 1 PM and 2 PM to 6 PM. Cash only.

H2O (624-143-1219; Guerrero and Madero) This boutique sells swimwear as well as evening dresses and women's sportswear. Open Monday through Saturday 9 AM to 8 PM and Sunday 11 AM to 5 PM.

No Worry's (624-143-8575; Boulevard Marina) For a wide variety of casual resort clothing and beachwear. Open daily from 9 AM to 10 PM.

Try out a new look from one of the street stylists working near the marina.

Take time out from shopping to enjoy some local music.

Home Furnishings

Diaz de Luna (624-144-4976; Plaza San Basilio, Local #9,) This shop features desert-style art, furniture, and accessories. Open Monday through Friday 9 AM to 7:30 PM and Saturday 9 AM to 4 PM.

El Callejón (624-143-3188; Hidalgo #3914) Here you'll find a nice selection of home furnishings such as lamps and fabrics as well as Mexican furniture. Open Monday through Saturday 9:30 AM to 7 PM.

Jewelry

Cabo Silverado (624-143-6454; Boulevard Marina, Local #4) This shop offers a large selection of silver jewelry. Open daily between 8:30 AM and 10 PM.

Diamonds International (624-105-0810; Lazaro Cárdenas between Guerrero and Madero) A diverse array of designs and watches can be found in this branch of the international jewelry concern. Open daily 9 AM to 9 PM.

La Mina de Taxco (624-144-4531; Hidalgo between Boulvard Marina and Zapata) This shop specializes in silver jewelry and gifts from Taxco. Open daily 9 AM to 9 PM.

2

SAN JOSÉ DEL CABO AND THE CORRIDOR

Twenty miles northeast of the bustling streets of Cabo San Lucas—and a world away—lies the quiet colonial village of San José del Cabo. There are roughly two parts to this quaint place: the hotel zone where you'll find lodging along a series of beautiful beaches and the downtown area with its clean, tree-lined streets and interesting shops and restaurants. The two areas are connected by Boulevard Antonio Mijares. Located just off the airport road from Cabo San Lucas, San José experienced somewhat of a boom of its own when Cabo San Lucas exploded in the 1980s. Despite this growth, the town has managed to retain its provincial charm and even build on it with an influx of cafés and galleries. Its main square, located on the site of an old mission, is larger and more attractive than Cabo's, with a well-preserved gazebo in the center and a cathedral just beyond it.

Given its serene charms, San José is not the ideal location for those travelers looking for rowdy beach clubs or late-night parties. This is a relaxing place with a slower pace than that of Cabo San Lucas. In the hotel zone, you'll find a tranquil estuary where the silence is broken only by the sounds of the many birds that call it home and the occasional ATV that rumbles through. It's a wonderful place to have an early-evening walk.

The stretch of coast that runs between San José del Cabo and Cabo San Lucas is referred to commonly as the Tourist Corridor or simply the Corridor. Here, along the southernmost stretch of Mexico 1, the Carretera Transpeninsular (Transpeninsular Highway), are sprawling beach resorts, golf courses, and breathtaking views of the ocean. This 20-mile stretch and San José are perfect places to relax or jump off and explore the natural beauty of the East Cape, the pristine stretch of coastline to the northeast.

GENERAL INFORMATION

Police
624-0361
Emergency dial 066

Federal Highway Police
624-146-0573

Ambulance
624-142-2770

Medical Service
624-142-0056

Taxi Service
CABO SHUTTLE
624-142-3939

The main square in San José del Cabo

History

In April 1730 a Jesuit missionary named Nicholas Tamaral founded the mission of San José to convert the Pericu people who inhabited the area. He chose a spot overlooking the Rio San José, 3 miles north of where the town is currently situated. However, because this spot was swarming with mosquitoes, Tamaral quickly moved the mission to the mouth of the estuary. The Pericu tolerated Tamaral until 1734, when he issued an injunction condemning the practice of polygamy, a long-held tradition in Pericu society. After Tamaral punished a Pericu shaman for violating this decree, the natives rebelled, burning the mission and killing Tamaral.

The Spanish returned to the area in 1737, establishing a presidio manned by 30 soldiers to quell the rebellious natives. The nearby Rio San José served as an important source of fresh water for the military outpost as well as for Spanish galleons arriving from the Philippines. This establishment had a significant impact on the native population, for within 30 years, nearly all of the Pericu had died in skirmishes with the Spanish or from European diseases. Those who survived were moved to missions farther north.

Still, San José remained an important military post. During the Mexican-American War, U.S. marines from the U.S. frigate *Portsmouth* occupied the presidio for a short time. However, the Mexican Navy, led by José Antonio Mijares, laid siege to the Americans and ultimately forced them out. San José's town square and main boulevard are named after Mijares to commemorate this victory.

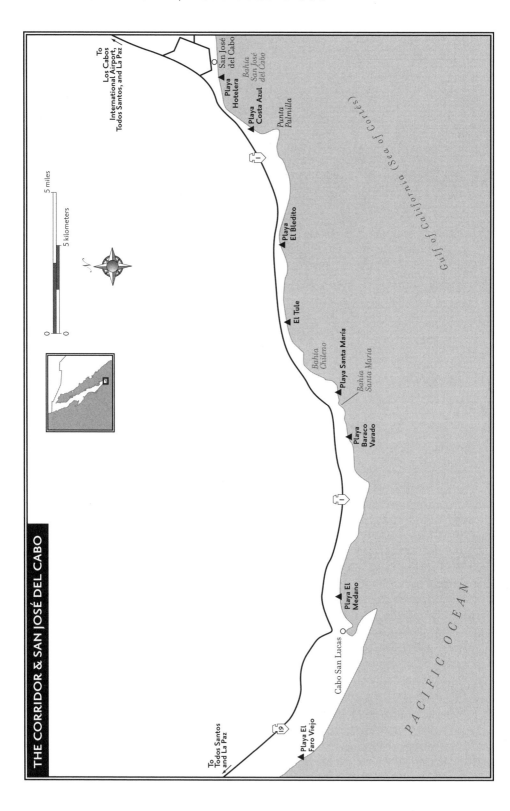

THE CORRIDOR & SAN JOSÉ DEL CABO

To
Los Cabos
International Airport,
Todos Santos, and La Paz

San José
del Cabo

Playa
Hotelera

Bahía
San José
del Cabo

Playa
Costa Azul

Punta
Palmilla

Gulf of California (Sea of Cortes)

5 miles

5 kilometers

Playa
El Bledito

El Tule

Bahía
Chileno

Playa Santa María

Bahía
Santa María

Playa
Baraco
Varado

Playa El
Medano

Cabo San Lucas

To
Todos Santos
and La Paz

Playa El
Faro Viejo

PACIFIC OCEAN

CAR RENTAL COMPANIES

Avis
Los Cabos International Airport
Phone: 624-143-2422
Open daily 7 AM to 8 PM.

Budget
Los Cabos International Airport
Phone: 624-146-5333; fax 624-146-5188
Open daily from 8 AM to 11 PM

Dollar
Boulevard Mauricio Castro
Phone: 624-142-0100; fax 624-142-1098
Open daily from 7 AM to 8 PM

Meliá Cabo Real
Phone: 624-144-0200; fax 624-142-1098
Open daily from 8 AM to 6 PM

Hotel Presidente
Phone: 624-142-2011; fax 624-142-1098
Open daily from 8 AM to 6 PM

Hertz
Los Cabos International Airport
Phone: 624-142-5088; fax 624-142-1812
Open daily from 8 AM to 10:30 PM

Regina Westin Hotel
Phone: 624-142-9113; fax: 624-142-5088
Open daily from 8 AM to 6 PM

National
Los Cabos International Airport
Phone: 624-146-5021; fax: 624-142-1099
Open 24 hours daily

Hotel Casa Del Mar
Phone: 624-145-7700
Open daily 8 AM to 7 PM

Hotel Hilton
Phone: 624-145-6531
Open daily 8 AM to 7 PM

Hotel Sheraton Hacienda Del Mar
Phone: 624-145-6125
Open daily 8 AM to 6 PM

Thrifty
Boulevard San José #2000A
Phone: 624-142-2380
Open daily 7 AM to 9 PM.

San José International Airport
Phone: 624-142-5030
Open daily 7 AM to 11 PM.

As the region's mining industry gave out in the late 19th century, San José lost much of its population. By 1940, when the town church was rebuilt, only a few farmers and fishermen stayed in the area. San José remained a forgotten backwater until the second half of the 20th century, when sportfishermen began to discover what the cape region had to offer. Since the '70s, FONATUR has sponsored several tourism development projects along San José's seashore. Residents, too, have done plenty to develop the town by restoring its 18th-century architecture, preserving its colonial character.

GETTING AROUND

The Los Cabos airport is actually much closer to San José del Cabo than Cabo San Lucas. Bus transport from the airport into town is available, but taxis are also readily obtainable and much more convenient. Once you arrive in town, San José provides plenty of pleasant vistas and window shopping for strolls. Since downtown San José is several miles away from most of the town's hotels, taxis are the best way of getting back and forth from your hotel. Taxis are not metered, so be sure to agree on a price with your driver before getting in. This is a situation in which you can save yourself some money if you speak a little Spanish.

There is also no shortage of car rental agencies inside the main airport terminal and in San José. Since the Los Cabos area is full of beaches, restaurants, and other places you'll want to visit, having your own car is much more convenient than buses, taxis, and even prearranged tours. Renting a car also makes day trips to Todos Santos much easier. One tip: If you plan on renting a car while you're in Los Cabos, save yourself some money and book the car in advance.

WEATHER

The weather in San José del Cabo is almost always warm and sunny. Located in a tropical-arid desert, the area has low humidity that makes it ideal for beachgoing, scuba diving, and other outdoor activities. The average temperature varies throughout the year, with summer highs in the mid 90s and dipping to the mid-70s in winter. In the evening temperatures fall into the mid- to low 60s during the winter, but summer lows only cool down to the high 60s to mid-70s. Visitors generally don't have to worry about rain since the area averages only 10 days of rain and less than 12 inches of precipitation annually. Even though September is considered to be the rainy season, the region usually only sees three or four rainy days during this month and fewer than 5 inches of rain for the whole month. However, San José del Cabo is particularly exposed to relatively rare summer storms called *chubascos,* which roll in from the southeast. These infrequent hurricane swells can bring torrential rain and even floods—though these storms can also make for some great surfing.

ACCOMMODATIONS

In contrast to Cabo San Lucas, accommodations in San José del Cabo are geared toward an older crowd, and room rates and hotel ambiance reflect this. You'll find very few truly inexpensive hotels here and even fewer that cater to young partiers. There are several boutique hotels in town and a few others in the hotel zone, though most hotels here are large resorts. With a few exceptions, the hotels along the Tourist Corridor are sprawling resorts built to minimize their guests' need to leave the hotel grounds. Even the smaller hotels here have more than 50 units. Notable exceptions are the Cabo Surf Hotel, Los Nidos Hotel, and Vista Azul Suites, but even these hotels are generally expensive. However, these hotels do offer a unique combination of seclusion and easy access to the golf courses that have become such big business here.

Budget Hotels

EL DELFIN BLANCO

Manager: Aza Franzen de Lopez
624-142-1212
www.eldelfinblanco.net
Pueblo La Playa, San José del Cabo
Credit Cards: MC, V (for reservations)
Special Features: On-site activities

A collection of thatched-roof bungalows set along the beach in a seaside village make up this hotel. Two of the bungalows have private bathrooms, while three feature shared baths. In all, the hotel can accommodate a group of up to 15 people. Rates: $39 to $50 for double occupancy.

MARISOL PETIT HOTEL

Owners: Marisol Garcia Figaredo
624-142-4040; fax 624-142-2050
www.marisol.com.mx
Paseo San José, San José del Cabo
Credit Cards: MC, V
Special Features: Satellite TV, ocean view

This pretty little boutique hotel is located in the hotel zone near the beach in San José. It features eight rooms decorated in pale colors with Mexican art. Rooms feature satellite TV, two double beds, and a balcony with an ocean view. The property also has a beauty salon and a convenience store. Room rates include a continental breakfast. Rates: $55 to $75.

Midrange Hotels

EL ENCANTO INN

Manager: Blanca Pedrin Torres
624-142-0388; fax 624-142-4620
www.elencantoinn.com
Morelos #133, San José del Cabo
Credit Cards: MC, V
Special Features: On-site spa service, Internet access

This small hacienda-style hotel features 26 intimate rooms set around a garden courtyard. Guests may choose either the garden wing of the hotel or the pool wing. Rooms are decorated in various styles, each with attention to detail and a Mexican feel. The pool itself is heated for year-round use, and the pool area is equipped with wireless Internet access. The hotel also offers two-hour in-room body treatments and Swedish massages. Rates: $89 for a standard room double occupancy. Suites are more expensive.

TROPICANA INN

Manager: Jorge Hijar Estrada
624-142-2311; fax 624-142-1590
www.tropicanacabo.com
Boulevard Antonio Mijares 30, San José del Cabo

Credit Cards: MC, V, AE
Special Features: Swim-up bar, restaurant

Comfortable and quaint, this hotel features 40 Colonial-style air-conditioned rooms. The rooms in this hotel have *saltillo* tile floors and arched doorways for a particularly Mexican feel. Most are furnished with two double beds. The rooms are built around a tiled courtyard with a pool that has a swim-up bar in the middle. The property also features a beautifully appointed palapa guesthouse — perfect for a romantic getaway. Rates: $81 to $138 from May through October and $90 to $146 from November through April.

Luxury Hotels

CASA NATALIA

Owners: Nathalie and Loic Teneoux
624-142-5100; fax 624-142-5110
www.casanatalia.com
Boulevard Antonio Mijares 4, San José del Cabo
Credit Cards MC, V, AE
Special Features: Beach club, pool service, concierge service

Located in the heart of San José, this boutique hotel features 18 luxury European-style suites. Its tranquil setting of waterfalls, tropical flowers, and dozens of palm trees seemingly slows down time. Rooms are individually decorated with unique local artwork and equipped with a private terrace and a personal hammock. Every morning guests are served a full breakfast on these terraces. The hotel also has a full-service gourmet restaurant on site that provides unique dishes. Exclusive beach club shuttle transportation and in-room spa service are also available. Children under 13 are not allowed. Rates start at $230 for double occupancy.

CROWNE PLAZA LOS CABOS

Manager: Mike Van Der Croft
624-142-9292 or 1-866-365-6932 (U.S.);

fax 624-142-9299
www.crowneplaza.com
Paseo San José, San José del Cabo
Credit Cards: MC, V, AE
Special Features: Offers an all-inclusive rate, concierge service

This 333-room resort hotel located in the hotel zone is one of the newest on the cape and certainly one of the most beautiful in San José. The rooms are spacious—each has a view of the Sea of Cortés—and some have easy wheelchair access. The high-ceilinged lobby has bright and colorful furnishings and opens onto the main pool area, where you will find poolside service and an aqua bar. The hotel tries to offer something for everybody, including several large meeting rooms for business and a baby-sitting service for parents looking to get away for a while. Also available: a workout room, high-speed Internet access, and five pools, including a children's pool and one set aside for adults only. The one thing this hotel is short on is nightlife (which is common in San José del Cabo). There is live music three times a week, but those shows are usually sparsely attended. If you're looking for nightlife, see the concierge to arrange transportation to Cabo San Lucas. Several on-site restaurants provide a variety of cuisines from Italian to a sushi bar. The hotel is located across the street from the San José Golf Course. See the golf concierge to make arrangements. Snorkeling, deep-sea fishing, and whale-watching tours are also located conveniently nearby. The waters directly in front of the hotel can be treacherous, so be sure to look out for red flags warning you to stay out. Rates: $216 to $329 for double occupancy.

INTER-CONTINENTAL PRESIDENTE LOS CABOS RESORT

General Manager: Michael Oney
624-142-9229; fax 624-142-0232
www.loscabos.interconti.com

Paseo San José, San José del Cabo
Credit Cards: AE, MC, V
Special Features: Offers an all-inclusive rate, concierge service

One of the hotel zone's older resorts. Its layout is spread out over a large area, so it does not have the tall, grand stature of the newer resorts. The rooms are also a bit smaller, though manageable. Not every room has a view of the water, so be sure to make that request when making reservations. Upgrading to a room with a terrace and hammock is also well worth the extra cost. The hotel has three pools, each with a different "personality." A "quiet pool" is for adults only and is ideal for relaxing and reading. The "family pool" is perfect if you are traveling with children. And the "activities pool" is where you will find loud music and the activities director leading games such as bingo and water volleyball. Six restaurants are on site. Breakfast is served buffet style, with all-you-can-eat waffles, omelets, and pastries. Be sure to try the watermelon *agua fresca,* a traditional Mexican refreshment. For night owls, the lobby bar closes at midnight. For nightlife later than that, you will have to take a taxi into Cabo San Lucas. The hotel offers an 8 PM shuttle that costs $15 per person and returns at 1 AM. Rates average $474 for double occupancy.

POSADA REAL LOS CABOS

Manager: Vicente Landeros Velazquez
624-142-0155; fax 624-142-0460
Paseo San José, San José del Cabo
Credit Cards: MC, V
Special Features: All-inclusive rate, tennis courts, satellite TV

Located in the hotel zone, this all-inclusive beachfront resort is affiliated with the Best Western hotel chain. It features 148 rooms overlooking the beach. The rate covers all meals, snacks, and unlimited domestic drinks and cocktails. The property has a

Enjoying the serenity of the estuary in San José del Cabo

swimming pool and a Jacuzzi as well as an on-site professional putting green, tennis courts, two bars, two restaurants, and beach volleyball. Rates: start at $140 for double occupancy.

ROYAL SOLARIS LOS CABOS
Manager: Gilberto Bermudez
624-145-6800; 1-800-557-7684 (U.S.); fax 624-145-6811
www.clubsolaris.com
Paseo San José, San José del Cabo
Credit Cards: MC, V, AE
Special Features: Gym, tennis court, spa, juniors club, theater

This mammoth all-inclusive hotel-zone resort features four hundred air-conditioned rooms. All rooms are furnished with one double and one king-sized bed, satellite TV, and a balcony. Not all rooms have an ocean view, so be sure to request one that does when making reservations. The property is equipped with a slew of amenities. Some of them are common, such as swimming pools, a game room, a spa, tennis courts, and four restaurants with bars. Oth-ers are rather uncommon, such as a mini water park and a theater offering live shows. Rates: $163 to $276 for a standard room double occupancy.

SUITES LAS PALMAS
Manager: Enrique Navarro
624-142-2131; fax 624-142-4442
www.suiteslaspalmas.com
Km 31 Mexico 1, San José del Cabo
Credit Cards: MC, V, AE
Special Features: Satellite TV, heated pool

Guests of this 69-unit resort hotel are offered a variety of accommodation options. Standard rooms are furnished with a king-sized bed or two queen-sized beds. Standard one-bedroom suites are equipped with a queen-sized bed and a sofa bed as well as a kitchenette. All rooms have a balcony and satellite TV. Rates: $94 to $130 double occupancy.

TOURIST CORRIDOR RESORTS
Cabo Surf Hotel
Owner: Mauricio Balderrama
624-142-2666 or 858-964-5117 (U.S.); fax

624-142-2676
www.cabosurfhotel.com
Playa Acapulquito, Km 28 Mexico 1, Tourist
Corridor
Credit Cards: MC, V, AE
Special Features: Surfing beach, Internet
access, satellite TV

Located right on Playa Acapulquita, this
hotel features 19 air-conditioned rooms
with two double beds or one king-sized
bed. Each room also has Internet access and
satellite TV. The hotel is aptly named since
the beach it sits on is great for surfers of all
skill levels, and the world-famous Costa
Azul break is also nearby. Those guests not
raring to get out in the waves can enjoy a
pool and Jacuzzi in a garden courtyard facing the beach. This area also provides for
stunning photo opportunities. Also on site
is the 7 Seas Restaurant (142-2666), a fine-
dining restaurant that features seafood
dishes and a view of the beach. Rates: $250
to $595 per night plus 13 percent tax and $7
per night service charge.

CASA DEL MAR GOLF RESORT & SPA
Manager: Karla Colin
624-145-7700 or 1-888-227-9621; fax 624-
144-0034
www.casadelmarmexico.com
Km 19.5 Mexico 1, Tourist Corridor
Credit Cards: MC, V, AE
Special Features: On-site spa, on-site gourmet restaurant

This golf resort and luxury spa hotel features 56 Colonial-style units overlooking
the Sea of Cortés. The hotel is conveniently
located near the best golf courses in Los
Cabos, and guests receive preferred tee
times and course discounts. The on-site spa
offers many services to help you rejuvenate
after playing a round of golf. The hotel
grounds are beautifully fashioned like a
hacienda, with a stone fountain at the center of a garden courtyard and an arched
pathway opening onto the sea. Rooms fea-

ture marble tile bathrooms and in-room
Jacuzzis. The on-site El Tapanco Restaurant
(144-0030) offers gourmet Mexican cuisine
on a terrace overlooking the pool area and
an air-conditioned dining room. Rates
average $434 for double occupancy.

DREAMS LOS CABOS ALL SUITES RESORT
Manager: Francisco Silva
624-145-7600; fax 624-144-0216
www.dreamsloscabos.com
Km 18.5 Mexico 1, Tourist Corridor
Credit Cards: MC, V, AE
Special Features: Spa, fitness center, three
pools, five restaurants

This luxurious 194-suite hotel is constructed around a large oasis-style pool area
that is lined with palm trees among three
swimming pools and two swim-up bars.
The property also features a full-service spa
and a fitness center. Five on-site restaurants offer a variety of cuisines. Portofino
offers Italian specialties, Himitsu serves
Pan Asian, the Seaside Grill near the pool
offers casual dining, Oceana has international seafood specialties, and El Patio is a
patio restaurant that is open for breakfast,
lunch, and dinner. Twenty-four-hour room
service is also available, as are all-inclusive
rates. Rooms are luxuriously furnished in
European decor. Junior suites are furnished
with one king-sized bed or two double beds
with a sitting room and a balcony overlooking the sea. They are also equipped with a
fully appointed kitchenette. Rates: start at
$265 double occupancy.

FIESTA AMERICANA GRAND LOS CABOS
Manager: Eduardo Cruz del Rio
624-145-6200 or 1-800-343-7821; fax
624-145-6202
www.fiestamericana.com
Cabo del Sol, Km 10.3 Mexico 1, Tourist
Corridor

Credit Cards: MC, V, AE
Special Features: Spa, kids' club, fitness
center, laundry service, money exchange

Luxury accommodations for all types of
travelers are offered at this 250-room
resort. Air-conditioned rooms are spacious
and equipped with private balconies facing
the pool area. The hotel itself is constructed
in an arc shape around an oasis pool area
consisting of five swimming pools and a
beach club. This area gives way to a wide
beach on the Sea of Cortés. Additionally, the
hotel offers three restaurants, a full-service
spa, a kids' club, and two lit tennis courts.
Guests also receive discounted golf rates.
The on-site Viña Del Mar Restaurant (145-
6200, ext. 8234) has an international menu
and a Mexican buffet on Tuesdays. Rates:
$270 to $350 double occupancy.

HACIENDA DEL MAR RESORT & SPA
Manager: Marcelo Moretti
624-145-8000; fax 624-145-8002
www.sheratonhaciendadelmar.com
Km 10 Mexico 1, Tourist Corridor
Credit Cards: MC, V, AE
Special Features: Two championship golf
courses, full-service spa, kids' club, high-
speed Internet

This 270-room resort is housed in a huge
hacienda-style building on 28 acres overlooking the Sea of Cortés. Rooms, which are
decorated in a warm Mexican decor, have a
private balcony and come equipped with
high-speed Internet access and a Jacuzzi
tub. The hotel offers guests four restaurants
with a choice of buffet meals, casual poolside service, or gourmet dining. Twenty-
four-hour room service is also available.
The hacienda buildings tower over a pool
area that opens onto the beach, while the
property is surrounded by the Cabo del Sol
golf courses. The on-site Cactus Spa offers
European-style treatments to help you relax
after a tough day on the greens. Rates: $329
to $399 from December through March and

$239 to $279 from April through November.

HILTON LOS CABOS RESORT
Manager: Lee Chipman
624-145-6500; fax 624-144-0628
www.hiltonloscabos.com
Km 19.5 Mexico 1, Tourist Corridor
Credit Cards: MC, V, AE
Special Features: Fitness center, kids' center

Situated on a bend on the west side of El
Bledito Beach, this Mediterranean-style
resort features 375 rooms with balconies
overlooking the Sea of Cortés. Junior suites
are nicely appointed with king-sized beds
and separate dressing areas, and bathrooms
are equipped with deep Jacuzzi tubs. Guests
have several dining options, including 24-
hour room service. The Fenicia Restaurant
offers Mediterranean cuisine and live music,
La Hacienda serves Mexican and American
dishes in an informal atmosphere, while the
Sun Fun Hut swim-up bar offers fresh sushi
at noon. The hotel is conveniently located
near several of the best golf courses in Los
Cabos. The resort also has a large spa, two lit
tennis courts, and a kids' club. Rates: $214 to
$330 double occupancy.

HOTEL LOS NIDOS INN
Owner: Karl Klaesson
624-144-0588 or 1-877-417-9658
(U.S./Canada)
www.losnidos.com
Km 18 Mexico 1, Tourist Corridor
Credit Cards: MC, V, AE
Special Features: Personal accommoda-
tions, large suites

This small bed-and-breakfast inn may
seem out of place among the huge resorts of
the Corridor, but it has a relaxing atmosphere and places an emphasis on privacy
and quiet luxury. It features six individually
appointed suites organized around a swimming pool patio. There is a palapa bar next
to the pool, and the whole patio is surrounded by manicured gardens. Suites are

furnished with a king- or queen-sized bed or a queen and a twin. Rates: $95 to $149 double occupancy.

HOTEL TWIN DOLPHIN

Manager: David Halliburton
624-145-8191; fax 624-145-8196
www.twindolphin.com
Km 12 Mexico 1, Tourist Corridor
Credit Cards: MC, V, AE
Special Features: Wireless Internet, tennis courts, fitness center, spa

The 50 rooms of this hotel—relatively spacious and nicely appointed in a desert decor—are spread throughout a secluded 160-acre property in front of Santa Maria Beach. There is wireless Internet access throughout the property. The pool area features a Jacuzzi and a swim-up palapa bar. The on-site La Tortuga Restaurant (145-8190) serves Mexican seafood. On Saturdays they offer a Mexican buffet. Rates: start at $385 double occupancy.

LAS VENTANAS AL PARAÍSO

Manager: Luis Fernandez
624-144-2800; fax 624-144-2801
Km 19.5 Mexico 1, Tourist Corridor
Credit Cards: MC, V, AE
Special Features: Spa, fitness center, satellite TV

This 61-unit hotel offers large suites on a secluded and spacious property next to the Cabo Real golf course. Guests arrive to complimentary tequila and are given free access to a spa and fitness center. The on-site Restaurant at Las Ventanas (144-2800, ext. 8201) offers Mediterranean and Mexican specialties along with a long wine list and live music nightly. The Seagrill Restaurant (144-2800, ext. 8205) serves Mexican seafood specialties in an elegant setting. Reservations are required. Rates: start at around $600 per night double occupancy plus 12 percent tax and 15 percent service fee.

LOS PATIOS

Manager: Carlos Ramos Conchouso
624-145-6070; fax 624-145-6071
www.lospatioshotel.com
Km 4 Mexico 1, Tourist Corridor
Credit Cards: MC, V, AE
Special Features: Beach club, poolside service, conference center

Here, 76 air-conditioned units are sited around a spacious pool area. Rooms are colorfully appointed in an ocean decor. Junior suites are furnished with either a king-sized bed or two queens; all have a private terrace, patio, or balcony with a relaxing hammock. The on-site El Tabachin Restaurant offers international specialties either on an outdoor patio or in an air-conditioned dining room, with a Sunday breakfast buffet. Rates: $70 to $85 double occupancy.

MARBELLA SUITES

Manager: Carlos Escobosa
624-143-6268 or 1-866-654-6160 (U.S.);
fax 624-143-6265
www.marbellasuites.com
Lot 20, El Tezal, Km 3 Mexico 1, Tourist Corridor
Credit Cards: MC, V, AE
Special Features: Free phone service to U.S., fitness center, Internet service

This hacienda-style hotel offers spacious suites situated along a cliff overlooking the Sea of Cortés. Rooms are equipped with balconies, kitchens, and Internet service. Not all rooms have a view of the sea, so be sure to request this when making reservations. Rooms are built around a central pool patio area where you will find a poolside bar. The Marbella Beach Club Restaurant (144-1057) is an open-air palapa restaurant, serving breakfast, lunch, and dinner, with nice views of the sea. Rates: $150 to $300 double occupancy.

MELIÁ CABO REAL

Manager: José Gomez Collazo
624-144-2222 or 1-800-336-3542; fax
624-144-0189
www.caboreal.com/meliacaboreal.htm
Km 19.5 Mexico 1, Tourist Corridor
Credit Cards: MC, V, AE
Special Features: All-inclusive rates, kids'
club, swim-up bar

This 349-unit mammoth hotel has a great
location at the edge of El Bledito Beach.
Nearly all rooms have an ocean view and are
furnished with either two double beds or
one king. Guests are offered an all-inclusive experience, which includes an all-day
unlimited buffet and a la carte dining in
four restaurants plus unlimited drinks and
cocktails in three bars. The property also
features a lagoon-style swimming pool with
an oceanfront Jacuzzi. For further diversion, the hotel has two tennis courts, a fitness center, and a health spa. Rates: start at
$272 double occupancy.

ONE & ONLY PALMILLA

Manager: Andre Boersma
624-146-7000; fax 624-146-7001
www.oneandonlyresorts.com
Km 27.5 Mexico 1, Tourist Corridor
Credit Cards: MC, V, AE
Special Features: Golf course, spa, satellite TV

Located right on Palmilla Beach, this hotel
features 172 balconied units that enjoy
ocean views plus flat-screen satellite TVs.
Amenities include butler service and twice-
daily maid service. The hotel features an
executive conference center and a full-
service spa. The hotel grounds are also
home to the Palmilla Golf Club. Rates: start
at $475 double occupancy.

SUITES TERRAZAS DE POSITANO

Managers: Virginia and Vito Parlato
624-143-9383
www.suitesterrazasdepositano.com
Plaza Positano, Km 3.7 Mexico 1, Tourist

Corridor
Credit Cards: MC, V
Special Features: Boutique hotel, private
terraces, ocean view

This boutique hotel is among the smallest
and most affordable hotels along the Corridor. It features eight air-conditioned suites,
each with a private terrace overlooking the
ocean. Rooms are furnished with one king-
sized bed or two twins. Suites also have fully
equipped kitchens and breakfast nooks. An
on-site deli restaurant offers Mexican coffee and plenty of healthy choices. Rates: $77
to $85 double occupancy.

VISTAZUL SUITES & SPA

Manager: Loren Iriarte
624-144-4727; fax 624-144-4799
www.vistazulsuites.com
Km 3.5 Mexico 1, Tourist Corridor
Credit Cards: MC, V, AE
Special Features: Spa, satellite TV

Located just off the highway east of Cabo
San Lucas, this boutique spa hotel offers 20
suites and 8 studios arrayed in front of an
attractive desert courtyard. Standard rooms
feature a queen-sized bed and a balcony
overlooking the courtyard. One- and two-
bedroom suites are also available. The on-
site spa offers a variety of services,
including Swedish massage, shiatsu, hot-
stone massage, deep-tissue massage, and
Temazcal, an ancient Mexican purification
ritual. Rates average $120 double occu-
pancy.

WESTIN LOS CABOS BEACH & GOLF RESORT

Manager: Patrick Sanchez
624-142-9000 or 1-800-937-8461; fax
624-142-9010
www.westin.com/loscabos
Km 22.5 Mexico 1, Tourist Corridor
Credit Cards: MC, V, AE
Special Features: Private balcony, satellite
TV, kids' club

In a tribute to Cabo's most famous land-mark, this interesting arch-shaped hotel rises out of the desert and towers over a wildly shaped swimming pool area that seems to teeter on a cliff above the Sea of Cortés. Rooms are furnished with one king-sized bed or two doubles and have a private balcony with an ocean or partial ocean view. The hotel features a kids' club for children 4 to 12 years old. For adults, there are tennis courts, business activities center, and a full-service spa. The hotel's Arrecifes Restaurant (142-9000 ext. 8319) offers fine cuisine with Asian, Mexican, and French influences as well as a full bar and live music daily. La Cascada Restaurant—open for breakfast, lunch, and dinner—offers fresh seafood and traditional Mexican recipes. The La Playa poolside restaurant serves more casual fare. Rates: $415 to $579 for a standard room double occupancy.

RV Parks

BRISA DEL MAR RV RESORT
624-142-2935
Km 28 Mexico 1, Tourist Corridor

This RV park is the only one in the Los Cabos area that is located right on the beach. They offer 120 sites with full hookups as well as clean bathrooms with flush toilets, a swimming pool, and boat-storage facilities. A convenience store is located on the property, and they also have bike and water sports equipment rentals. Rates: $20 to $30 per night for RV sites with full hookups and $11 per night for tents. Cabanas with kitchenettes are also available for $60 per night.

VILLA SERENA RV PARK
624-143-0290; fax 624-143-0511
Km 7.5 Mexico 1, Tourist Corridor

Situated on a hill overlooking Cabo San Lucas Bay, this property features 54 spaces with full hookups. It also has a pool and Jacuzzi as well as a laundry room and bath-rooms. Extended and permanent stays can be arranged with the management. Rates: $21 per night.

DINING

For being such a small town, San José del Cabo offers many fashionable restaurants and good, reasonably priced eateries. For the most part, you'll find them along Boule-vard Antonio Mijares and Calle Zaragoza, near the town's main plaza. Perhaps it's due to the fact that San José proudly retains its traditional feel, or maybe it's because San José caters to a different crowd, but you won't find any of the overbearing peddlers

Relaxing in a Hammock

There's nothing quite like relaxing in a beachside hammock with a cool beer in your hand, listening to the waves lap against the shore. However, for the inexperienced hammock sitter, you're likely to won-der what the big deal is all about if you don't know what you're doing. After straddling the hammock in the center and then lifting up your legs, with your head up on one end and your butt in the middle, pressing almost to the ground, you'll probably be there only a minute or two before realizing that it's actually not all that comfortable.

But it's easy to fix this back-wrenching posture. By lying in the hammock diagonally, with your head as far to one side as you can get it, the center of your body going across the center of the ham-mock, and your feet either at the edge or hanging off the other side, you will find that your weight is spread out across the hammock webbing instead of it being concentrated at the butt. Suddenly you will find yourself comfortably lost in contemplation, drifting away into a hang-loose haze.

drumming up business in front of these restaurants such as are present in Cabo San Lucas. The quiet culture that distinguishes San José carries over to its restaurants. Most restaurants in the Tourist Corridor are affiliated with the large resorts, but visitors to the area should try to check out a few independent places before they leave, including Zipper's Bar & Grill, Mama Mia, Lattitude 22+ Steakhouse, and Sunset Da Mona Lisa to watch the sun go down.

Mexican

DAMIANA RESTAURANT BAR & PATIO

624-142-0499
Boulevard Antonio Mijares #8, San José del Cabo
Price: Moderate
Serving: L, D
Wheelchair Accessible: With difficulty

Located in a mid 18th-century hacienda, this restaurant retains the feeling of long ago with a lofty beamed ceiling and Mexican folk art on the walls. Inside the restaurant there are two small salons with only a few tables, and the patio in back is dominated by a huge bougainvillea. At night the tree is lit, giving the patio a romantic radiance. The menu features international and Mexican cuisine, with seafood specialties such as imperial shrimp and bay scallops ceviche. You won't find a more perfect restaurant for a romantic night out. This restaurant is popular with the locals, so if you plan on eating here from November to May, be sure to make reservations in advance. Open daily 10:30 AM to 10:30 PM.

EL CHILAR RESTAURANT

624-142-2544
Benito Juárez #1490, San José del Cabo
Price: Moderate
Serving: L, D
Wheelchair Accessible: With difficulty

Since you're in Mexico, you'll want to enjoy some authentic Mexican cuisine. In this rustic and cozy restaurant, Chef Armando Montano does his best to make you feel at home in his country. Murals of the Virgin of Guadalupe adorn the walls, and the open kitchen adds a casual atmosphere. Though the chef's dishes are a little less than traditional, the creativity of his menu more than makes up for it. He changes the menu every month, but you're sure to find several imaginative offerings such as grilled flank steak with chipotle-based pumpkin-seed sauce and baby squash or duck enchiladas with a sweet and creamy white-mole sauce. The restaurant has a wide selection of wines and tequilas, with suggested pairings to your meal. At night the tables are lit by candles—just the right touch for travelers on a romantic vacation. Open Monday through Saturday 3 PM to 10 PM.

EL COMAL

624-142-5508
Plaza La Casa de Don Rodrigo, Boulevard Antonio Mijares, San José del Cabo
Price: Moderate
Serving: L, D
Wheelchair Accessible: Yes

This attractive Mexican restaurant—tucked off San José's main street behind several *artesenía* shops—offers up wonderful takes on traditional Mexican cuisine. The menu is filled with interesting dishes from all over Mexico. The restaurant is housed in a historic building from the 1800s; however, meals are served on a gorgeous outdoor patio with handmade chairs and fragrant trees providing shade and atmosphere. Open daily 11 AM to 3 PM for lunch and 6 PM to 10 PM for dinner.

JAZMIN'S RESTAURANT

624-142-1760
Morelos between Zaragoza and Obrogón, San José del Cabo
Price: Moderate to Expensive

Serving: B, L, D
Wheelchair Accessible: Yes

Located near the historic cathedral of San José, this colorfully decorated Mexican restaurant offers an interesting menu of vegetarian and seafood specialties as well as several traditional *carne* dishes. The menu also features drinks from the restaurant's full bar as well as a nice kid's menu. Open daily 8 AM to 11 PM.

VILLA SERENA RESTAURANT & BAR

624-145-8244
Km 7.5 Mexico 1, Tourist Corridor
Price: Moderate
Serving: B, L, D
Wheelchair Accessible: Yes

This Mexican seafood restaurant is located in the Corridor 5 miles east of Cabo San Lucas. The palapa dining area provides nice views of the sea as you feast on traditional and down-to-earth Mexican fare. The service is welcoming, and the drinks are very good. Open daily 7 AM to 10 PM.

Asian

BAAN THAI

624-142-3344
Morelos s/n Comonfort, El Centro, San José del Cabo
Price: Moderate
Serving: L, D
Wheelchair Accessible: No

This Pan-Asian restaurant has an extensive menu of soups, wok dishes, and curries. The smell of the Far Eastern spices alone is enough to lure you to the table. Here you'll dine on a meal that evokes such exotic cultures as those of Thailand, Laos, and China—a meal that you won't soon forget. They have a very good wine list, as well. Although it's not far off the main square, this restaurant is notoriously hard to find, so you may have to ask directions. If you're taking a cab, your driver can certainly point you in the right direction. Reservations are recommended. Open daily 12 PM to 10:30 PM.

Cafés

CENTRAL GOURMET

624-104-3274
Plaza La Europea, Km 6.7 Mexico 1, Tourist Corridor
Price: Inexpensive to Moderate
Serving: B, L, D
Wheelchair Accessible: Yes

For a nice change of pace, this Corridor café offers signature sandwiches and gourmet pizza, not to mention sushi. Cap things off with a darn good cup of coffee. Delivery is available. Open 8 AM to 10:30 PM Tuesday through Sunday.

CORRE CAMINOS CAFÉ

624-142-3510
Plaza La Misión #1A, San José del Cabo
Price: Inexpensive
Serving: B, L, D
Wheelchair Accessible: Yes

This Internet café and bakery is a great place to get started in the morning with an espresso drink and a fresh-baked pastry. For later on in the day, they also have gourmet sandwiches.

DELIGHT CAFÉ GOURMET

624-144-6043
Las Tiendas de Palmilla Local A-101, Km 27.5 Mexico 1, Tourist Corridor
Price: Inexpensive
Serving: B, L, D
Wheelchair Accessible: Yes

Located within a shopping center in the Corridor, this European-style coffeehouse features gourmet coffee, espresso drinks, and freshly baked pastries. Open daily 7 AM to 9 PM.

GATO EN LA LUNA
624-144-6159
Las Tiendas de Palmilla Local A-102, Km
27.5 Mexico 1, Tourist Corridor
Price: Moderate
Serving: B, L, D
Wheelchair Accessible: Yes

This Corridor Internet café offers wonderful
gourmet fare as well as specialty wines and
other drinks. Open Monday through Saturday 7 AM to 7 PM and Sunday 9 AM to 5 PM.

HABANERO'S
624-142-2626
Plaza Misión, Boulevard Antonio Mijares,
San José del Cabo
Price: Moderate
Serving: L, D
Wheelchair Accessible: Yes

Chef Tadd Chapman offers varied dishes of
Mexican fusion cuisine at this local hotspot.
The menu includes tacos, burritos, and
organic salads for lunch and steak and
seafood with signature sauces for dinner.
Call ahead for reservations, or expect to
wait. Open daily 11 AM to 10 PM.

ZIPPER'S BAR & GRILL
624-172-6162
Km 28.5 Mexico 1, Tourist Corridor
Price: Inexpensive to Moderate
Serving: L, D
Wheelchair Accessible: Yes

This well-known Corridor bar and grill
offers Mexican and American fare on a patio
overlooking the Sea of Cortés. They also
feature live music every Friday night and
satellite TV for all major sporting events.
Open daily 11 AM to 10:30 PM.

Steak and Seafood

LA PANGA ANTIGUA
624-142-4041
Zaragoza #20, San José del Cabo
Price: Expensive

Serving: L, D
Wheelchair Accessible: With difficulty

The menu at this elegant steak-and-seafood
restaurant is based largely on the freshest
local seafood available. The fine menu
items are prepared by an award-winning
chef and served on an intimate patio courtyard. Open daily 11:30 AM to 10:30 PM.

LATTITUDE 22+ ROADHOUSE
624-143-1516
Km 4.5 Mexico 1, Tourist Corridor
Price: Inexpensive to Moderate
Serving: B, L, D
Wheelchair Accessible: Yes

Show up at this popular Corridor steakhouse
ready for a casual meal and a good time. The
walls are covered with old fishing memora-
bilia, providing the perfect atmosphere for
hanging out and enjoying a fine meal. And
you'll be doing plenty of that with food this
good and so reasonably priced. Live music is
featured Thursday through Saturday nights.
Open Wednesday through Monday 8 AM to 11
PM (kitchen closes at 10 PM).

THE TULIP TREE
624-146-9900
Plaza José Green, Boulevard Antonio
Mijares, San José del Cabo
Price: Moderate
Serving: D
Wheelchair Accessible: Yes

This steak-and-seafood restaurant specializes in generous portions of traditional fare
at reasonable prices. Besides the surf and
turf, they offer pastas, soups, salads, and a
full bar. Meals are served in a pleasant
courtyard setting. Open daily 5 PM to 10 PM.

Italian

ALFREDO DI ROMA
624-142-1001
Boulevard Antonio Mijares s/n, San José del
Cabo

Price: Moderate to Expensive
Serving: D
Wheelchair Accessible: Yes

Located in the Inter-Continental Presidente resort, this restaurant almost makes you forget that you're in Mexico. Unlike busy high-end restaurants, the atmosphere in Da Antonio practically convinces you that you are having dinner in a small Italian villa with a view of the Mediterranean. Though large enough for family gatherings, Alfredo di Roma has an intimate ambiance that also makes it perfect for romantic dinners. The Palermo, Sicily–born chef prepares a variety of Italian dishes, though seafood is the specialty here. You'll find it in many of the dishes, such as the *insalata tiepida di mare* (warm seafood salad with lime dressing), *linguine ai frutti di mare* (linguine with seafood), and the *risotto all pescatora* (risotto with seafood). Finish your meal with one of the elaborate Italian deserts and an espresso, complemented by the amazing view. Reservations are recommended. Open daily from 6 PM to 11 PM.

PASSAPAROLA
624-146-3825
Plaza José Green, Boulevard Antonio Mijares, San José del Cabo
Price: Inexpensive to Moderate
Serving: L, D
Wheelchair Accessible: No

This Italian bistro is located in downtown San José, upstairs from Banamex. They offer pastas, wine, and espresso drinks at reasonable prices. Open daily 1:30 PM to 10 PM.

SUNSET DA MONA LISA
624-145-8160
Km 5.5 Mexico 1, Tourist Corridor
Price: Expensive
Serving: B, L, D
Wheelchair Accessible: No

This fine-dining Italian restaurant is located in the Corridor in a building with multilevel glass-enclosed terraces especially designed for enjoying the sunset. The view of the famous arch of Cabo San Lucas provides the perfect setting for a romantic dinner. Open daily from 8 AM to 11 PM.

International
FRENCH RIVIERA RESTAURANT
624-104-3125
Plaza Del Rey, Km 6.5 Mexico 1, Tourist Corridor
Price: Expensive
Serving: L, D
Wheelchair Accessible: Yes

Despite the inauspicious name, this stylish French restaurant located in the Tourist Corridor offers some of the most elegant cuisine in Los Cabos. French master chef Jacques Chretien combines fresh seafood, organically grown produce, and a French sensibility to create such dishes as braised red snapper with potatoes au gratin and steamed seafood with onion flan and mushrooms with fried calamari. Open daily from 12 PM to 4 PM and 5 PM to 10:30 PM for dinner.
A bakery spinoff of this restaurant, located on the corner of Miguel Hidalgo and Doblado in San José, is called the French Riviera Restaurant & Bakery (142-3350). It's open daily 7:30 AM to 10:30 PM.

LOCAL EIGHT
624-142-6655
Plaza Misión, Boulevard Antonio Mijares, San José del Cabo
Price: Expensive
Serving: L, D
Wheelchair Accessible: No

This fine-dining restaurant serves international cuisine with an emphasis on seafood. Dishes such as Cajun blackened snapper and Tagarashi tuna demonstrate how far flung its influences are. They also offer a generous wine list. Dinner is served on an intimately lit patio. Open Monday through Friday 11 AM to 10:30 PM and Saturday and Sunday 6 PM to 10:30 PM.

MAMA MIA

624-142-3939
Km 29.5 Mexico 1, Tourist Corridor
Price: Moderate
Serving: B, L, D
Wheelchair Accessible: Yes

With a menu that offers plenty of Mexican fare, Italian food, international cuisine, and a Saturday night barbecue, this restaurant is hard to define. It's located in a large thatched-roof palapa on the beach and offers live music every night. The atmosphere here is definitely one of revelry. Every day has a theme, including Tuesday's Mexican fiesta, Thursday's karaoke party, and Sunday's breakfast buffet to name a few. Open daily 8 AM to 10 PM.

BARS AND NIGHTLIFE

OK, San José del Cabo doesn't have anywhere near the nightlife that you'll find down the road in Cabo San Lucas. However, the bars and lounges that the town does have generally cater to an older crowd. Most people beyond their mid-20s who are looking for nightlife should be able to find a spot that suits them in San José. If you are staying in the Tourist Corridor and would like to remain there for nighttime diversions, your options are generally limited to resort lounges and a number of restaurants that keep their bars open late.

CACTUS JACK'S

624-142-5601
Boulevard Antonio Mijares at Juárez

This fun-loving bar and grill is a popular hangout that stays open late on the weekends and features Karaoke some nights. Open Wednesday through Monday 9 AM to 4 AM.

ESCALA KARAOKE SPORTS BAR

624-142-5155
Boulevard Antonio Mijares

How often do you get to have a combination of karaoke and sports? This bar has eight TVs for all major sporting events as well as DJ music along with live music and dancing on Saturday nights. Open daily 10 AM to 4 AM.

LA SANTA WINE BAR

624-142-5601
Miguel Hidalgo and Álvaro Obregón

Located in an old building with a beamed ceiling and quarry-stone walls, this stylish lounge carries more than 130 wines from around the world. They also offer a nice menu of tapas. Open Monday through Saturday 6 PM to 2 AM.

SHOOTERS SPORT BAR

624-146-9900
Manuel Doblado and Boulevard Antonio Mijares

This sports bar is located upstairs at the Tulip Tree Restaurant. They have pool tables, satellite TV to go along with "cheap drinks and good eats."

BEACHES

San José and the Corridor have no equivalent to Médano Beach, the party beach in Cabo San Lucas. The long beach that fronts the resorts of San José's hotel zone is wide and beautiful, but because of its rough surf and strong undertow, it is unsuitable for swimming and thus pretty deserted. The Corridor, though, has several beaches that are located in protected coves and provide great swimming and snorkeling. While a few of them have some services located nearby, for the most part they're pretty secluded, especially when compared to Médano Beach. This is not to say that these Corridor beaches are empty. Buses and tour groups usually begin bringing in crowds in late morning, so early morning generally provides the best snorkeling and swimming.

PLAYA HOTELERA This single expansive stretch of sand runs west from the estuary past all the hotels on the hotel zone until it reaches the Mayan Resorts Golf Course and the beach of Costa Azul. But unlike Médano Beach in Cabo San Lucas, Playa Hotelera is not commonly regarded as a swimming beach because it has a fairly brutal shore break. Furthermore, because nearby tour companies lead horseback-riding tours along this beach—particularly the eastern end near the estuary—the sand is sometimes littered with horse droppings. For these reasons you won't find many people along this beach, and vendors are pretty much nonexistent here. Visitors to the resorts that line this beach generally appreciate it solely for its view and rely on hotel pools for swimming.

COSTA AZUL A bend in the coast marks the end of Playa Hotelera and the beginning of Playa Costa Azul. This half-mile stretch of beach is world famous for its surf break, which carries the same name. To reach this beach, take exit Km 28.5 off Mexico 1, and turn right at the bridge. The beach is just a few meters beyond. For nonsurfers, perhaps the only reason to come here is to eat at Zippers (624-172-6162), a palapa restaurant overlooking the ocean at the southwest end of this beach. They serve American-style food daily from 11 AM to 10 PM. Farther west, just past the rocky bluffs, you'll find Playa Acapulquito, also known as "Old Man's Beach," which is a good beach for inexperienced surfers. However, because this is an easy-access beach with plenty of parking, it does tend to get crowded, particularly on weekends.

PLAYA PALMILLA Located off the Km 27 exit on Mexico 1, this beautiful white-sand beach is quite different than either Costa Azul and Playa Acapulquito, which lie just to the east. Here a protrusion of rocks creates a protected cove that makes this beach safe for swimming. For this reason, Playa Palmilla attracts families and snorkelers. The beach itself stretches for about a mile, with plenty of palapas to provide shade. If you're interested in snorkeling or scuba diving, a dive shop is located just off the east side of the beach, along with a restaurant that has snacks and cold drinks and a restroom for patrons.

PLAYA BLEDITO This somewhat secluded beach is located in front of the Meliá Cabo Real and the Hilton Los Cabos beach resorts off exit Km 19.5 on Mexico 1. You can access the beach by going through the resorts. The wide, crescent-shaped stretch of sand has a man-made breakwater that diminishes waves and undertow, making it a great place for families looking to get away from the crowds of their resort pools. But you should still use caution, particularly during the late summer and early fall storm season. Just to the east of this beach is Playa La Concha, which has a tide pool, restaurant, showers, and equipment rental.

PLAYA EL TULE With its waves and secluded location, this beach is often overlooked by tourists. It's a good surfing beach with a right reef break that has its biggest swells during the wintertime. However, watch out for the boulders that are scattered about in the surf. Playa El Tule has easy access, and camping is allowed here—an option best achieved with a four-wheel-drive vehicle. To get here, look for the EL TULE sign at around km 16.2 on Mexico 1.

PLAYA CHILENO This beach—located at km 14 on Mexico 1, just west of the Hotel Cabo San Lucas—is an excellent place for diving and snorkeling. Chileno is also one of the most popular beaches among locals, so it can get crowded on weekends. On the beach's western end, you'll find a reef that is abundant with tropical fish, and on the east end there are tide pools that are great for kids. There are restrooms with showers and some palm trees set back from the beach, but it's a good idea to bring a beach umbrella if you have one. Get here in the morning before the tour buses arrive, and you'll find the beach empty—for a few hours, at least, you can have it to yourself. However, toward the afternoon, it does tend to fill up.

PLAYA SANTA MARIA The beautiful horseshoe-shaped cove known as Playa Santa Maria is a protected marine sanctuary and offers some of the best snorkeling in Los Cabos. To get here from the highway, look for the beach access sign around Km 13, near the Twin Dolphin Hotel, and follow the dirt road to the parking area. Once again, arrive early to beat the

Swimming is fantastic at Playa Chileno.

Get to the beach early to beat the crowds.

crowds and for the best snorkeling. Tour operators often bring clients here around 10 AM. There are no services here and very little shade, so come prepared.

PLAYA LAS VIUDAS If Playa Santa Maria is too crowded for your taste, scramble over the rocks on the west end of the beach to reach Playa Las Viudas, also known as "Widow's Beach" or "Twin Dolphin Beach." Or locate this picturesque beach from Km 12 on Mexico 1. After you exit onto the beach access road, head down a rough dirt stretch for almost a half mile before reaching the beach. This is a lesser-known beach, free of crowds and vendors, making it a great place to come for a secluded picnic and soaking up the sun. Dogs are also allowed here, though here again there are no facilities and almost no shade, so bring your own gear.

PLAYA BARCO VARADO A Japanese freighter once crashed into the rocks at this site. The rusting wreckage of the freighter remains on the rocks, providing an interesting backdrop to the ocean view near Cabo Del Sol Hotel and the finishing hole of the resort's golf course designed by Jack Nicklaus. If you decide to explore the waters near the wreck, use caution. There's a strong undertow here. Access this beach through the Cabo Del Sol Hotel entrance off exit Km 11 on Mexico 1.

RECREATION

San José del Cabo and the Tourist Corridor is a playground that straddles the desert and the sea, providing activities that feature the best of both worlds. The area is world famous for both its sport fishing and golfing. Since the late 1980s, the Corridor has become tattooed with courses designed by the biggest names in golf, including Jack Nicklaus and Robert Trent Jones. These courses are generally well kept and provide spectacular vistas of the ocean and desert. Not a golfer? All along the coast you'll find wonderful opportunities for snorkeling and diving as well as surfing. Inland, the desert roads and mountains provide a great setting for hiking, horseback riding, and piloting ATVs.

Unlike most places in on the east coast of Baja California Sur, San José del Cabo is not great for kayaking. Ocean waves slam along its shores, making San José beaches a dangerous place to set off. The exception to this is the estuary, where you will find a calm lagoon rich with wildlife, making it an excellent kayaking destination.

The deserts and mountains around San José provide a great setting for mountain biking. Bikes can be rented in town for about $5 an hour or $20 a day. However, you should not head out to Los Cabos's remote back roads alone, and you should always have a detailed map and plenty of supplies.

Another activity that has been growing in popularity in Los Cabos in recent years is rock climbing. Several local outdoor tour groups offer guided climbing tours of the area.

Does hanging onto a cable suspended over a river gorge appeal to you? If so, for a quick thrill, head out to the Costa Azul Canyon just north of Mexico 1 from Playa Costa Azul for a zip-line ride over the river canyon.

Diving and Snorkeling

The waters all along the coast of Los Cabos offer excellent diving and snorkeling opportunities, many accessed easily and just minutes from the hotels along the Corridor. The relatively calm waters of Playa Chileno and Playa Santa Maria offer dives that are spectacular yet

Playa Santa Maria is just one of the many beautiful beaches in "The Corridor."

close by and appropriate for inexperienced divers. For more experienced divers, the far-ther-out Gorda Banks offers a deep-water experience that includes the large sport fish that have made Los Cabos famous. And for an amazing day trip appropriate for divers of all skill levels, Cabo Pulmo along the East Cape offers one of the most unique diving experiences in Baja California.

CHILENO BAY This dive spot is located in front of Playa Chileno. Here, a web of finger-shaped reefs covered in tree coral awaits. This reef formation begins right at the shore of the beach and extends out into the bay for about a half mile. The reef is home to a wide assortment of tropical sea life, such as starfish, sea fans, sponges, and sea urchins. The reef also attracts large numbers of schooling tropical fish and occasionally sea turtles and nurse sharks. This dive spot is appropriate for snorkelers and divers of all skill levels, beginning with a drop to about 30 feet then gradually plunging to around 80 feet.

SANTA MARIA REEF This dive spot in front of Playa Santa Maria is ideal for underwater photographers. Located within Santa Maria's sheltered cove, this site is home to colorful gorgonians, including sea fans that line the cove's rock walls, as well as hard and soft corals, octopuses, and eels. Tropical reef fish are in abundance here, plus the occasional bat ray, sea bass, and sea turtle. Appropriate for intermediate divers, this dive drops to around 40 feet.

WHALES HEAD POINT This point at the west end of Playa Barco Varado is formed by a large cliff that juts out of the bay. The cliff drops 20 to 30 feet into the water, depending on tidal

Snorkelers at Playa Chileno

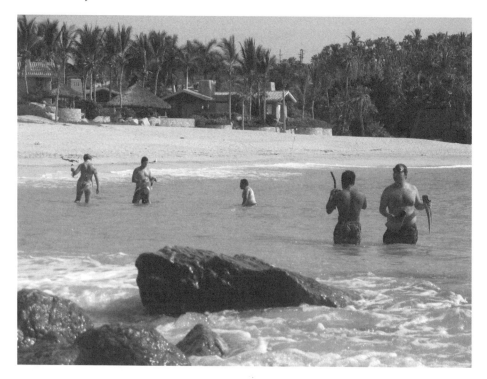

conditions. It features dazzling rock formations that are the habitation of nurse sharks, sea turtles, octopuses, and the occasional guitarfish. This dive, which drops to depths from 30 to 60 feet, is appropriate for intermediate to advanced divers.

THE BLOWHOLE This dive spot—located near Playa Chileno—features a rock formation with a hole about 25 feet below the surface that, as the current surges through, shoots water out an opening at the top. When this happens, as the name suggests, it resembles a whale spouting from its blowhole. The underwater site itself is a labyrinth of rocks and canyons. The rock walls are covered in gorgonians and large coral heads. The area is inhabited by small nurse sharks and guitar fish along with a variety of rays. This is an intermediate dive, with depths of 40 to about 100 feet.

GORDA BANKS Many wonderful dive sites can be found farther afield along the East Cape, and most of the diving guides of Los Cabos offer trips to these places. One of these dive sites is known as Gorda Banks, a seamount some 50 miles south of the cape that necessitates a two-hour boat ride to reach it. The tip of this seamount lies at a depth of about 110 to 120 feet, and it's covered with bushes of black coral. Marine life commonly seen on this deep-water dive includes dorado, tuna, wahoo, marlin, and even hammerhead and giant whale sharks. This dive is for advanced divers only because of the depths and currents.

CABO PULMO NATIONAL MARINE SANCTUARY This East Cape diving location features the only live coral reef in the Sea of Cortés and more than 350 species of marine life. Getting to this remote location requires a two-hour drive from Los Cabo, but there are nearly 20 prime dive sites that are appropriate for beginning to advanced divers.

Fishing

San José del Cabo and the East Cape offer plenty of great sportfishing opportunities. Here you can find reef *panga* fishing close to the shore as well as excellent offshore fishing. You also have your choice between Pacific waters and great spots in the Sea of Cortés. Discovered in the 1950s, the Gorda Banks in particular offer excellent prospects to catch marlin, wahoo, and tuna. The inshore fishing seasons for cooler-water fish such as yellowtail peaks between March and June. The season for roosterfish, cabrilla, and various species of snapper peaks between April and July. The chances of catching wahoo and snook are the best during the warmer months of July through October. A catch-and-release policy is encouraged by most fishing charters.

Golf

Over the last decade, Los Cabos has become one of North America's premier golf destinations. This is due in large part to a California developer named Don Koll who, in 1990, commissioned Hall of Fame golfer Jack Nicklaus to design 27 holes of golf at the Palmilla resort in San José del Cabo. Since then, Nicklaus has gone on to design two other golf courses in the area (El Dorado Golf Club at Cabo Real and Cabo del Sol), and other well-known golfers have also designed courses here. Los Cabos has been the site of the PGA Senior Slam Tournament since 1995, and golfing has grown to be the number-two attraction in Los Cabos, with panoramic ocean views lending themselves to create an incredible golfing experience. Most of the courses are fairly new and in very good condition. All these courses are located in the Tourist Corridor, within 20 minutes from just about any hotel in the area.

Golfing the day away in the Corridor

CABO DEL SOL

624-145-8200; U.S. Tee Time Reservations: 1-877-944-2226
Km 7.5 Mexico 1

This is actually comprised of two golf courses, which are closer to Cabo San Lucas than San José del Cabo. The 18-hole Ocean Course was designed by Jack Nicklaus and was the location of the 1998 Senior Slam. The front nine is 3,597 yards, the back nine is 3,440 yards, and the course has a par-72 rating. The Desert Course, designed by Tome Weiskopf, is farther inland but ocean views are guaranteed from every hole. Carts are available. Greens fees for the Ocean Course are $350 from October through June and $250 from July through September. Green fees for the Desert Course are $185 to $220 from October through September and $165 from July through September. Twilight rates are also available at the Desert Course.

CABO REAL

624-144-0040; U.S. Tee Time Reservations: 1-877-944-2226
Km 19.5 Mexico 1

This 18-hole Robert Trent Jones–designed course is located about halfway between Cabo San Lucas and San José del Cabo. Offering very nice ocean views, the course has a front nine of 3,943 yards, a back nine of 3,452 yards, and a par-72 rating. Greens fees are regularly $176 and $115 during the summer. Carts are available.

CABO SAN LUCAS COUNTRY CLUB

624-143-4653; U.S. Tee Time Reservations: 1-877-461-3667
Lázaro Cárdenas

This 18-hole course is located just outside downtown Cabo San Lucas on the north side of Mexico 1. It was designed by Roy Dye with a front nine of 3,651 yards, a back nine of 3,596 yards, and a par-72 rating. This course features seven lakes, with natural desert and mountain terrain. Greens fees are $182 before 2 pm and $125 after 2 pm. Fees include a cart.

EL DORADO COUNTRY CLUB
624-144-5451, 1-800-393-0400 (U.S.)
Km 19.5 Mexico 1

This is the latest Jack Nicklaus–designed course in Los Cabos. The front nine is 3,440 yards, the back nine is 3,610 yards, and the course has a par-72 rating. The 18-hole course has four lakes and five holes overlooking the Sea of Cortés. Greens fees are $246 for daytime hours and $168 for twilight hours.

PALMILLA GOLF CLUB
624-144-5524; U.S. Tee Time Reservations: 1-800-637-2226
Km 27.5 Mexico 1,

This 18-hole course was the first designed by Jack Nicklaus in Mexico. It was also the site of the 1997 Senior PGA Senior Slam. Totaling 6,900 yards, it has a par-72 rating. Greens fees are regularly $185 and $90 during the summer.

Off-Roading
ATV tours with either seaside vistas or in the mountains have become a popular way to spend a day in Los Cabos. In the San José area, the local mountains and dirt roads north of town offer a particularly good setting for off-roading. Tour operators are available through-

A tour guide rolls his quad through San José del Cabo.

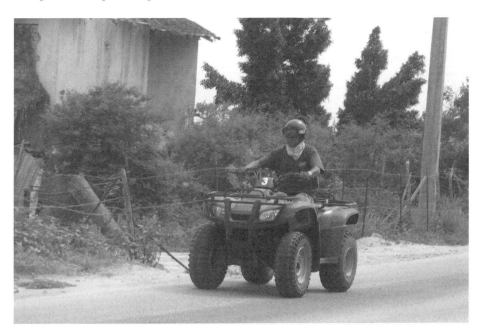

out San José and the East Cape who will guide you through desert arroyos, sand dunes, and even through the heart of town. Other off-road options include dirt-bike rentals and guided tours, horseback riding, and even extended multiday Hummer tours. An abundance of relatively flat terrain around San José is great for dirt bikes, particularly along the unpaved roads of the East Cape.

Hiking

Several locations near San José del Cabo are great for hiking. The estuary is an obvious first choice for a nice, relaxing day hike. For a more demanding jaunt, the Sierra de la Laguna Mountains to the north of San José will provide you with a challenging adventure. The trails to these mountain passes are easily accessible, though they narrow out and become more difficult to follow as you climb in elevation and the terrain becomes rockier. Along the way, the vegetation quickly changes from desert to forest. Guided day hikes and ecotours include hot springs and waterfalls near Santiago, a small village an hour to the north. These pools provide a great location for relaxing and having a picnic. Other hiking tours feature fossil fields and old mining ghost towns. Make sure you have good footwear and plenty of water. Because the dry temperatures can get so hot during the day and fall so precipitously at night, you should have at least 2 liters of water per person per day as well as warm clothing for the evening. Also be aware that from July through October, rains can cause flash floods and wash out hiking trails. Hiking is best in the winter, with comfortable temperatures in the 70s.

Surfing

The Tourist Corridor provides several surfing spots that are appropriate for all skill levels. This area picks up southerly and southwesterly swells, though westerly swells are blocked by the tip of Cabo San Lucas. When there is a swell, the most famous break along the Corridor is Costa Azul at Km 28.5 on Mexico 1. A surf shop here rents boards and gives advice. However, fame has also brought crowds, and chances are you'll be fighting for position if you surf here. Less experienced surfers should head just to the west to Playa Acapulquito, where a right-breaking swell offers good surfing for beginners. At El Tule—at Km 16.2 on Mexico 1, roughly the center of the Corridor—expert surfers will find a fast break that goes both ways. Closer to Cabo San Lucas just in front of the Misiones del Cabo Hotel, a left-point break provides decent-sized waves. This also should be left to more experienced surfers.

Whale Watching

From January to March, visitors to Los Cabos are treated to the sight of gray whales spouting offshore as they make their 6,000-mile journey to their winter homes in the warm waters of the Sea of Cortés. These bottom-feeding animals are gentle voyagers that tend to stay close to shore. They once traveled the coasts of Europe and Asia but are now confined to the North Pacific from Alaska to Mexico. These whales seek shelter in the protected, shallow lagoons of San Ignacio, Ojo de Liebre, and Magdalena Bay, where they birth their calves. In the lagoons the calves learn survival skills as they prepare to make the summer journey back to Alaska. Although several other species frequent this area, grays are the most common. The visible tip of the whale breaking the surface of the water as it exhales is usually the first sign of whale activity. Lucky whale watchers may catch sight of these giant mammals breaching as they propel themselves almost completely out of the water.

Tour Companies

BAJA RIDE

624-120-5335; cell 624-122-0203
www.bajaride.com
Km 28 Mexico 1, San José del Cabo

This tour company specializes in off-road
motorcycle and quad adventures. Half-day
tours run around $150, and full-day tours
are $225. Groups are guided through desert
valleys and mountain terrain as well as
trails along the Pacific Ocean and the Sea of
Cortés. Three- and four-day tours are also
available from October through June. Or if
you just want to ride around town, scooters
are available for rental.

BAJA WILD

624-172-6300
www.bajawild.com
Km 28 Mexico 1, San José del Cabo

This company operates a wide variety of
outdoor tours. On water, they offer full- and
half-day kayak snorkeling combination
tours on the East Cape as well as half-day
trips in Cabo San Lucas Bay. They also offer
surfing lessons along the Corridor as well as
whale-watching expeditions. Inland, they
offer hiking adventures that take you to the
desert canyons and waterfalls north of
San José as well as ATV and rapelling
adventures.

BAJA XPLORER EXPEDITIONS

624-142-4082
www.bajaxplorer.com
Retorno #8 s/n Col. Magisterial, San José
del Cabo

This company offers wave-runner tours of
the Cabo coast. From January through
March, they also offer whale-watching
expeditions in which you can view whales
from the close-up view of your own wave
runner. They also book tours to Todos Santos and dolphin-swimming adventures.

CANOPY COSTA AZUL

624-105-9311; fax 624-105-9312
www.canopycostaazul.com
Cañon Costa Azul, San José del Cabo

This facility is located just north of Mexico 1
from Playa Costa Azul. The company operates more than 3 miles of zip line suspended over the Costa Azul river canyon.
Zip-line tours include ecological information. You should wear comfortable clothing,
and a small backpack is allowed. Tours are
not physically demanding, but the company
advises that people with severe back or neck
problems, heart concerns or other disabili-
ties should carefully evaluate if the ride is
"suitable for their particular condition."
Riders must be at least seven years old and
weigh less than 250 pounds.

DESERT PARK

624-144-0127
www.desertpark.net
Km 19.5 Mexico 1, San José del Cabo

This tour company offers ATV nature tours
through 25 miles of rugged trails in the
Cabo Real Private Nature Reserve. They
have a training course so that you can get
comfortable riding your Honda ATV quad
before setting off along the nature trails.
Jeans or long pants and sneakers are highly
advisable.

GRAY LINE LOS CABOS

624-146-9410 or 206-331-3812 (U.S.); fax
624-146-9412
www.graylineloscabos.com
Plaza San José Suite 1, San José del Cabo

This is a full-activities management company that books everything from scuba diving adventures and ecotours to cultural
events and bar-hopping tours. They can
also arrange transportation, from a transport van to limousine service.

MIKE DOYLE SURF SCHOOL

624-172-6188 or 858-964-5117 (U.S.); fax
624-142-2676
www.cabosurfshop.com
Km 28 Playa Acapulquito, San José del Cabo

Perched above Playa Acapulquito, this surf
school is open from 8 to 8 daily. One hour of
personal instruction runs about $65. A surf
shop here rents surfboards, boogie boards,
and snorkel gear.

NOMADAS DE BAJA

624-146-9612
www.nomadasdebaja.com
Calle Zaragoza s/n Col. 1 de Febrero, San
José del Cabo

This adventure-tour group offers all types
of outdoor excursions around the Los Cabos
that focus on presenting the unique atmosphere of Baja in an authentic way. This
includes kayaking, mountain biking, scuba
diving, and Jeep safari tours. They also offer
desert, mountain, and ocean adventures
farther north on the Baja peninsula.

PANCHITO TOURS

624-143-8532
www.panchitotours.com
Col. Cerro de los Venados #19, Cabo San Lucas

This company offers city van tours of Los
Cabos. The four-hour tour takes you to historical missions, beaches, golf courses, and
other notable locations. Panchito also offers
snorkeling, kayaking, and whale-watching
adventures.

TRANSCABO GROUP

624-146-0888 or 1-866-403-5987
(U.S./Canada); fax 624-146-1486
www.transcabo.com
Km 43 Mexico 1, San José del Cabo

This is a private transportation company
that can provide you with high-class transportation around southern Baja. They can
also book adventure tours of all types.

Jet skiing along the Corridor

Other Attractions

SAN JOSÉ ESTUARY Estero San José, the San José Estuary, is the largest body of fresh water in southern Baja, and its 2,000-plus acres of marshland provide a home to 150 species of birds. In addition to birds, this large lagoon is a sanctuary for insects, aquatic mammals, turtles, many species of fish, and more than 300 types of flora. You can observe this abundance of life while kayaking or just wandering down the path. You can also explore this area by horseback, mountain bike, or even ATV. Open daily from dawn until dusk.

CACTI MUNDO
624-146-9191
Boulevard Antonio Mijares

This unique botanical garden features an incredible variety of cacti and other rare plants. For more than 15 years, the nurseries of Cacti Mundo have successfully reproduced and conserved these rare species. Today the circular-shaped garden contains about 5,000 plants representing 850 different species.

SHOPPING

San José del Cabo is known for its shopping, and here you'll find *artesenía* and interior-design products of good quality in the shops along Calle Zaragoza and Boulevard Antonio Mijares. However, this good quality is often accompanied by high prices. Along the Tourist Corridor, shopping is mostly confined to resort gift shops. But a few malls offer good shopping, in particular Las Tiendas de Palmilla at Km 27.5 on Mexico 1, the Carretera Transpeninsular (Transpeninsular Highway).

Arts and Crafts
Forja Casa y Jardin (624-143-9383; Km 4 Mexico 1, Tourist Corridor. Though quarters are cramped, you'll find a nice selection of traditional Mexican pottery and ironwork at competitive prices. Open daily 10 AM to 6 PM.

Copal (624-142-3070; Plaza Mijares 10, San José del Cabo) A selection of traditional *artesenía,* such as colorful carved animals from Oaxaca and masks from Guerrero Negro. Though the prices are much higher than they would be in those places, they are not unreasonable. Open daily 9 AM to 10:30 PM.

Curios Carmela (624-142-1117; Boulevard Antonio Mijares 43, San José del Cabo) A large assortment of Mexican handcrafts, such as glassware, pottery, and woven hammocks, are available here at very reasonable prices. Open daily 10 AM to 7 PM.

Clothing and Swimwear
Big Tony (624-142-0744; Zaragoza, San José del Cabo) This surf shop offers casual beachwear and swimsuits at reasonable prices. Open daily 9 AM to 9:30 PM.

Casa Vieja (624-144-6161; Las Tiendas de Palmilla, Local B-204, Km 27.5 Mexico 1, San José del Cabo) A unique selection of styles for men and women by Mexican designers. Accessories include handbags, scarves, and shoes. Open Monday through Saturday 10:30 AM to 9 PM.

Plenty of fine artesenia can be found in San José del Cabo.

Tropica Calipso Swimwear (624-144-6158; Las Tiendas de Palmilla, Local A-125, Km 27.5 Mexico 1, San José del Cabo) This swimwear shop offers an extensive selection of swimwear in a variety of styles, colors, and print designs as well as accessories. Open daily 9 AM to 9 PM.

Home Furnishings

Adobe Design (624-142-4281; Plaza San José, Km 32 Mexico 1, Tourist Corridor. A first-rate collection of antique and modern Mexican-style furniture. You 'll also find a variety of Adobe-style decorations such as ironwork, pottery, and Mexican tile. Open Monday through Friday 9 AM to 8 PM.

Antigua de Mexico (624-144-6121; Las Tiendas de Palmilla, Local A-107, Km 27.5 Mexico 1, Tourist Corridor.) This store offers plenty of knickknacks along with contemporary and Mexican Colonial-style furniture from Jalisco. Open Monday through Saturday 9 AM to 6 PM.

Casa Maya Los Cabos (624-142-6611; Km 32.5 Mexico 1, Tourist Corridor.) Custom-made antique-wood and forged-iron furniture along with a selection of tapestries and window treatments. However, not all pieces are flawless. Open Monday through Friday 9 AM to 7 PM and Saturday 9 AM to 5 PM.

Jewelry

La Mina (624-142-3747; Boulevard Antonio Mijares #33, San José del Cabo) Here find silver and gold jewelry designs embedded with diamonds and other precious stones. Open daily 9 AM to 9 PM.

Legacy Jewelers (624-144-6038; Las Tiendas de Palmilla, Local 202-B, Km 27.5 Mexico 1, Tourist Corridor) This fine-jewelry shop offers gold jewelry designs embedded with precious gemstones. Open daily 10:30 AM to 6 PM.

Silver Toños Taxco (624-142-6470; Boulevard Antonio Mijares, San José del Cabo) A wide variety of jewelry and silver knickknacks from Taxco. Open daily 9 AM to 9 PM.

The town square in Todos Santos

3

SIDE TRIPS ON THE CAPE

Most visitors to Baja's cape region never make it outside the Tourist Corridor of Los Cabos, and some don't even leave their hotel's grounds. These travelers likely have a very well-defined set of expectations for their visit to the region, which the facilities in Los Cabos are perfectly designed to meet. However, for travelers wanting to step outside of Cabos's tourist world and reach for something unexpected, the Cape region has plenty to offer. Depending on just how adventurous you want to get, the Cape is filled with places rich in history, intrigue, and culture. Furthermore, each region of the Cape has a distinct personality created by geography and historical circumstances. For example, the towns along the East Cape provide amazing vistas and wonderful opportunities for sportfishing and diving. The town of Todos Santos is an oasis of art and enchantment with famous surfing beaches located nearby and several boutique hotels devoted to relaxation and healing. Whether it's off-roading, windsurfing, or just getting into an RV and getting away from it all, the Cape is an adventure waiting to happen.

Todos Santos

If you arrive in Todos Santos by bus, you may step off onto the street in front of the PEMEX gas station wondering why you took the time to come to such a rustic little town. To begin with, few of its dusty streets are even paved, and walking down the roads off Degollado, where the bus drops you off, it's easy to feel as though you are lost in some back neighborhood. However, just under the surface (actually, just down the street, on Benito Juárez) is a place filled with beautiful boutique hotels, interesting art galleries, and wonderful restaurants. With approximately six thousand residents, this town, which sits on the Tropic of Cancer, is southern Baja's foremost artists' colony, where many prominent artists showcase their work.

HISTORY

In 1724 the Jesuit missionary Father Jaime Bravo established a farming community here to take advantage of the fertile ground and underwater springs. His purpose was to provide supplies to the nearby community of La Paz. He also established a church and called it Todos Santos, or "All Saints."

The town was a success and within a few years was shipping hundreds of burro-loads of provisions east to La Paz. Within a quarter century the population of the town had outstripped that of La Paz. Todos Santos reached mission status in 1749 and was renamed Nuestra Señora del pilar de Todos Santos. In 1840 Todos Santos was secularized, but the

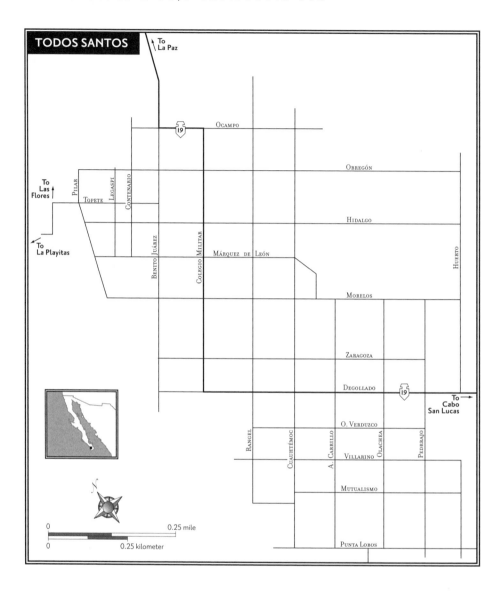

town continued to thrive due to sugarcane production. By the late 19th century, the town was supporting eight sugar mills.

After World War II sugar prices fell sharply, and the freshwater spring that fed Todos Santos dried up. The town appeared to by dying and by the mid-'60s, all the mills in town had shut down. Todos Santos remained an insignificant dot on the map until the 1980s, when the natural spring suddenly began flowing again, allowing a large quantity of crops to once again be grown here. Also in the '80s the road between Cabo San Lucas and San Pedro was paved, and suddenly tourists began to pop up. The road also brought in artists who were drawn to the town by its authenticity, solitude, and mysterious manner. Over the last decade developers and American expatriates have picked up on the town's colonial charm and have polished it just a bit. Its historic feel is so well-known that Mexico's National

Institute of History and Anthropology has declared the town a national monument, and restoration guidelines are strictly enforced.

GETTING THERE

Todos Santos is roughly an hour's drive from both La Paz and Cabo San Lucas. The trip from either town is fairly straightforward, though, as always, driving Mexico 1, the Carretera Transpeninsular (Transpeninsular Highway), at night is not recommended. Bus service from each city is also available and generally runs about every hour. If you are traveling to a hotel along the El Pescadoro, such as La Alianza, inform the bus driver, and he will let you out within walking distance of your destination. Taxis are another option for getting here, and the fare can usually be bartered down to around $100. Because Todos Santos is generally noticeably cooler than either Los Cabos or La Paz during the summer and warmer during the winter, you may find it more pleasant than those places.

Within Todos Santos, the town is small enough that walking can get you pretty much anywhere you want to go except the beach. The buses that pass through town on their way to Cabo San Lucas can provide inexpensive transport to the more popular beaches. Just let the driver know where you want to get to, and he will let you out at the proper mile (or in this case *kilometer*) marker. Getting back, just wave down a bus heading toward town, and the driver will stop for you. A few makeshift taxis in town will also take you out to the beach, and you can make arrangements to be picked up at a later time. Round-trip transport to Playa Cerritos runs around $40. Be sure to set all prices before you accept a ride since there are no meters.

ACCOMMODATIONS

Because Todos Santos is just an hour away from both Cabo San Lucas and La Paz, most people treat it as a day trip. However, if you do plan on staying over, be sure to make arrangements for your accommodations in advance. There aren't a lot of hotels in Todos Santos, and they're spread out and tucked away. This means that they're not only hard to find but also they'd often be booked up once you get there. Many are actually large private residences owned mostly by expatriate Americans who have converted part of their property into vacation rentals or small, attractive boutique hotels that are perfect for relaxation.

ALEGRIA INN
Manager: Elena Moreno
612-145-0700; fax 612-145-0292
www.alegriainn.net

La Cachora, Todos Santos
Credit Cards: None

Located in a Mexican hacienda on a large plot of land, this hotel has a small patio pool adjacent to an old mango grove. With seven units available, it is a rather intimate hotel with personal service. The rooms are nicely appointed with *saltillo* tile and hand-carved Mexican furniture. The daily maid service is accompanied by fresh flowers, and a massage therapist is available to provide you with a variety of treatments. Rates: $125, $165, or $185, depending on the room.

CASA BENTLEY
Owner: Bob Bentley
612-145-0276
www.casabentleybaja.com
38 Calle del Pilar, Todos Santos
Credit Cards: MC, V (through PayPal)

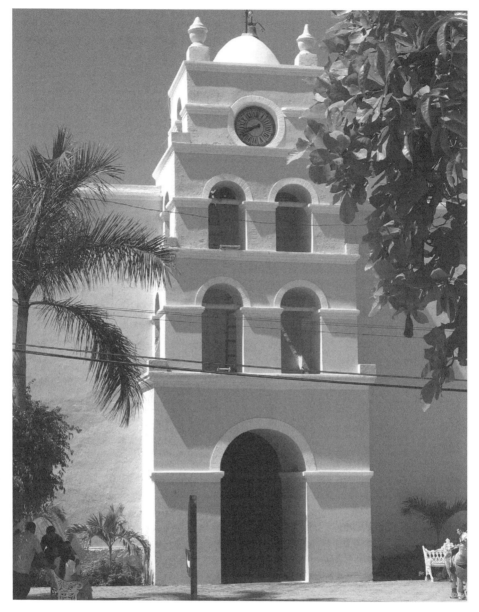

Nuestra Señora del pilar de Todas Santos

This rustic hotel with its blue-tile pool and quarry-stone walls has six attractive units, individually decorated with local art. They are furnished with either king- or queen-sized beds and fine Egyptian-cotton linens. The gardens that surround the pool area and trickling fountains create a relaxed atmosphere to enjoy after a long day of perusing the shops of Todos Santos or surfing the waves of the nearby Pacific beaches. The hotel itself is conveniently located off the main plaza, close to shops and restaurants and not far from the beach. Rates: $90 to $250 from October 16 through May 15 and $90 to $170 from May 16 through October 15. Lower rates are available for stays longer than four nights.

CASA RAYO DEL SOL
Manager: Happy Moreno
612-145-0472
La Poza, Todos Santos
Credit Cards: None

This vacation rental is a three-bedroom, two-bath palapa house located a short distance from the beach. The house has a large living room as well as a full kitchen and breakfast nook plus a washer and dryer as well as satellite TV. Bedrooms are furnished with king- and queen-sized beds. Rates: $250 nightly and $1,500 weekly.

THE GARDEN CASITA
Owners: Howard and Janice Ekman
612-145-0129
Mutualismo, Todos Santos
Credit Cards: None

This guesthouse vacation rental combines the rustic feel of exposed brick walls and a thatched palapa roof with modern amenities such as a DVD player and wireless Internet. The bedroom is furnished with a queen-sized bed, and a separate loft area has a double bed. The property also features an enclosed patio courtyard with fruit trees and tropical gardens. Rates: $85 nightly and $395 weekly November through July 14; $55 nightly and $325 weekly July 15 through October.

HACIENDA TODOS LOS SANTOS
Owner/Manager: Karen Rodriguez Bremer
612-145-0547
Benito Juárez, Todos Santos
Credit Cards: None

This hacienda compound offers three guesthouses, two equipped with full kitchens and all with a private garden terrace or patio and spacious bathrooms. Each house is well maintained and beautifully appointed. Bedrooms are furnished with either queen- or king-sized beds. A pool on the property is perfect for lounging on warm evenings. This hotel is located at the south end of Calle Benito Juárez. Rates average $122 per night.

HOTEL CALIFORNIA
Owners: John and Debbie Stewart
612-145-0525
Calle Juarez, Todos Santos
Credit Cards: MC, V

No, this is not the Hotel California made famous by the 1970 Eagles hit of the same name. However, that's one of the many rumors that surround this boutique hotel. After all, it is located off a dark desert highway around the corner from a mission. What is certain is that the Hotel California, which sits in the heart of downtown Todos Santos, is a luxurious retreat with 11 colorfully appointed rooms and plenty of desert ambiance. Among these rooms is a large penthouse with a rooftop garden terrace offering ocean and mountain views. The hotel's La Coronela Restaurant also provides good food with a warm atmosphere. Rates: start at $85 for a standard room double occupancy.

HOTEL SANTA ROSA
Manager: Heraclio Antonio Manriquez Carrillo
612-145-0394
www.hotelsantarosa.com.mx
Calle Agustin Olachea and Col. San Vicente, Todos Santos
Credit Cards: None

Located a block and a half south of Degollado, this attractive eight-room hotel may seem a little bit off the beaten path, but the town is so small that it isn't much of an issue. Rooms are nicely appointed and furnished with one or two queen-sized beds and a hideaway bed as well as a fully equipped kitchen. The rooms face a good-sized pool area and include a Jacuzzi. The hotel is also equipped with wireless Internet access. Rates: start at $50 per night. Discounted rates are available for stays longer than seven nights.

JARDIN DEL PILAR CASITA SUITES
Owner: Rick Switzer and Rosalie Parker
612-145-0386
www.jardindepilar.com
Calle Pilar between Topete and Hidalgo, Todos Santos
Credit Cards: None

This hotel offers two privately gated suites located right off the historic district. These suites are actually small houses that are well-kept and nicely appointed with colorful fabrics and original art. They are

equipped with kitchenettes, CD stereo systems, and wireless Internet access. Behind them is a private patio area with lush gardens and a small pool that is perfect for relaxing. Rates: $105 to $120 per night. Discounted rates are available for stays longer than seven nights.

LA ALIANZA GUEST QUARTERS
Owner: Degora McIntire
612-108-0436
www.bajaturtle.com
Km 19 Mexico 19, at El Pescadero
Credit Cards: None

This secluded six-room hotel located 10 minutes south of Todos Santos overlooks vast orchard fields and is a short walk away from San Pedrito Point, one of the most popular surfing spots in Baja. The rooms are tastfully decorated with a blend of tradiional and modern decor and come with a

The garden pool at the Todos Santos Inn

king-sized, queen-sized, or two twin beds. The grounds provide views of both the mountains and the ocean. Rates: start at $95 to $110 from June through September, $115 to $130 from October through May, and $135 to $150 during Easter week and between December 15 through January 7.

LAS PALMAS TROPICALES

Manager: Wendy Cain
www.tropicalcasitas.com
Mexico 19, El Pescadero
Credit Cards: None

This hotel offers four secluded beachfront casitas overlooking San Pedrito Point, a sea turtle preserve and one of Baja's most famous surfing spots. Getting to the beach from this hotel requires walking out your front door. The casitas are individually decorated with a Mexican desert decor. Three have one bedroom, and one is a two-bedroom unit; all bedrooms are furnished with a queen-sized bed. Rates: $75 to $140 per night, depending on the casita.

TODOS SANTOS INN

Manager: John Stoltzfus
612-145-0040
www.todossantosinn.com
Calle Legasi #33, Todos Santos
Credit Cards: MC, V

Calling a hotel the most charming in Todos Santos is really saying something because there are several beautiful hotels here. But it would be hard to beat the luxurious elegance offered at the Todos Santos Inn. A converted 19th-century sugar baron's hacienda, this hotel from the outside is a squat brick building that is only interesting because it looks so old. But this changes once you step inside the well-maintained courtyard with its brick arches and stone fountain. Follow the stone walkway down to the lush garden area, and you'll find a beautiful pool and the La Popa Wine Bar. This is also the setting for the daily colonial breakfast. The rooms are fur-

A typical room at the Todos Santos Inn

nished with a large net-draped bed and heavy antique furniture. For extra-secluded comfort, check out the garden suites located down by the pool. Throughout, this hotel evokes the feel of colonial Mexico, a place with lots of history. This ambiance is completed by the bullet holes found in the faded frescoes of the lobby. Rates: $125 for terrace rooms ($165 December 20 through January 6). Junior suites and garden suites are more expensive.

RV Parks

EL LITRO TRAILER PARK

612-125-0121
Calle Olachea at Mexico 19, Todos Santos

These facilities offer RV spaces with electricity, water, and sewer along with flush toilets and hot showers. There are also tent spaces available with lots of shade. Rates: $10 per night for RVs and $4 for tents. First come, first serve. Guards are on duty 24 hours a day.

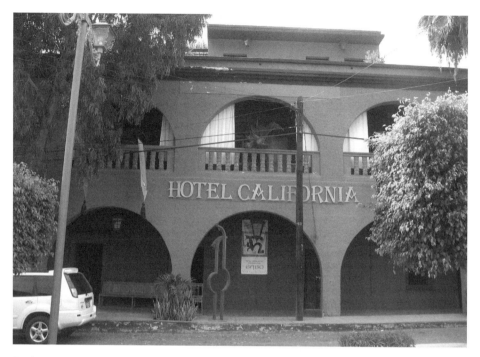

The famous Hotel California

LOS CERRITOS RV PARK
Km 64 Mexico 19, Todos Santos

This is an old worn-down government campground located on one of the best beaches in the area. Facilities are slightly primitive, with flush toilets, full hookups, and cold water showers. Getting to the site is no small feat, either. It is 1 mile down a narrow dirt road with exposed stones and potholes and should be taken slowly. However, it is steps away from miles of wide-open beaches. Rates: $4 to $5 per night.

DINING

Though the variety of food is limited in Todos Santos, the town has several good choices. The vast majority of food purveyors understandably offer Mexican food, with plenty of seafood items on the menu. Eateries range from street-side vendors to casual establishments to elegant sit-down dining. For a change of pace, there are a couple of Italian restaurants in town—and, of course, there is always Shut Up Frank's, a beach-style sports bar and grill located at the west end of town.

CAFÉ SANTA FE
612-145-0340
Calle Centenario #4
Price: Expensive
Serving: L, D
Wheelchair Accessible: Yes

This fine-dining restaurant features a full bar and elegant Italian dishes made with fresh seafood, organic vegetables, and homemade pastas. Meals are served in a lush courtyard setting. Open Wednesday through Monday 12 PM to 9 PM. Closed parts of September and October.

FONDA EL ZAGUÁN
612-131-6769
Juarez between Topete and Hidalgo

Price: Moderate
Serving: L, D
Wheelchair Accessible: Yes

Located just east of the historic district, this Mexican restaurant offers a delicious menu of vegetarian and seafood specialties. Open Monday through Saturday 11:30 AM to 9 PM.

LOS ADOBES DE TODOS SANTOS

612-145-0203
Calle Hidalgo between Juárez and Militar
Price: Expensive
Serving: B, L, D
Wheelchair Accessible: Yes

This elegant restaurant located in an unassuming hundred-year-old adobe building on the north side of town offers a gourmet take on traditional Mexican dishes. Meals are served on a shaded open-air patio that abuts a desert garden. On the other end of the garden is a spa offering a variety of treatments. Open Monday through Saturday 8:30 AM to 9 PM and Sunday 8:30 AM to 5 PM.

PANCHO BANANO

612-145-0885
Hidalgo #11, between Juárez and Militar
Price: Moderate
Serving: B, L, D
Wheelchair Accessible: Yes

Across the street from Los Adobes is Pancho Banano, and the contrast couldn't be more startling. This restaurant's owner can sometimes be seen standing out front drumming up business, declaring to the occasional passerby that *"Pancho Banano es muy rico!"* This down-to-earth restaurant serves standard Mexican fare and fresh-fruit drinks. Meals are served on plastic tables on a concrete patio facing the street. This establishment also doubles as a cyber-cafe, with several computers available for a nominal fee. Open daily 7 AM to 9 PM.

RESTAURANT LAS FUENTES

612-145-0257
Degollado and Militar
Price: Moderate
Serving: B, L, D
Wheelchair Accessible: Yes

A large menu of seafood and continental specialties are offered here as well as a full bar. Meals are served on an attractive outdoor palapa patio. Open daily 7:30 AM to 10 PM.

RISTORANTE LE TRE GALLINE

612-145-0274
Topete and Benito Juárez
Price: Moderate
Serving: L, D
Wheelchair Accessible: Yes

This restaurant offers authentic northern Italian cuisine, featuring fresh pastas and breads as well as homemade desserts and real Italian espresso. Open Monday through Saturday noon to 10 PM.

SHUT UP FRANK'S

612-145-0707
Degollado and Rangel
Price: Moderate
Serving: L, D
Wheelchair Accessible: No

This sports bar and surf restaurant combines American flavor with Baja style. The menu includes steaks, burgers, giant burritos, and several vegetarian offerings. Show up for happy hour Monday through Friday 4 PM to 6 PM. Open Monday through Saturday 10 AM to 10 PM and Sunday 10 AM to 8 PM.

TEQUILA SUNRISE

612-145-0073
Benito Juárez across from Hotel California
Price: Moderate
Serving: L, D
Wheelchair Accessible: Yes

Located just across the street from the Hotel California, this Mexican restaurant has a surfing and classic-rock theme. Sitting here among the pictures of Don Henley and Glen Frey, one gets the feeling that the restaurant staff would rather hang themselves than listen to "Witchy Woman" one more time. That said, this is a fun place with friendly service, good food, and a great chicken chimichanga. The walls are papered with dollar bills and the signatures of previous patrons. Be sure to try a margarita on the rocks, made with fresh-squeezed limes. Open daily 10 AM to 9 PM.

BEACHES

Todos Santos is located on a hill just inland from the Pacific Ocean. Although some beautiful beaches lie within a not-unmanageable walking distance, these beaches aren't safe for swimming—though they are very good for strolling, whale watching, skim boarding, fishing, and other activities that don't involve you exposing yourself to heavy shore breaks and dangerous rip currents. Farther south along the coast, there are miles of beautiful white-sand beaches that are great for swimming, surfing, and just playing in the water. These beaches are accessible through rugged, unmarked dirt roads. Still, keep in mind that the Pacific Ocean is always a dangerous place to swim, and there are no lifeguards around to save you if you get in trouble. Rip currents occur almost everywhere along this coast, and people drown in these waters.

San Pedrito is a popular beach with surfers.

The Los Cerritos Surf Shop on the beach at Los Cerritos attests to the good surfing to be found here.

Town Beaches

You can access beaches within 20 minutes' walking distance from downtown Todos Santos. Heading northwest down Topete out of the historic district and down through a palm valley will bring you to La Cachora, a wide beach that is great for a stroll or watching the sun set. Farther down you will come to La Poza, a beautiful beach that has a freshwater lagoon inhabited by a number of birds. Neither of these beaches is ideal for swimming because of a heavy shore break and a strong undertow and riptides.

PUNTA LOBOS This beach access road is at marker Km 54 on Mexico 19. The dirt road is clearly signed, and is the beach is about 2.5 kilometers (about 1.5 miles) down the road. Punta Lobos is also sometimes referred to as Fisherman's Beach because local fishermen launch their *pangas* from this beach every morning and return in the afternoon with their catch. It's interesting to watch them negotiate the waves. If you are interested in going out with these men, you can often arrange it with them, though that requires a certain proficiency in Spanish. This beach is also a decent place to swim, but you should do so with caution, and keep in mind that there are no lifeguards to save you if you get into trouble.

LAS PALMAS (SAN PEDRO) This small stretch of beach is located down a dirt access road that's about 2.6 kilometers from Km 57 on Mexico 19, across from the SAHR experimental station. It is secluded and surrounded by a palm grove with a freshwater lagoon. Las Palmas is good for swimming and bodysurfing, but you should do so with caution. Access to the beach is through private property, and the gates are open only between 6 AM to 9 PM; camping is not permitted. If you drive here, be aware that car break-ins have been reported at Palm Beach, so leave your valuables back at your hotel!

SAN PEDRITO Located 3.1 kilometers down a dirt road from Km 59 on Mexico 19, this beach has long been a favorite spot among surfers. The waves get pretty formidable here, and the area is not suitable for beginning surfers. A popular RV and camping park that was

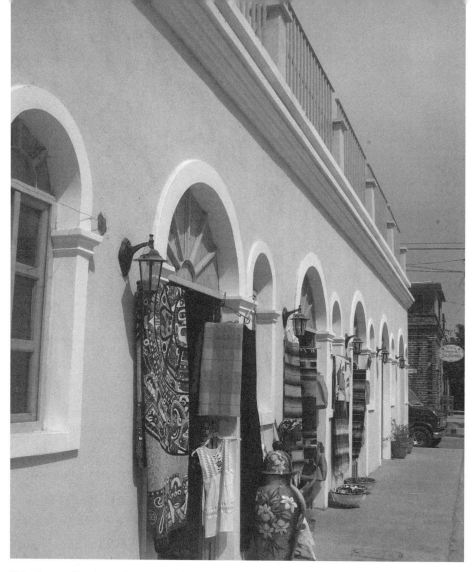

Todos Santos offers plenty of street-side shopping.

located here was recently sold to a developer with plans to build a resort hotel, so camping is no longer permitted, though day visits are.

LOS CERRITOS Another popular camping and surfing spot, this beach is about 8 miles south of Todos Santos, off Mexico 19 at Km 64. The turnoff is easy to miss, so watch for the markers, and follow the rocky dirt road 2.6 kilometers down to the ocean. Despite its seclusion, the dirt parking area will likely be packed with RVs and tents. Set back from the beach there is even a palapa surf shop renting boards, though you would not describe this pristine crescent-shaped beach as crowded. The parking area opens onto miles of open sand.

SHOPPING

Todos Santos is Baja's art center, and as such, Benito Juárez and the streets of the historic district are some of the most interesting in Baja. Aside from fine art you'll find handmade textiles, surf shops, and *artesenía* from around Mexico and Latin America.

Cactus Folk Art (612-145-0771; Calle Juárez across from Hotel California, Todos Santos) This shop offers a variety of arts, crafts, and jewelry, including interesting pieces such as lamps and vases made of leather over clay with metal inlays.

Charles Stewart Gallery & Studio (612-145-0265; www.charlescstewart.com; Centenario and Obregón, Todos Santos) Charles Stewart was the pioneer who established Todos Santos as an artists' colony. This gallery located in the artist's refurbished home sells his oil and watercolor paintings.

Curios Tony (612-145-0356; Juárez e/ Morelos and Zaragoza, Todos Santos) This shop has a good selection of Mexican arts and crafts, such as Talavera pottery from Puebla and *artesenía* from Oaxaca.

El Tecolote Libros (612-145-0295; Benito Juárez and Hidalgo, Todos Santos) An extensive selection of new and used books, including hard-to-find books in English.

Ezra Katz Fine Art Gallery (612-137-3473; Benito Juárez and Hidalgo, Todos Santos) Located next to the bookstore, this gallery offers works by a variety of artists.

Galería de Todos Santos (612-145-0500; www.galeriadetodossantos.com; Topete and Legaspi, Todos Santos) This gallery features several beautifully intimate pieces by numerous artists.

Todos Santos has a wide variety of traditional Mexican artesenía.

Galería Wall (612-145-0527; www.catherinewallart.com; Benito Juárez #4, Todos Santos) Pieces by artist Catherine Wall. Much of her art is inspired by Mexican culture and life in Baja California.

Jill Logan Galería (612-145-0151; www.jilllogan.com; Benito Juárez and Morelos, Todos Santos) Located in an attractively gated building, this gallery handles the diverse works of artist Jill Logan.

La Galera (612-145-0215; Obregón e/ Juárez and Centenario, Todos Santos) This shop offers a wide variety of custom-designed jewelry and home furnishings.

Los Cerritos Surf Shop (612-137-7343; Rangel and Degollado, Todos Santos) Rent surfboards and other gear here. Surfing lessons and a variety of tours are also offered. A second shop is right off Playa Los Cerritos.

Mangos (612-145-0451; Calle Centenario e/ Topete and Obregón, Todos Santos) This shop offers a wide variety of *artesenía,* including Mexican folk art, wood carvings, Talavera pottery, and Guatemalan textiles.

West Cape

Despite the presence of Mexico 19—a well-maintained paved road that runs along the coast from Todos Santos all the way to Cabo San Lucas—the West Cape is by far the least developed area of the Cape region. The eastern side is dotted with small towns along the coastal dirt road, and several centuries-old villages lie along Mexico 1, which passes through the Central Cape. The western side is pounded by tumultuous Pacific waves, and little is to be found here except turtle nesting gounds, a few small hotels, and a couple of campsites. However, this dearth of settled population may actually be what makes this area attractive to developers. After all, with a new resort going in at Playa San Pedrito in the north and the new Sunset Beach Pueblo Bonito timeshare facility towering near Cabo Falso in the south, the cape's Pacific coast seems to be teetering on development. Movements are gathering—particularly in Todos Santos—to resist such development and keep the beaches pristine and accessible to those willing to give a little to experience them.

BEACHES

CABO FALSO   About 2 miles west of Cabo San Lucas you'll come upon Cabo Falso, a wide strip of beach that is a protected nesting ground for sea turtles. Because of this, visitors aren't permitted within 165 feet of the surf. However, the nearby dunes have become a popular spot for adventure tourists on ATVs. In the hills above the beach is the El Faro Viejo lighthouse. Now abandoned, this lighthouse signaled ships off the coast of Cabo from 1895 until 1961. Not much of it remains, but it does provide spectacular views of the ocean, which makes it a popular ATV and horseback-tour destination.

PLAYA MIGRIÑO   Up over the Sierra de la Laguna foothills, at the Km 94 turnoff on Mexico 19, you will come upon Playa Migriño. In the winter this is a popular surfing and camping beach, though the water here can be dangerous.

LA CANDELARIA   Up in the rugged foothills of the Sierra de la Laguna Mountains north of Cabo San Lucas is the small Indian pueblo of La Candelaria. This village is home to fewer

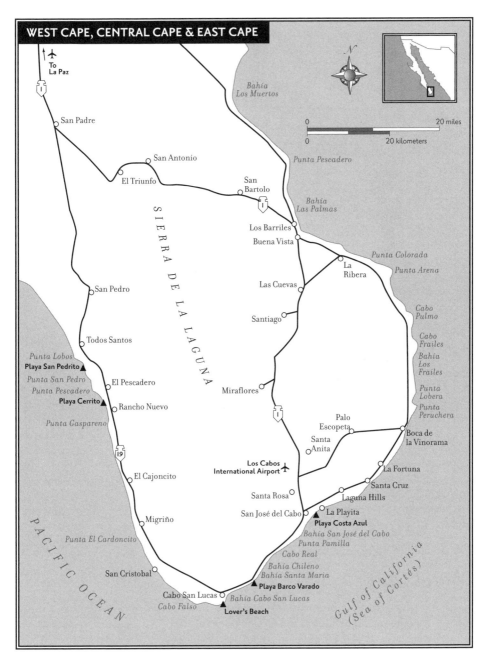

WEST CAPE, CENTRAL CAPE & EAST CAPE

To La Paz

San Padre

San Antonio

El Triunfo

Bahía Los Muertos

Punta Pescadero

San Bartolo

Bahía Las Palmas

Los Barriles
Buena Vista

Punta Colorada
Punta Arena

La Ribera

Las Cuevas

S I E R R A   D E   L A   L A G U N A

San Pedro

Santiago

Cabo Pulmo

Cabo Frailes
Bahía Los Frailes

Todos Santos

Punta Lobos
Playa San Pedrito

Punta San Pedro
Punta Pescadero
Playa Cerrito

El Pescadero

Rancho Nuevo

Miraflores

Punta Lobera
Punta Peruchera

Punta Gaspareno

Palo Escopeta

Boca de la Vinorama

Santa Anita

El Cajoncito

Los Cabos International Airport

La Fortuna

Santa Cruz

Laguna Hills

Santa Rosa

Migriño

San José del Cabo

La Playita
Playa Costa Azul

Bahía San José del Cabo
Punta Pamilla

Punta El Cardoncito

Cabo Real

Bahía Chileno
Bahía Santa Maria
Playa Barco Varado

San Cristobal

P A C I F I C   O C E A N

Cabo San Lucas
Cabo Falso

Bahía Cabo San Lucas

Lover's Beach

Gulf of California (Sea of Cortés)

0   20 miles
0   20 kilometers

N

---

than one hundred inhabitants, but a local school draws children from nearby environs. This enigmatic village is known for its *curanderas* and its clay pottery. *Curanderas* are healers who purportedly wield "white magic," but in reality they've merely gained knowledge about medicinal herbs, which is probably necessary for living in such a remote area. The town's famous clay pottery is made from earth dug up from the local hillsides. This "ranchware" is popular among foreign collectors.

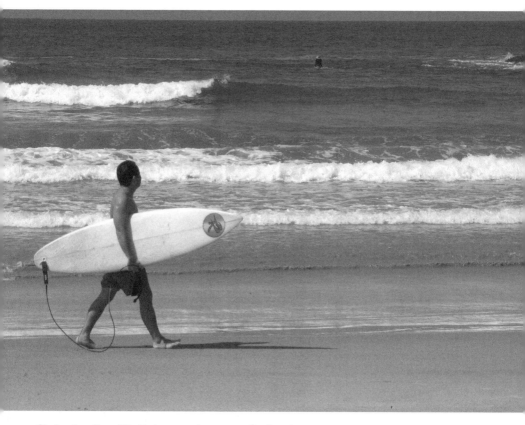

The beach at Playa Migriño is yet another great surfing location.

To get to La Candelaria, you have to take a dirt road that goes due north from Mexico 19 near Playa Migriño. This unsigned turnoff is less than a half mile north of the main Playa Migriño turnoff. The road is suitable only for 4WD vehicles and can be treacherous after it rains.

Central Cape

One irony of Todos Santos's ascendance as a tourist destination is that the towns of the central cape had a head start of more than a decade when the Carretera Transpeninsular was completed in the early 1970s. Each of these towns has a unique history and definite charm that is genuinely Mexican. However, each of them has, for the most part, gone undiscovered while the rest of the cape's locations—accessible by paved roads—have boomed. This is fortunate for those looking for an authentic experience. And as places like Todos Santos become more "boutiquized" with new resorts going up on nearby beaches, the towns of the Central Cape will surely have their day in the sun.

Miraflores

Miraflores is a quaint, centuries-old village located approximately 25 miles north of San José del Cabo off Mexico 1 and about halfway to the coastal village of Los Barriles. This small ranching and farming community is well known for producing quality leatherwork, so if you're interested in purchasing leather goods such as saddles, this is the place for you. Another reason for making the short drive to Miraflores are the natural hot springs located just outside of town. This quiet, tranquil area is a good place to spend a half day relaxing in the lush hills and taking in a way of life that seems to belong to another era. For off-roaders, a popular dirt trail goes north from Miraflores through the village of Agua Caliente and on to Santiago, where it reconnects with Mexico 1.

Santiago

About a 30-minute drive up the highway from San José, Santiago is the perfect place to get away from loud American tourists. This is the largest town on the Central Cape, with a population of nearly three thousand. Founded by an Italian missionary, Santiago is a colonial puebla that dates back more than 280 years. This authentic town sits on a hill a little more

than a mile west of Mexico 1. It is known as a sleepy place, with fruit orchards, ranches, and, on the west side of town, the only zoo in Baja California Sur. It is also an important regional source for palm leaves used in making palapa roofs. Walking through Santiago's quiet streets, you'll be amazed that this place is in the same neighborhood as a tourist trap like Cabo San Lucas.

Desert blooms in the Central Cape

San Bartolo

San Bartolo is a picturesque tropical village of palapa-roofed homes in the hills 10 miles north of Los Barriles. This pleasant town owes its lushness to a spring-fed creek that runs along the nearby hills and provides San Bartolo with an abundant supply of fresh water. This is a great place to stop and buy avocados, mangos, and homemade candy from the roadside stands.

San Antonio and El Trifuno

Located 20 miles north of San Bartolo, these two towns have plenty of history. Originally ranches were scattered through these hills before silver was discovered at the site of San Antonio in 1748, which soon became a minor mining town. The town's biggest distinction came in 1829 when Loreto was destroyed by a hurricane and San Antonio was briefly designated the capital of the Californias. However, the capital was transferred to La Paz the following year. Amazingly, San Antonio was once a city of ten thousand. Today, the population stands at around a mere eight hundred residents. The unusual church, which dates to 1825, and the buildings that remain from the town's colorful past make for an interesting photo op to break the monotony of driving between La Paz and Los Cabos.

Fishermen have long flocked to the beautiful waters of Baja California Sur. Jason MacBeth

In 1862 gold and silver deposits were discovered 4.5 miles to the north, setting off a minor rush. Within 15 years, seven gold and silver mines had popped up around the new town of El Trifuno. The "triumph" for which El Trifuno was named lasted a little beyond the end of the last century. However, in 1918 a hurricane flooded the mines, ending their heyday. In less than a decade, both towns were all but abandoned.

Today, El Trifuno is a town of only about four hundred residents. Some of them are still involved in small-scale mining, though the local economy is now based on minor production of tourist wares like woven baskets.

East Cape

The East Cape retains the feel of what southern Baja California must have been like three decades ago, before developers turned Cabo San Lucas into a tourist mecca. For the most part, much of this region is still only visited by off-roaders, yachtsmen, and deep-sea fishermen. More recently, other groups such as long-distance kayakers have begun to find adventures along Baja's East Cape. For adventurous travelers looking for a day trip, a graded dirt road that follows the coast out of San José del Cabo takes you along a series of small pueblos and secluded beach hotels. Keep in mind, though, that this road is in terrible shape, with certain stretches rutted and pocked with exposed rocks—and the seclusion that you set out to find can be a horrible burden should your vehicle break down. However, this treacherous stretch of road provides some of the most spectacular vistas to be found in all of Baja. The farther you dare to go, the more removed you become from civilization, and the closer you get to an isolated desert paradise. The road hits pavement between Punta Arena and La Ribara and again about 10 miles north near Buena Vista, where it hooks up with Mexico 1. This region may represent the near future for the East Cape because here is where you will find new development and an influx of expatriate Americans. If and when this road along the East Cape shore is ever paved, this gorgeous stretch will surely see development. For now, it offers a view of what southern Baja used to be.

Cabo Pulmo

Since 1993 Cabo Pulmo Bay, including Cabo Frailes Bay, has been part of a marine preserve that is home to more than 350 different species of aquatic life. It is also the home to the only living reef in the Sea of Cortés—a fact that draws divers from around the world and diving tour companies from Los Cabos and La Paz. This environment is extremely sensitive, and care should be taken not to damage the reef in any way while visiting.

The bay acts as a natural shield to shelter the coral from the elements, allowing them to grow in abundance. The combination of clear water and a rich ecosystem results in one of the premier locations on the cape for scuba diving and snorkeling. Kayakers also come through for the opportunity for close contact with sea lions as well as great whale watching from January through March.

Baja's desert can be surprisingly beautiful.

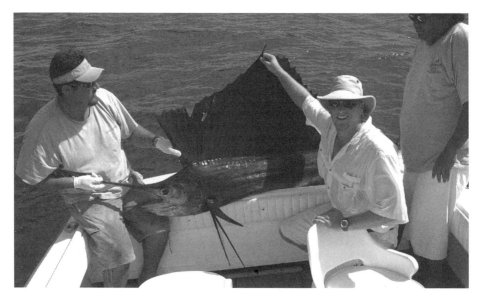

The East Cape, well-known for its marlin fishing, draws fishermen from all over world. |ason MacBeth

Los Barriles and Buena Vista

About an hour out of Cabo San Lucas along Mexico 1, the road skirts the Sea of Cortés before turning back inland until it reaches La Paz. This is where you will find the twin villages of Los Barriles and Buena Vista. This secluded stretch of beach currently seems to be in the process of becoming a booming beach town. Houses are popping up along the beach, and the word is out that this is one of the premier big-game fishing spots in the world. The waters here teem with marlin, wahoo, dorado, and yellowfin tuna. Despite the development, the area retains the laid-back pace that made Baja famous in the first place. The calm, clear turquoise water here is a comfortable 70 to 80 degrees as is the air temperature during winter months, though nights do tend to be cool.

ACCOMMODATIONS

HOTEL PLAYA DEL SOL
Managers: Bob and Chacha Von Wormer
1-877-777-8862 (U.S.)
www.loscabosguide.com/hotels/
ecplysol.htm
Calle de la Playa, Los Barriles
Special Features: Pets OK

This hotel is located right on Bahia Las Palmas and offers 26 air-conditioned rooms at very reasonable rates—amenities include three meals a day, and pets are permitted. Most of the hotel staff speaks English and are very helpful. The hotel features a bar inside and one next to a freshwater swimming pool that has a beautiful view of the sea. Rates start at $65 per night.

LOS BARRILES HOTEL
Manager: Giovanni Ruiz
624-141-0024
www.losbarrileshotel.com
Calle de la Playa, Los Barriles

This hotel offers 20 rooms, each with two queen-sized beds and a large bathroom. The rooms are attractively appointed and situated around a patio pool area. Internet access is available on the premises. The hotel also offers storage for boats and RVs. Rates: $49 for a room with one bed and $59 for a room with two beds.

PALMAS DE CORTEZ HOTEL

Managers: Bob and Chacha Von Wormer
624-141-0050 or 1-877-777-8862 (U.S.)
www.loscabosguide.com/hotels/
ecpalmas.htm
Calle de la Playa, Los Barriles

This hotel is something of an unexpected oasis on the East Cape. Situated right on a beautiful beach, it has amazing views of the sea. It also has an impressive pool area that faces the Sea of Cortés. The hotel offers a number of condos and suites in addition to 28 regular rooms. Accommodations include three meals a day. Rates: $75 for a single room with one person and $120 for a double room with double occupancy.

MARTÍN VERDUGO'S RESORT AND RV PARK

Owner: Martin Verdugo
624-141-0054
www.verdugosbeachresort.com
Playa Bahía de Palmas, 1 mile north of Los Barriles

This attractive hotel and RV park is located right on the water and offers 72 lots with full hookups as well as 25 tent sites, a few of which have electricity and water. The property has flush toilets, laundry facilities, and hot showers. If you prefer, stay in one of the 20 modern, air-conditioned rooms—some with kitchenettes. For diversion, there is a roof garden restaurant and cocktail lounge as well as a pool, a palapa bar, and steel mats for launching boats over the sand.

4

La Paz

On the surface, La Paz isn't much of a tourist town. After all, it doesn't have sprawling golf courses or resort-lined beaches. On first glance, it's more of a bustling port city with a few college kids mixed in and a bit of a graffiti problem. Located on a large bay on the Sea of Cortés, La Paz is the capital of Baja California Sur, and with a population of approximately 250,000, it's also the largest city in the state. Having such a population base, La Paz has trappings that are rare elsewhere in Baja, such as a theater, a number of museums, and a university—not to mention the best health care on the peninsula.

Even as the tourism industry in Baja has boomed over the last 30 years, La Paz has remained obscure to most visitors. For a brief period in the 1960s, this city seemed to be on the cusp of becoming the latest big resort destination south of the border. At the time, Puerto Vallarta and Acapulco were Mexico's chic tourist towns, bustling with sunbathers and high-rise hotels crowding the shoreline. However, La Paz's reputation for world-class sport fishing and tranquil coves was well known. Hollywood stars Bing Crosby and Desi Arnaz owned homes nearby, and John Wayne regularly flew in with friends here for fishing trips. Yet when the Mexican government set about developing tourist centers in the 1970s, La Paz was passed over for a backwater town 90 miles to the south called Cabo San Lucas. This was perhaps because La Paz was already a busy industrial center: The town would likely have had a hard time developing a true resort identity in the midst of existing characteristics of local industry, such as the smoke-bellowing Pemex refinery on the edge of town and the cargo ships that seem to be perennially docked in port. While La Paz may not have the prefabricated, easily accessible tourist experience of Los Cabos, to visitors willing to put forth the effort of exploration it offers breathtaking beauty combined with the authentic feel of a provincial Mexican town.

HISTORY

This region has had human inhabitants since as early as 10,000 b.c. These first residents of Baja were likely fishermen and gatherers who collected seeds, roots, and berries and lived in nearby caves. The remnants of this civilization can be found in cave paintings a short distance from La Paz. One of the first Europeans to visit the area was Hernán Cortés, who arrived in May 1535—well after gaining fame and fortune. At the time the Baja Peninsula was thought to be a large island, and legends held that it was controlled by warrior women who used men only to procreate and who had huge stores of gold and pearls. In reality, La Paz was inhabited by wandering bands of Guaicura and Pericú. Cortés called the area Santa Cruz and attempted to use it as a base from which to conquer Baja—the first of many efforts

The Malecón (seaside esplanade) in La Paz

to subdue Baja by force that failed due to the harsh desert conditions. In 1596 Sebastian Vizcaino gave the area its modern name, which means "The Peace," in an effort to lure settlers. However, supply problems and a fire soon forced the abandonment of the settlement. The entire Baja peninsula subsequently remained free of Spanish settlements for the next hundred years, until Loreto was established in the north in 1697. During that time, Spain continued to send ships along its famous Manila trade route from the Philippines to the northwest coast of America south to Acapulco and back again. English, Dutch, and French pirates used the bay of La Paz as a staging ground to launch raids on the Spanish galleons laden with supercargos of silk, spices, and gold. Francis Drake and Thomas Cavendish are just a couple of the many famous pirates who took refuge in the waters of La Paz.

The history of La Paz has been equally tumultuous in recent centuries. European diseases quickly decimated the region's Native populations as Mexican ranchers and fishermen gradually moved into the area. In 1811 these new residents founded a town and called it La Paz after the bay. In 1829, after Loreto was destroyed by a fire, the capital of Baja California Sur was moved to La Paz, where it has remained ever since. In March 1847, during the Mexican-American War, an American warship landed in La Paz and imposed surrender on its inhabitants. Afterward, a battalion from New York known as the "baby regiment" was stationed in the city to keep the peace but left after the Treaty of Guadelupe-Hidalgo ceded the southern portion of the Californias back to Mexico. Soon afterward, however, American general William Walker invaded La Paz and declared it to be part of his new government, the Republic of Sonora. He had been dissatisfied with the treaty and hoped to add another state to the United States to counter the growing abolitionist movement. But his expedition was short-lived, as he left abruptly on hearing that an army was on its way to liberate La Paz.

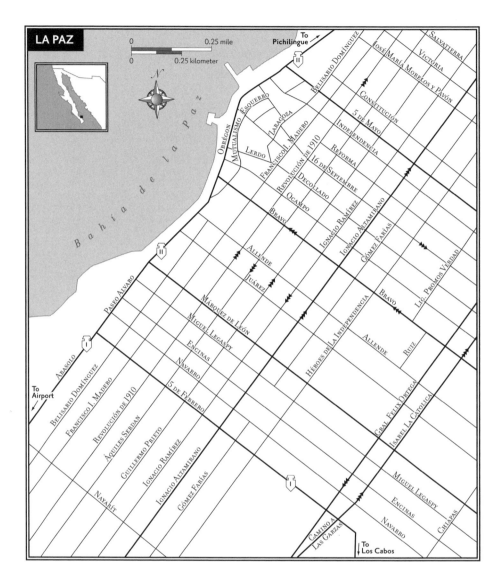

For many years La Paz was a center for pearl fishing. In fact, the city is the setting for both John Steinbeck's novella *The Pearl* and Scott O'Dell's novel *The Black Pearl*. In the late 1930s the pearl industry was wiped out due to disease and overharvesting. Later, the city banked its economic security on being a duty-free port as well as agricultural trade with the Mexican mainland. The city also developed as a vacation destination for Mexicans from the mainland as well as wealthy Americans, but it remained inaccessible to most Americans until the Carretera Transpeninsular (Transpeninsular Highway)—Mexico 1—was completed in 1973.

Baja California Sur was given statehood in 1974, and La Paz was made the state capital. Linked by air, highway, and ferry to mainland Mexico and the United States, the city has continued to grow, particularly over the last decade.

GENERAL INFORMATION

Emergencies

Dial 066

Both public and private hospitals handle emergencies for foreigners. You'll need to pay for services when you're discharged, so get a receipt in case you want to collect on your insurance. Look in the phone book for specialists.

Police

612-122-6610

Boulevard Luis Donaldo Colosio Murrieta and Avenida Álvarez Rico

Fire Department

612-122-0054

Corner of Isabel la Católica and Melitón Abáñez

Post Office

Corner of Revolución and Constitución

Tourist Office

612-122-0199

Paseo Álvaro Obregón between Calle 5 de Mayo and Independecia

GETTING THERE

La Paz is a unique blend of authentic Mexican living and first-class recreation. Not only does it have a relatively close proximity to the United States, but it also has an infrastructure that few other Mexican cities enjoy. The city has an abundance of transportation services, including ferry, bus, and direct air service.

La Paz is 950 miles south of Tijuana and 140 miles north of Cabo San Lucas, making it highly accessible by way of Mexico 1. You can drive to La Paz from Cabo in just a few hours and from Loreto in about four hours. The drive can be made from San Diego in about 24 hours if you drive straight through, though this is not recommended since it is dangerous to drive Mexico 1 at night.

The city's Manuel de Leon Airport is located about 7 miles south of the city off Mexico 1. Although it is a small airport, it has adequate facilities, such as two bars, car rental kiosks, an ATM, and a couple of gift shops. It is served by the Mexican airlines Aero California and Aeroméxico as well as such major American carriers as American Airlines, America West, Continental, and Delta. Connecting flights come from Los Angeles, Tucson, and Mexico City.

If you are in the market for a cheaper option, La Paz also lies directly on Baja Caifornia's bus routes that run from Los Cabos all the way north to Tijuana. One-way bus travel from the Tijuana bus terminal is about $90 on Baja's major bus line, Autotransportes de Baja California (ABC). This is not the overcrowded Mexican bus experience with rustic mariachis and roosters in the aisles as portrayed in Hollywood films. These buses have large reclining seats and TVs that generally play movies in English. Still, even with these comforts, the drive is quite long.

If you are traveling to or from mainland Mexico, La Paz is near the principal ferry port in Baja Califonia, located at Pichilingue 10 miles north of town. Ferries provide vehicle and passenger service between the mainland cities of Mazatlan or Topolobompo every day of the week. The ferry trip to Mazatlan takes about 18 hours, depending on wind, weather, and currents, and transit to Topolobomo takes about 10 hours. Third-class travel runs about $20, while a two-person cabin with a private bathroom is an additional cost of around $62. Transport for a small car runs about $225; larger vehicles cost about $290.

Taking the Ferry

Because the Baja Peninsula is cut off from the Mexican mainland by the Sea of Cortés, the southern region of the peninsula is the most isolated in the country. Most Mexicans view this state very similarly to the way most Americans view the state of Alaska.

La Paz is the touch point along the southern peninsula where ferries arrive from across the sea with supplies and passengers from the mainland. These ferries can be a great way to experience other parts of Mexico, particularly if you are driving through Baja. From La Paz, you can make your way to either Topolobampo or Mazatlan. There used to be ferry service between Cabo San Lucas and Puerto Vallarta, though that service is no longer available. You can book passage at the ferry terminal, though reservations are recommended. During peak seasons, you should try to book your ferry reservations between one week and one month in advance. Traveling with a pet is not recommended for ferry travel because your pet must remain in your vehicle for the duration of the trip—and since you are not allowed on the car deck, your dog, for example, can't be walked throughout the 10-to-18-hour voyage. But if you must take the voyage with a pet, you'll need a recent International Health Certificate, and have your vehicle prepared with water and newspaper and leave your windows slightly open.

The voyage between La Paz and Topolobampo takes 10 hours while the trip between La Paz and Mazatlan takes 18 hours. A variety of accommodations are offered, from a simple seat to a private cabin with a TV and private bath. These accommodations can be quite pricey, though, because passengers pay general seating first and the cost of the cabin is assessed on top of that. Also, you'll have to wait in separate lines for vehicle tickets and passenger tickets. Arrive early and get your passenger ticket first (after having your vehicle weighed) since the good seats tend to sell out.

Be aware that Baja has a special trade-zone status in which drivers don't have to pass through customs. However, when you board the ferry, you'll pass through customs, and you may have to pay duty fees. If you are transporting a vehicle, it will need to be weighed as you go through customs. The fees for taking your vehicle into the interior of Mexico run around $16.90 plus a deposit of $400 to guarantee that you will leave the country with your vehicle.

GETTING AROUND

The *malecón* (seaside promenade) in La Paz provides a beautiful backdrop for an evening stroll, but to truly enjoy what La Paz has to offer, you will need some form of transportation. This is because only a couple of hotels in the city are located on the beach, and even the in-town beaches are difficult to reach by walking. The cheapest option is the bus station on Paseo Álvaro Obregón between Calle 5 de Mayo and Independencia. From here, buses run continuously to the beaches north of town as well as to the closer beaches. The trip out to Tecolote costs about $2 and takes around 45 minutes. You can also use this bus station to depart to other destinations from Cabo to Tijuana. Taxis are also readily available all along

CAR RENTAL COMPANIES

Car rentals are available at the airport as well as at the larger hotels. In town, the following offices are available.

Baja California Auto Rental
612-125-7662
Avenida Obregón #826, La Paz
Rent sedans and station wagons
Open daily 8 AM to 7 PM

Alamo
612-122-3681
www.goalamo.com
Avenida Álvaro Obregón 942-A between
Manuel Pineda and Marquez De Leon
Open daily 7:30 AM to 7 PM

Avis
612-122-2651, 612-124-6312 (airport)
www.avis.com
Airport location open daily 24 hours
Avenida Álvaro Obregón past Pineda.
Open Monday through Saturday 8 AM to 8 PM
and Sunday 8 AM to 4 PM

Budget
612-123-1919, 612-124-6433 (airport),
or 1-800-322-9975 (U.S.); fax 612-125-6686
www.budget.com
Airport location open daily 7 AM to 11 PM
Obregón 1775, La Paz; between Hidalgo and
Morelos
Open daily 7 AM to 9 PM

Felix Car Rental
612-121-6369; fax 612-121-6254
Carretera a Pichilingue Km 2.5, La Paz; east of
central La Paz, on the main road.
Suburbans and minivans available.
Open daily 8 AM to 7 PM

Hertz
612-122-5300, 612-124-6330(airport), (800)
654-3030 (U.S.)
www.hertz.com
Airport location open daily 8 AM to 10:30 PM (airport)
Obregón 2130-D, La Paz, Baja California Sur,
Mexico
Open Monday through Friday 8 AM to 8 PM, Saturday 8 AM to 7 PM, and Sunday 8 AM to 6 PM

Thrifty
612-125-9696 or 612-124-6365 (airport)
www.thrifty.com
Paseo Obregón at Lerdo de Tejada
Open daily 7 AM to 11 PM

the *malecón*. It's a common practice here to rent a taxi to take you to the outlying beaches and make arrangements for the taxi to return at a set time to pick you up. If you would rather drive yourself, all the major car rental companies have offices somewhere along the *malecón*.

WEATHER

La Paz has pleasant temperatures almost all year round. From December through March, average daily temperatures reach the high 70s while nightly lows average in the mid- to upper 50s. Temperatures climb into the high 80s in May and June, with nightly lows just the lower to mid-60s. August and September are really the only uncomfortable months, as average daily highs creep into the mid- to upper 90s and nightly "lows" stay in the mid-70s. These two months are also considered the rainy season as it's the only time of year when precipitation gets much above an inch. Water temperatures tend to stay in the mid-60s from December through June and climb into the mid-80s from August through October.

ACCOMMODATIONS

La Paz offers a wide variety of accommodations, from multibed hostels to secluded luxury resorts. For a beach town, however, there is a dearth of beachfront hotels. Only La Concha Beach Resort has beach access. There has been discussion in recent years of building a resort at Playa Balandra, though this has been fiercely opposed by local residents and environmental groups. Certainly a hotel at that location would take a lot away from what makes it special. Most of the hotels in La Paz are located along or near the *malecón*. What these hotels lack in beach access, they gain in convenience to restaurants and bars.

Budget Hotels

GARDENIAS HOTEL

Manager: Graciela Olmos
612-122-3088; fax 612-125-0436
www.hotelgardenias.com.mx
Aquiles Serdan #520
Credit Cards: None

This rustic hotel is located in the heart of La Paz, six blocks from the cathedral and three blocks from the *malecón*. It is an older hotel, which is apparent from the moment you step into the lobby with stained-glass windows that are definitely a throwback to seventies decor. However, it is clean and a good value for less than $50 a night. Each of the 56 air-conditioned rooms are furnished with two full-sized beds and a color TV. Its restaurant-bar is open from 7 AM to 3 PM, serving a nice menu of Mexican food. The hotel also has an old-style rectangular

swimming pool with a diving board and plenty of on-site parking. Rates: start at around $41 double occupancy.

HOTEL PERLA

Manager: Laura Coronado
612-122-0777 or 1-800-716-8799 (U.S.);
fax 612-125-5363
www.hotelperlabaja.com
Paseo Álvaro Obregón 1570
Credit Cards: None
Special Features: Swimming pool, Jacuzzi, kids' play structure, restaurant, nightclub.

This hotel opened in 1940 and claims to be the oldest in La Paz. Conveniently located right in downtown La Paz, the hotel has 110 air-conditioned rooms, all equipped with cable TV and a minibar. Only about one-quarter of the rooms have a view of the *malecón,* so be sure to request that when making reservations. The hotel's Terraza Restaurant opens for breakfast at 5 AM to accommodate guests heading out on fishing expeditions. It specialized in international cuisine but serves a buffet-style meal on some nights consisting of seafood, chicken, and steak. A separate nightclub on the property called La Cabaña is open from 9 PM to 3 AM. Rates: start at around $67 double occupancy.

Midrange Hotels

LOS ARCOS HOTEL

Manager: Jose Rafael Garcia
612-122-2744 or 949-450-9000 (U.S.); fax 612-125-4313
U.S. Fax: (949) 450-9010
www.losarcos.com

Paseo Álvaro Obregón 498
Credit Cards: MC, V
Special Features: On-site masseuse, two swimming pools, sauna

This is one of the oldest and most popular hotels in La Paz. As you walk down the *malecón,* this distinctive hotel is hard to miss with its 22 bayview rooms jutting toward the street. It has 93 standard rooms along with 15 suites and 24 bungalow cabanas. Most of the rooms are a bit narrow and even a little cramped, though the suites have plenty of space. There are also two pools on the property, one of which is in a private garden set aside for the cabanas. The on-site Bermejo Restaurant serves breakfast, lunch, and dinner. Additionally, a coffee shop is open for breakfast. The Los Pelicanos Bar offers live entertainment and nice sunset views. This hotel also has two conference rooms suitable for banquets or wedding receptions. Rates: $80 to $115 double occupancy.

ARAIZA INN PALMIRA

Manager: Josue Villarreal
612-121-6200 or 1-877-727-2492 (U.S.); fax 612-121-6227
www.araizainn.com.mx
Boulevard Alberto Aramburo s/n
Credit Cards: MC, V, AE
Special Features: Tennis court, gym, swimming pool, wireless Internet.

This hotel offers five different accommodation packages, from standard rooms with two double beds to the master suite equipped with a queen-sized bed in a separate bedroom, 27-inch TV, and a refrigerator. The hotel also has a cafeteria that serves a buffet breakfast, lunch, and dinner as well as room service. The El Rollo Disco Bar is also located on the premises, complete with colorful lights and a giant-screen TV. If you're in the mood to check out the city, the hotel offers scheduled transportation to downtown La Paz. Rates: start at around $71 for a standard room double occupancy.

EL ÁNGEL AZUL

Owner: Ester Ammann
612-125-5130
www.elangelazul.com
Independencia #518
Credit Cards: MC, V
Special Features: Historic monument, wireless Internet, night guard.

Once the town's courthouse, this building situated in the heart of La Paz is considered a historic monument by the INAH (National Institution of Anthropology and History). Today, it is a tastefully renovated hacienda-style bed-and-breakfast hotel with a beautiful courtyard garden. The air-conditioned rooms, all with private baths, are decorated in a colorful Mexican style. Three historical rooms are furnished with one queen-sized bed and one single bed, while the hotel's six standard rooms are furnished with a double bed plus a single. The mini suite can accommodate up to five guests, as it is furnished with four beds, one of them a queen. The main suite on the second floor is furnished with a queen-sized bed. This hotel only accepts children older than 12 and no pets. Breakfast is served daily, and a bar is available to guests. This is a great hotel for a relaxing stay since it is a quiet place despite its convenient downtown location. Rates: start at $85 for a standard room double occupancy.

LA CASA MEXICANA INN

Owner: Arlaine Cervantes
612-125-2748
www.casamex.com
Calle Bravo 106
Credit Cards: MC, V (through PayPal)
Special Features: Deluxe continental breakfast, wireless Internet

A Spanish art-deco inn located one block from the Sea of Cortés in downtown La Paz, this small hotel features five elaborately decorated rooms in a beautiful white stucco cottage. Each room has its own unique attributes ranging from El Jardin, a secluded room decorated with vibrant Guatemalan fabrics set off a garden courtyard, to Vista Paz, an open suite decorated almost entirely in white with a private terrace and a view of the sea. Each room is air-conditioned and has wireless Internet access. A deluxe continental breakfast is included with the price of your stay and each room has a refrigerator in case you want to sneak up an extra helping for later. Rates: $65 to $85, depending on the room.

CLUB EL MORO
Director: Ricardo Curiel
612-122-4084
www.clubelmoro.com
Km 2 Carretera a Pichilingue
Credit Cards: MC, V
Special Features: Pool, satellite TV.

This hotel features striking white-Moorish architecture in a setting of landscaped gardens. Six different accommodation options are available, from a standard room with a king- or queen-sized bed to a two-bedroom suite with queen-sized beds. All rooms are equipped with air-conditioning, satellite TV, and a private terrace. The Café Gourmet Restaurant serves a variety of breakfast specials as well as delicatessen sandwiches for lunch. The grounds also include a Jacuzzi, pool, and a palapa bar. Located just over a mile out of town, the hotel is slightly set apart from the action. However, buses pass on a regular basis during daylight hours. Rates: $73 for a standard room with one queen or king bed.

CLUB HOTEL CANTAMAR SPORTS LODGE
Owners: Aguilar Family
612-122-1826; fax 612-122-8644
www.clubcantamar.com
Paseo Álvaro Obregón 1665
Credit Cards: MC, V

Special Features: Specializes in diving and other water sports, satellite TV

This hotel and diving facility is located near the ferry terminal at Bahía Pichilingue north of town. The four-story lodge has 35 standard rooms, 4 suites, and a 4-unit apartment complex. These apartments are two bedroom, two bath with kitchenettes and private balcony. All rooms have a tasteful desert-themed decor with Mexican-tile floors, rustic furniture, and satellite TV. Other amenities include a swimming pool with a swim-up bar and a view of the sea, a dockside restaurant, and a 35-slip marina. The lodge offers diving packages for stays of 3 to 10 nights and include lunch and transportation to and from the airport. Rates: $85 for a standard room double occupancy.

HOTEL HACIENDA DEL CORTEZ
Owner: Ogden Gutierrez
612-122-4011; fax 612-122-0663
Calle Nuevo Reforma
Credit Cards: MC, V
Special Features: Swimming pool, bar, laundry service, private parking.

This hotel was previously the Posada de Engelbert, built by the pop crooner Engelbert Humperdinck in the 1950s as a resort for the Hollywood crowd. Today it is a renovated Colonial-style hotel located south of the *malecón* and the Marina de la Paz. It has 26 good-sized air-conditioned rooms decorated with heavy wooden furniture and Mexican fabrics. A garden courtyard features a swimming pool and a view of the Bay of La Paz. Adjacent to this is a restaurant that serves up traditional Mexican fare. Rates: average $157.

HOTEL MEDITERRANE
Manager: Jack Danylchuck
612-125-1195
www.hotelmed.com
Allende 36
Credit Cards: MC, V

Where this intimate, Greek-themed family-owned hotel falls short with amenities it makes up with character and convenience. This no-frills hotel may seem lacking to anyone looking for a four-star experience. The nine individually designed rooms are each named after a Greek island. While they are relatively small, each room is equipped with a refrigerator and wireless Internet access. One room is located on the ground floor, but most are upstairs, accessed by a narrow stairway, as is the rooftop terrace that overlooks the *malecón* (this hotel is not recommended for anyone who uses a wheelchair or a walker). The hotel restaurant is not fancy but serves delicious Swiss and Italian cuisine at a modest price. Hotel Mediterrane is convenient walking distance from the center of the city of La Paz, although guests are offered the use of bicycles (and kayaks) at no additional charge. Those traveling by car must find parking on the street, which can be a bit of an inconvenience in this busy neighborhood. Rates: start at $75 double occupancy.

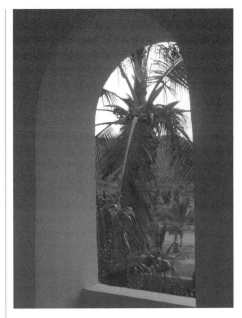

Sunset at Caimancito Beach in front of La Concha Beach Resort in La Paz

LA CONCHA BEACH RESORT AND CONDOS

Manager: Liliana Ruelaas
612-121-6161 or 1-800-999-2252 (U.S.);
fax (619) 294-7366 (U.S.)
www.laconcha.com
Km 5 Carretera A Pichelingue
Credit Cards: MC, V, AE
Special Features: Swimming pool, Jacuzzi, sports bar, gift shop.

This hotel is located right on Caimancito Beach 10 minutes from downtown La Paz. With 92 rooms and a slew of amenities, this old beauty does show its age a bit with missing roof tiles here and there in the hallway and rooms that are slightly less than roomy. However, the staff seems to constantly be doing upkeep, and it's a good option for travelers with kids on a family vacation as well as couples on a romantic retreat. The air-conditioned rooms have double or king-sized beds and a small private balcony, the poolside bar is great for kicking back, and the palm-shaded patio has easy access to a beach with calm water. Caimancito Beach is usually clean and beautiful, though there are times during the spring when it is covered with algae. During these times the pool is especially appealing. You can also check out a kayak from the front desk to go exploring. The front desk can make reservations for island tours, but you would be much better served by going to Tecolote Beach and making reservations on your own so that you can choose the best tour company for you. The hotel restaurant is adequate but not great. Better food can be had in town for less money. Rates: start at $80 for a standard room double occupancy.

POSADA LUNA SOL

Manager: Benjamin Duarte Robledo
612-123-0559 or 1-800-355-7140 (U.S.)
www.posadalunasol.com

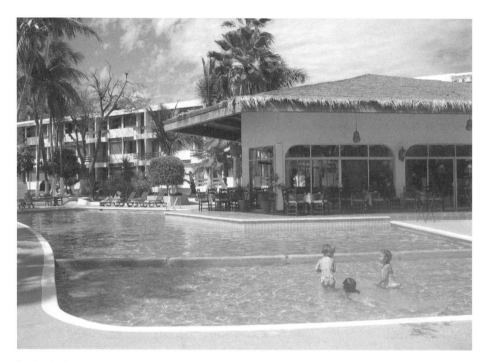

La Concha Beach Resort in La Paz

Topete 564
Credit Cards: MC, V

This charming Mexican inn is located a short walking distance from the *malecón*. Decorated in a Mexican Colonial with hand-painted tile murals, hand-woven fabrics, and heavy Mexican furniture, the hotel has 11 uniquely decorated rooms, most of which provide a view of the sea. A palapa terrace on the hotel's third floor provides a great place to relax and enjoy the sunset. Rates: start at $70 for a standard room double occupancy.

Luxury Hotels

HOTEL MARINA
Manager: Mario Hurtado de Mendoza
612-121-6254 or 1-800-250-3186 (U.S.);
fax 612-121-6177
www.hotelmarina.com.mx
Km 2.5 Carretera A Pichilingue
Credit Cards: MC, V

Special Features: Swimming pool, Jacuzzi, tobacco store, wireless Internet, tennis court

This hotel is located on the west side of La Paz on the Marina Palmira, which is actually a bit of a walk to get to downtown. However, all rooms have a view of the marina, which provides nice sunsets, as well. The hotel's Dinghy Dock Restaurant is located in front of the marina and also offers views of the yachts and the sunset while you dine. The pool area has a bar and is shaded by palm trees in a very attractive setting. An on-site spa offers massages, body treatments, facials, depilation, pedicures, and manicures. Other amenities include a ballroom, laundry facilities, bike rental, and on-site parking. Rates: start at $105 for a standard room double occupancy.

POSADA DE LAS FLORES
Owners: Guiseppe Marcelletti and Ursula Croci

612-125-5871
www.posadadelasflores.com
Paseo Álvaro Obregón 440
Credit Cards: MC, V, AE, D

This boutique hotel is all about ambiance. Located right across the street from the *malecón,* it offers great views of the sea. All rooms feature queen-sized beds and Colonial-style decor, with heavy wooden Mexican furniture, handwoven fabrics, and antiques. The tiled bathrooms include large marble showers and tubs. Rates: start at $150 to $180 for a standard room double occupancy.

RV Parks

AQUAMARINA RV PARK
Owners: Richard and Mary Lou Adcock
612-122-3761
Calle Nayarit 10

This 5-acre RV park features full hookups with plenty of water and electrical power, a swimming pool, and a boat ramp. It also offers large showers, a shaded terrace with tables and chairs, and a laundry room. Rates: $12 to $15 per night.

CASA BLANCA RV PARK
612-125-1142
Km 15 Mexico 1

Facilities at the RV park include flush toilets, a lounge, and a grocery store. There is also a tennis court and swimming pool for recreation. Rates: $15 to $20 per night.

DINING

Being a city of a quarter of a million people, La Paz offers a wide variety of cuisine. This is especially true along the *malecón,* where the city's largest concentration of restaurants is found. Unadventurous Americans can find several familiar fast-food joints here as well as an Applebee's that dominates its corner on Paseo Álvaro Obregón. However, you probably weren't attracted to La Paz for its familiar surroundings. And why get a fast-food burger when you can enjoy gourmet food for a fraction of the price of a similar meal in the United States? One of the great things to come out of the expansion of La Paz over the last decade is the emergence of some interesting and fine-dining establishments. Combine this with the fact that La Paz is not primarily a tourist town—which keeps prices scaled well below those at other tourist destinations. Travelers to La Paz will find a wealth of seafood obtained from the very waters that makes this place so beautiful. Additionally, you can dine on fine Sonoran beef, fresh chicken and pork, and vegetarian options. Furthermore, the city's wonderful atmosphere has drawn chefs from around the world specializing it Italian, French, Asian, and other cuisines. This adds up to an abundance of great choices. The biggest problem is deciding which one to try next.

Mexican

CARLOS 'N CHARLIE'S
612-123-4547
Paseo Álvaro Obregón and 16 de Septiembre
Price: Moderate
Serving: L, D
Wheelchair Accessible: Yes

This party-themed restaurant is brought to you by the same people who created Squid Roe and Señor Frog's. Open daily noon to 1 AM, they serve up traditional Mexican fare in addition to steak and seafood dishes. It features both indoor and outdoor seating, with a wooden deck that provides a great view of the sea. Although it feels a bit like a tourist trap, it's frequented by a good mix of tourists and locals.

EL ZARAPE

612-122-2520
Avenida México 3450
Price: Moderate
Serving: B, L, D
Wheelchair Accessible: Yes

This brightly decorated restaurant provides the perfect ambience for a Mexican adventure. Come here to sample the tastes of Mexico, particularly on Saturday evenings when they feature a buffet dinner with choices from the country's heartland. On Sunday evenings the buffet offers choices from all over Mexico and an excellent breakfast buffet is offered Tuesday through Sunday. Open daily 7:30 AM to midnight.

EL TASTE

612-122-8121
Paseo Álvaro Obregón and Juárez
Price: Moderate
Serving: B, L, D
Wheelchair Accessible: Yes

Situated at the west end of the *malecón,* this restaurant is popular with tourists and locals alike. Open daily 8 AM to midnight, it serves up steaks and seafood along with traditional Mexican specialties. However, breakfast is the best meal served here.

Steak and Seafood

LAS BRISAS DEL MAR

612-123-5055
Paseo Álvaro Obregón and Colegio Militar
Price: Moderate to Expensive
Serving: L, D
Wheelchair Accessible: Yes

This waterfront steak house located on the east end of the *malecón* offers delicious steak dishes along with fresh seafood and plenty of ambiance. The service is excellent, as well, and the view of the sea makes it a great place for a romantic dinner. Open Monday through Saturday 1:30 PM to 11 PM.

LA MAR Y PEÑA

612-122-9949
Calle 15 de Septiembre and Isabel la Católica
Price: Moderate
Serving: B, L, D
Wheelchair Accessible: Yes

Located on a quiet street in downtown La Paz, this small casual-dining restaurant has a distinctly Mexican atmosphere. It is decorated with wooden furniture and white tablecloths, with air-conditioning and ceiling fans to keep it bearable in the hot La Paz weather. The extensive menu is almost exclusively seafood dishes—and seafood is what this restaurant does well. From the ceviche to the Veracruz fish tacos to the lobster, seafood lovers are sure to find what they are looking for here. Visa and MasterCard accepted. Open daily 9 AM to 10 PM.

BISMARK II

612-122-4854
Degollado and Altamirano
Price: Moderate
Serving: B, L, D
Wheelchair Accessible: Yes

This home-style restaurant has been a popular La Paz eatery for many years. It's a bit out of the way, but the generous portions and wide variety of dishes make it worth the trip. Seafood is the specialty here, starting with the fresh ceviche appetizer to fresh dorado or halibut and enormous grilled lobsters. Visa and MasterCard accepted. Open daily 10 AM to 10 PM.

Pizza

LA FABULA PIZZA

612-122-4101
Paseo Álvaro Obregón 15
Price: Inexpensive
Serving: L, D
Wheelchair Accessible: Yes

This is Mexico's version of fast-food pizza. Nothing too great, but they have some good specials if you're looking for a cheap meal. Open daily 11 AM to 10 PM.

PIZZA A PEZZI
Paseo Álvaro Obregón 1773
Price: Inexpensive
Serving: D
Wheelchair Accessible: Yes

The Italian owners of this hole-in-the-wall pizza joint make the dough right in the restaurant. Standard pizza toppings are offered as well as some more interesting combos. There are a few tables inside as well as a few on the sidewalk out front. It seems to be a favorite with local college students. Open Monday through Saturday 6 PM to 11:30 PM.

Asian

LA COCHINITA
612-122-1600
Forjadores and Veracruz
Price: Inexpensive
Serving: L, D
Wheelchair Accessible: Yes

Here you'll find generous portions of Japanese fast food served with a hint of a Mexican twist. This joint is popular with the local college kids. Open daily 10 AM to 10 PM.

RESTAURANTE DRAGÓN
612-122-1372
16 de Septiembre and Esquerro
Price: Moderate
Serving: L, D
Wheelchair Accessible: Yes

Enjoy an after-dinner sunset stroll along the Malecón in La Paz.

This is probably the most popular Chinese restaurant in La Paz. It's located in the heart of the city's small Chinatown, and while not particularly expensive, it's not a place to dine in shorts and a tank top. The menu is mainly made up of Cantonese dishes. You'll enjoy some of the best spicy shrimp you've ever had at a fraction of the price you're used to. Open Wednesday through Monday 1 PM to 11 PM.

SEÑOR SUSHI
612-122-3425
Madero 1715
Price: Moderate
Serving: L, D
Wheelchair Accessible: No

Fifty different types of sushi are featured at this sushi restaurant. They are made with quality ingredients and fish fresh from the sea. Free delivery is offered within the Tourist Corridor.

SUSHI EXPRESS
612-122-1372
Madero and Degollado
Price: Inexpensive
Serving: L, D
Wheelchair Accessible: Yes

This inexpensive, clean establishment specializes in fresh and fast sushi and tempura dishes. Open Wednesday through Monday 1 PM to 11 PM.

Cafés

CAFÉ EXQUISITO
612-128-5991
Paseo Álvaro Obregón e/ Tejada and Bañnuelos
Price: Inexpensive
Serving: B, L, D
Wheelchair Accessible: Yes

If you're homesick for Starbucks, this is the place to come. You'll hardly know the difference, with its young baristas serving up

frappuccinos and pastries. They even have overpriced knickknacks to mull over while you wait for your order. Open 6:30 AM to 11 PM Monday through Friday and 8 AM to 12 PM Saturday and Sunday.

CAFFÉ GOURMET
612-122-6037
Esquerro and 16 de Septiembre
Price: Inexpensive
Serving: B, L, D
Wheelchair Accessible: Yes

A great place to come for dessert or to pick up a quick sandwich before heading out to the beach. The menu features a long list of coffee drinks as well as Italian sodas. Open Monday through Saturday 8 AM to 10 PM.

THE DOCK CAFÉ
612-125-6626
Topete and Legaspi 3040, next to Marina de la Paz
Price: Moderate
Serving: B, L, D
Wheelchair Accessible: Yes

Casual and elegant at the same time, this small restaurant has street-side eating with a view of the marina. The menu offers everything from hamburgers to fish and chips to Mexican dishes. Breakfasts are Mexican and American fare. There is occasionally live music in the evenings. Open daily 8 AM to 10 PM.

MAREIROS CAFÉ
612-123-5439
Paseo Álvaro Obregón, north of Oasis
Price: Moderate
Serving: B, L, D
Wheelchair Accessible: Yes

This restaurant located across the street from the *malecón* is probably the best Internet café you'll find in La Paz. Its simple but extensive menu offers coffee, pastries, sandwiches, and other light fare. Open 8 AM to 11 PM Monday through Saturday and 9 AM to 5 PM Sunday.

International

CAFFÉ MILANO

612-125-9981
Calle Esquerro 15
Price: Expensive
Serving: L, D
Wheelchair Accessible: Yes

Authentic Italian cuisine is served up in the comfort of a restored building that dates back more than a century. This fine-dining restaurant is located a block off the *malecón,* so it's near the city's nightlife. The menu offers a wide range of wines to go with such traditional favorites as homemade sausages or fresh seafood tossed in fresh pastas. Reservations are recommended, particularly for large groups or on weekends. Open Monday through Saturday 12:30 PM to 11 PM.

BOUGAINVILLEA RESTAURANTE

612-122-7744
Malecón de Vista Coral 5
Price: Expensive
Serving: L, D
Wheelchair Accessible: Yes

Located on the west end of the *malecón* just behind Estella del Mar restaurant, Bougainvillea specializes in California cuisine in addition to steak and seafood dishes. The service is upscale, and the restaurant's location can't be beat. Live music is offered on some nights. Visa and MasterCard accepted. Open daily 12 PM to 12 AM.

CAFÉ CAPRI

612-123-3737
Malecón de Vista Coral, between Márquez de León and Topete
Price: Inexpensive
Serving: L, D
Wheelchair Accessible: Yes

This restaurant is situated on the north side of the *malecón* and boasts both a beautiful vista and a romantic atmosphere. On its international menu you will find crepes, extensive drinks, and a variety of deserts. Patio dining is available, where you can catch a nice breeze and enjoy a light meal. Enjoy live music on Friday and Saturday nights. Open Tuesday through Sunday 7 AM to 12:30 AM.

LA DIVINA UVA

612-125-9977
Márquez de León and Abosolo
Price: Expensive
Serving: L, D
Wheelchair Accessible: Yes

If you're looking for a distinctive meal in an elegant setting, La Divina Uva is probably a pretty good bet. Located at the south end of the *malecón,* this fine-dining establishment has one of the finest waterfront views in La Paz. The best tables are outside on the patio, shaded by a palapa and several palm trees. The menu offers a wide range of interesting entrées with an international flair, including seafood, steak, and pork dishes. The bar has a good selection of wines and some of the finest margaritas and martinis in town. Open daily 3 PM to 12:30 AM.

GULA

612-106-7001
Pueblo Marinero Local 43
Price: Expensive
Serving: B, L, D
Wheelchair Accessible: Yes

Gula, which means "gluttony" in Spanish, is located in the neighborhood of Pueblo Marinero about 3 miles north of downtown. It overlooks the marina, providing a wonderful sunset vista as you enjoy a meal at this fine-dining establishment. The restaurant's motto is "This is where food becomes art," and the dishes are definitely presented that way with an amazing attention to detail.

Additionally, the restaurant's chef has created some of the most interesting and elaborate dishes to be found in La Paz. Open Tuesday through Sunday 8 AM to 10 PM.

KIWI RESTAURANT BAR
612-123-3282
Malecón between 5 de Mayo and Constitución
Price: Moderate
Serving: B, L, D
Wheelchair Accessible: Yes

This funky restaurant has a great location in the heart of La Paz. The menu offers a variety of international dishes, but seafood is the specialty here, particularly the lobster. Open daily 8 AM to midnight.

LA PAZTA
612-125-1195
Allende 36
Price: Moderate
Serving: B, L, D
Wheelchair Accessible: No

This small restaurant is next to the Hotel Mediterrane, just off the *malecón*. Echoing the decor of that hotel, La Pazta is done up in striking Mediterranean white stucco with a black-and-white tiled floor. The menu offers mainly a mix of Swiss and Italian dishes with pastas, pizzas, and fondues available. They also have a nice wine menu as well as real espresso drinks, a rarity in Baja. Breakfast offerings are sparse as it is mainly just a coffee bar at those hours. Open 7 AM to 11 PM Wednesday through Monday and 7 AM to 3 PM on Tuesday.

RESTAURANTE BERMEJO
612-122-2744
Paseo Álvaro Obregón at Hotel Los Arcos
Price: Moderate to Expensive
Serving: B, L, D
Wheelchair Accessible: Yes

Located in Hotel Los Arcos, this restaurant specializes in Italian cuisine and has some

seafood and steak dishes. It overlooks the *malecón,* so it's a great place to enjoy the view while dining. Open from 7 AM to 11 PM Monday through Saturday and 2 PM to 11 PM on Sunday.

LA TERRAZA
612-122-0777
Paseo Álvaro Obregón 1570
Price: Moderate
Serving: B, L, D
Wheelchair Accessible: Yes

This restaurant located in front of the Hotel Perla offers a varied menu of Mexican, American, and Italian dishes. It is definitely a tourist spot, though the benefit of that is that English is not a problem. For breakfast, try the omelet azteca, an omelet with chilaquiles. Or just have the pancakes. Open daily from 7 AM to 10:30 PM.

OASIS RESTAURANT AND BAR
612-125-7666
Paseo Álvaro Obregón 115
Price: Moderate
Serving: L, D
Wheelchair Accessible: Yes

This sidewalk patio restaurant specializes in continental fare with steak and seafood as well as some great Mexican dishes. There is usually live music in the evening, as well. Open from noon to midnight.

Vegetarian

EL QUINTO SOL
612-122-7274
Belisario Domínguez and Avenida Independencia
Price: Inexpensive
Serving: B, L
Wheelchair Accessible: Yes

Fruit salad isn't widely thought of as Mexican food, but it's a dish that has been perfected south of the border. This restaurant demonstrates this bit of trivia as well as other important but little-known staples of Mexican cuisine, such as fruit licuados, potato tacos, and torta sandwiches. This is also a well-stocked health-food store.

BARS AND NIGHTLIFE

A great night in La Paz starts at a café at dinner and ends many hours later. After a great meal, fun-seeking travelers stroll along the *malecón* or sit in the bars that line it and enjoy the sunset over the Sea of Cortés. The bars and clubs of La Paz are conveniently located here and stay open late into the night.

CHATITO'S AND PLANCHA'S MARTINI BAR
612-128-7787
Paseo Álvaro Obregón at the corner of Lerdo de Tejada

Located upstairs in the Seven Crown Hotel, this bar tends to attract a younger crowd. Its terrace is a great place to watch the sunset. Open daily 7 PM to 2 AM.

LA CABAÑA
612-122-0777
Paseo Álvaro Obregón 1570

This nightclub located in the Hotel Perla features Latin rhythms, so come ready to dance. There is a $4 cover on the weekends. Open daily 7 PM to 2 AM.

TEQUILA'S BAR AND GRILL
612-121-5217
Ocampo 310 at the corner of Mutualisimo

Enjoy plenty of great appetizers such as nachos and ceviche as well as some great dinner entrées. Combine that with a fun atmosphere and a long list of tequilas, and you'd better be prepared to catch a cab back to the hotel. Open Monday through Saturday 8 PM to 3 AM.

LAS VARITAS
612-125-2025
Independencia and Belisario Domínguez

This is defiantly a nightclub for the Latin set, with Latin rock, ranchero, and salsa all being heard here. Open daily 9 PM to 3 AM., and there is a $5 cover charge.

BEACHES

La Paz is an old working city that grew up around agriculture and industry rather than being designed for recreation and tourism. Consequently, the best beaches (and there are some good ones) are not really near town. This is not to say that the beaches near town aren't worth a visit. In recent years La Paz has worked to improve the quality of the beaches located near the *malecón* with daily cleaning crews, imported sand, and the construction of palapas. Unfortunately, the large cove where the city is located can create strong tidal currents, so most tourists choose to make the short drive—either in a rental car, bus, or taxi—to the outlying beaches north of town.

EL COROMUEL This first beach north of town is located within the harbor of La Paz and is therefore very convenient. Large palapas are available as are food and refreshment stands.

CAIMANCITO This beach is located directly in front of La Concha Beach Resort near Km 5 on Mexico 1. The best of La Paz's city beaches, it's lined with shade-providing palapas, and a rock reef within swimming distance offers decent snorkeling despite being so close to the city.

TESORO Located 8 miles out of town along the Pichilingue road, this calm beach is a good one for families and small groups. There is a small seafood restaurant here with plenty of palapas and moderate prices. If you're feeling active, you can also rent kayaks here.

PICHILINGUE This beach is located in a tiny cove and has a nice view of the ferry port and the *malecón*. Three good-sized palapas offer shade, and on the north end of the beach, an abandoned palapa restaurant can be used as a shady area for a large group. (A still-in-operation restaurant with a large patio area facing the water is located right on the beach.) Camping is allowed at this beach, which has clean bathrooms with flush toilets. However, these may not be stocked with toilet paper, so to be on the safe side (as is the case any time you're traveling in Mexico), you should probably bring your own.

BALANDRA If you were to ask around about which is the best beach in La Paz, your taxi driver, your waiter, and your tour guide are likely to reel off "Tecolote." This should be your first clue that Tecolote is not the best beach in La Paz. Even if Tecolote was not crowded with tourists, beachfront restaurants, and knickknack hucksters, it would still have a hard time beating out Balandra for beauty and tranquillity. Balandra is actually a series of secluded beaches located in a small bay with rock formations that lend themselves to exploration.

Balandra Beach—actually a series of beaches—is known for its beauty and tranquillity.

Aside from three large palapas, Pichilingue Beach has a beachside restaurant.

Decent snorkeling can be had here, and the water is shallow enough to allow an average-size adult to walk across the entire bay—though that would likely take an hour or so at its widest point. The drawbacks: no bathroom facilities and very little shade except for the occasional palapa. Drive north of town toward Tecalote, and watch for the sign to Balandra instructing you to take a left in the fork in the road. It is located about 5 miles beyond Pichilingue. Get here early to avoid crowds, particularly on weekends.

TECOLOTE This is the largest and most popular beach in La Paz, located 18 miles north of the city on a paved road. The white sand and calm water make the beach ideal for swimming. Two seafood restaurants offer good food and drinks as well as other beach necessities such as umbrellas and pay showers—keep in mind that you are expected to purchase something if you sit under a palapa. A large number of other vendors here offer a variety of refreshments and services, such as parasailing and Jet Skiing. This beach also has facilities for RV camping. It's also where you will come to rent and board *pangas* to take you to Isla Espíritu Santo, which is clearly visible in the distance.

The famed Mushroom Rock at Balandra Beach

Extending the Life of Mushroom Rock

Visitors to Balandra Beach north of La Paz have long been amazed by Mushroom Rock, located toward the north shore where the bay opens onto the Sea of Cortés. This 18-ton chunk of composite sedimentary rock has been sculpted by sea currents over the centuries into a 14-foot tall, 10-foot diameter teardrop that sits precariously atop a rock reef. The rock has been photographed so often that it has become a symbol of La Paz itself.

You can imagine the waves that were kicked up among La Paz's beach-loving community when the forces that had shaped this landmark finally destroyed it.

In 2005 Mushroom Rock was discovered toppled from its pedestal. While no one can be sure what happened, the most likely culprit was an unusually strong storm that brought strong winds and waves from the west.

A local movement was quickly organized to remount the rock. This proved a daunting task since the spot where Mushroom Rock sat is surrounded by shallow water, sharp rocks, and no access roads leading to it. A scaffolding frame of steel pipe was constructed around the site to support the rock as it was hoisted into position. A 4-foot-long steel shaft was drilled into the base to support the rock, which was further supported by smaller support rods, and then small rocks were glued around the base to hide the support rods. This extraordinary effort ensures that you and generations of visitors who come after you will continue to enjoy one of Baja's most amazing landmarks.

Tecolote is the largest and most popular beach in La Paz.

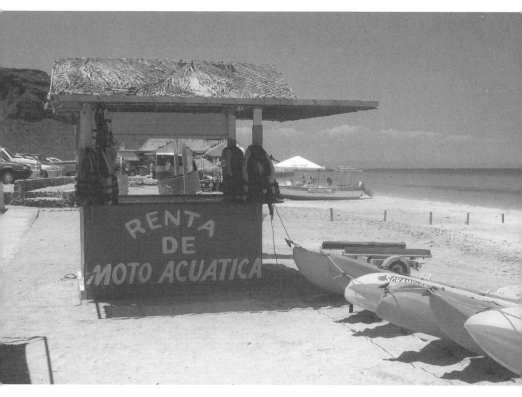

There is plenty to keep vacationers busy at Tecolote Beach.

PENÍNSULA EL MOGOTE On a map, this 7-mile appendage of land looks like a thumb enclosing the bay of La Paz directly across from the city. The southern shore of the peninsula is outlined by mangroves, while the north side facing the open sea offers long, empty beaches and clear water. The easiest way to reach this peninsula is by kayak since the access road is poorly maintained.

RECREATION

La Paz has been blessed with a seemingly unlimited assortment of natural resources that offer a number of recreational options. It has been a legendary spot for sportfishing for well over a half a century, and in more recent years snorkelers and divers have discovered it, as well. Whatever sport you're looking for, you'll find the city's tour agencies as well as your hotel staff to be more than accommodating.

Diving/Snorkeling

With its beautiful beaches and rocky offshore islands, La Paz is the ideal setting for scuba diving. The area has everything you could wish for in terms of underwater exploration, including shipwrecks, caves, sea mounts, and white coral reefs that are homes to more than 850 species of fish. Divers may also come across schools of hammerhead sharks, sea lions, giant manta rays, and even giant whale sharks. The beaches outside of town are great places

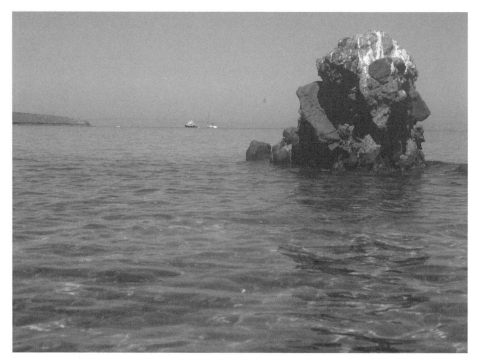

The clear water and composite rock reefs make Balandra Beach ideal for snorkeling.

for snorkeling, but the serious sea life is found offshore at Isla Espíritu Santo and other islands. For the best scuba diving, hook up with a local dive shop for a multiday trip. The warm months of May through November are when you'll find the clearest waters, with clarity down to 100 feet.

ROCAS LOBOS This dive site features several small caves and overhangs as well as a large number of coral heads. Here you'll immerse between corals and small coves, with depths that range from 20 to 100 feet. Rocas Lobos, which is very popular for night diving, was once home to a colony of sea lions. Although the sea lions have moved on, there is an abundance of life to enjoy here, including parrotfish and several species of ray.

GAVIOTA ISLAND WRECKS The offshore isle of Gaviota was once home to a colony of rare brown boobies, birds that have since disappeared from this area. This island is now the site of a 60-foot diving site in the bay of La Paz that features two sunken wooden boats. The ride from the city takes approximately 30 minutes, and for divers and snorkelers this island provides beautiful sandy beaches and a colorful abundance of sea life, including anemones, sergeant majors, and lobsters.

ROCAS TINTORERA Here, a series of underwater rock columns drop to 70 feet. Sea life commonly seen in this area includes octopuses, king angelfish, parrotfish, and moray eels.

Fishing

The waters off La Paz are teeming with fish, particularly the waters to the south. Generally speaking, fishing in La Paz is done from standard 22-to-26-foot *pangas*. However, because

The Salvatierra Shipwreck
In 1976 a cargo ferry named La Salvatierra sank after striking Swanee Rock, one of the few sites in the area with hard coral growth. The shipwreck victims were subsequently paid 50 pesos each in compensation, and La Salvatierra has become one of the most famous dive sites in La Paz. The ship now lies at a depth of approximately 60 feet and has become an artificial reef that attracts huge schools of fish, including baitfish, moray eels, and king angelfish.

La Paz is quickly becoming the location of choice among sportfishermen, larger boats are becoming more common at the city's three marinas. The two major fishing areas in La Paz are the offshore islands of Isla Espíritu Santo and Isla Cerralvo. Here you'll find yellowtail from November to March, roosterfish and tuna in the spring, and dorado, marlin, and sailfish from March through September. Red snapper, pargo, and wahoo are also plentiful. While there is good fishing to be had nearly all year round in La Paz, some of the best fishing is done in the brutally hot months of summer. Don't forget to pack a big hat and sunscreen.

Kayaking
La Paz offers wonderful opportunities for kayakers of all skill levels. For beginners, Playa Balandra is hard to beat, though other beaches closer to town also offer pleasant experiences, particularly Playa Caimancito. More advanced kayakers will have an unforgettable adventure launching from the northern beaches and heading out to Isla Espíritu Santo. Another option is to hire a *panga* to take you out to the islands in the morning and arrange to be picked up in the afternoon. For the truly ambitious, packages to kayak from Loreto to La Paz are available.

Bike Tours
Southern Baja has long been a popular destination for biking enthusiasts. The 230-mile Cape Loop begins in La Paz, goes through Todos Santos down to Los Cabos, then turns north through Los Barriles, San Bartlo, and El Trufino. The longest distance between hotels is 70 miles, plus there are ample camping sites. Several tour companies offer guided tours. For mountain bikers, many single-track dirt trails on the Pichilingue Peninsula north of La Paz go along the coast or through inland canyons. Multiday routes come out of Los Planes in the south. You can rent bikes and arrange tours on the *malecón*.

Off-Roading
Sure, La Paz is best known for recreational activities centered on its clear blue water. But Baja is also famous for off-roading through its rugged desert terrain, and some of the best off-road trails in Baja lie along the corridor between La Paz and Loreto. In fact, La Paz has often been the final leg of the world famous Baja 1000. Day trips or multiday tours are available along these famous trails in ATVs or dirt bikes. When heading out to the course, be sure that your passport and driver's license are on your person in case of a medical emergency. There have been rare instances in which an airlift to a San Diego hospital has been necessary, and this evacuation could be delayed without a passport due to new requirements.

Take an off-road tour through the desert outside La Paz.

Whale Watching

Whale enthusiasts from around the world come to La Paz for the chance to interact with the majestic gray whales that arrive yearly from January through March to bear their young. In addition to the gray whale, several other species are visible throughout the season, including the humpback whale, blue whale, fin whale, sperm whale, and orca. Schools of dolphins are also common throughout the winter months, and sea lions are present year-round. To learn more, visit the Whale Community Museum: 612-121-1693; Navarro between Altamirano and Farias; open 9 AM to 2 PM.

Tour Companies

As La Paz has grown as a tourist destination, serving tourists has become a big business there. Consequently, all manner of guides are vying for your business. While the businesses listed below have a certain degree of reputability, it's always best to discuss your expectations with the representative when making arrangements. This is particularly true when booking a trip from the *malecón* or your hotel. The last thing you want is to arrive at Tecolote Beach to find your captain cobbling together the engine on his *panga* right before you are to embark on an all-day tour. In the event something similar to this does happen, don't hesitate to back out and find another tour group. After all, there are plenty of 'em around.

BAJA ECOTOURS

612-124-6629 or 1-877-560-2252 (U.S.); fax 760-433-9863 (U.S.)

www.bajaecotours.com
La Paz
U.S. Office: 603 Seagaze Drive #732, Oceanside, CA

This eco-conscious company offers a variety of scuba diving and snorkeling trips tailored to your travel plans. Expeditions feature dives near the sea lion colonies at Los Islotes, at the Salvatierra shipwreck, and other popular locations.

BAJA EXPEDITIONS

612-123-4900 or 1-800-843-6967 (U.S.); fax 858-581-6542 (U.S.)
www.bajaex.com
La Paz
U.S. Office: 2625 Garnet Avenue, San Diego, CA

Whether whale watching, diving, or hiking, this company offers a wide variety of tours and cruises. You may choose to whale watch from the deck of their 80-foot boat or rough it on a multiday kayak adventure. Likewise, you can go diving for whale sharks based from your hotel, or live aboard a boat for a few days. Check their Web site for tour dates and availability.

BAJA OUTDOOR ACTIVITIES

612-125-5636
www.kayakinbaja.com
Centro, La Paz

This company offers multisport and combo trips: fly-fishing/sea kayaking or kayaking/remote hiking expeditions in May and October. In late January and February, they offer eight-day sea kayak expeditions to Isla Espíritu Santo with whale watching included. Trips are fully catered, and hotel accommodations are included. Half- and full-day excursions are also available.

BAJA QUEST

612-123-5320; fax 612-123-5321
www.bajaquest.com.mx
Rangel #10 (between Sonora and Sinaloa), La Paz

Specializing in marine adventure travel in Baja California Sur, this local company takes groups of up to 15 divers to popular spots in the area. Do a day trip, or book a trip for up to five days.

CLUB HOTEL CANTAMAR SPORTS LODGE

612-122-1826; fax 612-122-8644
www.clubcantamar.com

Dolphins off the coast of La Paz are a extra treat during a whale-watching cruise.

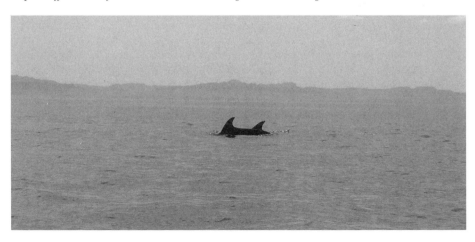

Paseo Álvaro Obregón 1665-2, Plaza Cerralvo, La Paz

This is a fully equipped dive center and resort. Stay in their hotel and take a day trip on their 22-foot *panga,* or live aboard and dive from their 90-foot vessel. They also provide whale-watching, kayaking, and sportfishing excursions.

THE CORTEZ CLUB

612-121-6120; fax 612-121-6123
www.cortezclub.com
Pichilingue Km 5 (at La Concha Beach Resort), La Paz

This is a full diving and water-sports center, complete with a private pier and a sunset bar. They offer everything from kayaking and windsurfing to Jet Skis and Hobie Cats. Instruction for sailing, windsurfing, and water skiing is available. They also have a fully equipped dive center and are ANDI, IANTD, TDI, PADI, and DSAT certified. Diving lessons are provided, and instructors are fully bilingual.

EL TECOLOTE TOURS

612-127-9494
www.eltecolote.net
Tecolote Beach, La Paz

This company is conveniently located right at Tecolote Beach and offers four-hour snorkeling tours of Isla Espíritu Santo.

FUN BAJA DIVING

1-800-667-5362 (U.S./Canada);
fax 780-389-2271
www.deepdiscoveries.com
La Paz
Canadian Office: P.O. Box 73, Mulhurst Bay, Alberta

This Canada-based tour company offers multiday camping expeditions to the secluded bays of Isla Espíritu Santo. Trips include gourmet meals and three-tank boat dives. They also offer whale-shark expeditions from June to November. Other package trips with various lodging options are also available.

KATUN TOURS

612-125-5636
www.katuntours.com
El Malecón in BOA's office, next to Hotel el Moro, La Paz

This company specializes in mountain-bike adventure tours, offering day trips as well as one- and two-week tours of Baja California Sur. Or just drop in, rent a bike, and ask for trail suggestions.

LA PAZ ATVS ADVENTURE

612-140-1620
www.lapazatvs.com
El Comitán, north of La Paz on Mexico 1

This company, located about 30 minutes north of La Paz, provides three-hour guided tours of the El Magote sand dunes outside La Paz. Tours cost about $75 per person ($90 for two people riding the same vehicle), and the ATVs are Honda Rancher 350 quads.

MAR Y ADVENTURAS

612-123-0559
www.kayakbaja.com
Topete 564 (at Posada Luna Sol Hotel),
La Paz

A variety of kayak expeditions—including combo snorkeling trips to Isla Espíritu Santos and whale-watching adventures—are offered by this company. Their tour guides are knowledgeable and professional and go out of their way to make sure you have a good time. They also rent to experienced kayakers.

THE MOORINGS

1-888-952-8420
www.moorings.com
La Paz
U.S. Office: 19345 US 19 N # 4, Clearwater, FL

This yacht-charter company offers boats from 38 to 50 feet. Typical week-long trips for qualified sailors begin at La Paz and continue north about 75 miles to Puerto Los Gatos and back, stopping at points along the way.

RAMA JAMA ADVENTURES

612-102-6175 or 760-346-3685
www.bajacharter.com
La Paz
U.S. Office: 45405 Via Corona, Indian Wells, CA

Enjoy a wide variety of activities with this water-adventure company. Explore hidden coves on kayak camping tours, dive beneath the surface to watch marine life, or sport-fish from their 26-foot boat. Opt for scuba and snorkeling day trips or live-aboard multiday dive trips. They also rent scuba equipment, and their PADI-certified dive instructors offer lessons, as well.

TAILHUNTER INTERNATIONAL

626-333-3355 or 1-877-825-8802 (U.S.);
fax 626-333-0115
www.tailhunter-international.com
Carretera a Pichilingue Km 5, # 205, La Paz

This company specializes in sportfishing of all types, catering to traditional anglers as well as to fly fishermen and spear fisher-men. They offer a variety of packages and have two fleets of pangas, one out of La Paz and one at Las Arenas on the northeast cape.

VENTANA WINDSPORTS

612-144-0065 or 1-800-998-5500 (U.S.)
www.ventanawindsports.com
Topete 2730-A, La Paz

Think of Ventana as a sort of a windsurfing bed and breakfast, located on the secluded La Ventana Bay 35 minutes east of La Paz on the other side of the Pichilingue Peninsula. They also have mountain bikes as well as yoga six days a week. However, windsports

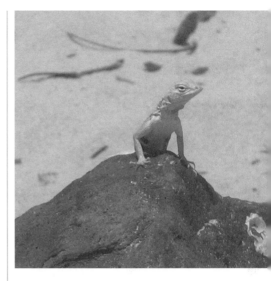

Baja is home to a wide range of desert animals like this lizard.

is the name of the game here, with wind-surfing as well as kite-boarding equipment. Instructions are offered, as well.

Other Attractions

MUSEO DE ANTROPOLOGÍA

612-125-6424; fax 612-122-0162
Calle 5 de Mayo and Altamirano
Open Monday through Friday 8 AM to 6 PM, Saturday 9 AM to 2 PM

This well-designed museum has three floors of exhibits that cover the anthropol-ogy of Baja California from prehistoric times through the colonial period and into modern times. For those interested in knowing more about the region's history, there are artifacts from the Native popula-tion as well as some dioramas depicting Native and colonial life. Although the labels are in Spanish only, you can't beat the admission fee: free.

CATEDRAL DE NUESTRA SEÑORA DEL PILAR DE LA PAZ

Calle 5 de Mayo and Revolución 1910

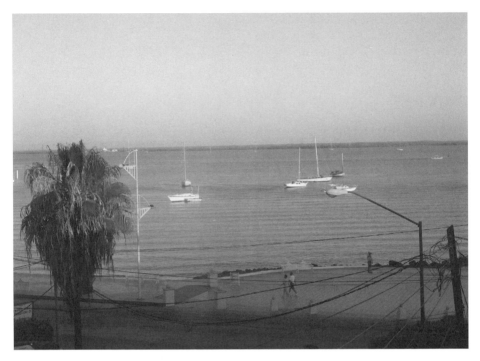

Morning in La Paz

This structure is on the site of a mission founded in 1720 by two Jesuit priests from Loreto, Juan de Ugarte and Jaime Bravo. The mission was quickly abandoned and moved south to Todos Santos due to lack of water and a rebellious Native population. The present cathedral was founded in 1861 by Dominican monks. The square in front of the building, known as Jardín Velasco or Plaza Constitución, features a high eight-sided kiosk of wrought iron. This is an ideal location for a romantic evening walk.

THE MALECÓN

This three-mile seawall is flanked by a wide promenade lined with statues, benches, and palm trees, making it one of the city's main gathering places. On warm evenings, the promenade is filled with couples and small groups of people enjoying the beautiful backdrop of the sea. Mornings find plenty of tourists and residents alike using the *malecón* for an early jog or bike ride. The only major drawback of the *malecón* is that it is difficult and at times even treacherous to access due to traffic on Paseo Álvaro Obregón, the busy street that parallels the promenade.

TEATRO DE LA CIUDAD

612-125-0207
Calle Farías and Calle Legaspy

This municipal theater is a 1,500-seat performing-arts facility that hosts musical, theatrical, and dance performances throughout the year.

MARINA DE LA PAZ

612-122-1646; fax 612-125-5900
Topete 3040

Marina de La Paz was the first floating marina in Baja California and only the second in all of Mexico. It began with only six slips but today can accommodate over 150 boats. It was remodeled in 2004 with all new docks and a Bazillian hardwood deck.

Pirates hid near the steep rocks of Isla Espíritu Santo to surprise Spanish galleons.

5

THE ISLANDS OF LA PAZ

The group of islands huddled north of the Pichilingue Peninsula is among the most important natural habitats in Mexico. These islands have the most pristine ecosystem in all of Baja California, providing a home for 500 species of fish, 31 species of marine mammals, and 210 species of marine and terrestrial birds. Additionally, this arid volcanic land rising abruptly out of the sea is home to 53 species of plants, including the world's largest cactus, which is endemic to the islands. Among the land animals found here—and nowhere else in the world)—are a variety of lizards, snakes, toads, and the endangered blacktailed jackrabbit.

Needless to say, with biodiversity like this, found in a gorgeous and easily accessible setting, the islands off the coast of La Paz are bound to attract visitors. In fact, these islands attract about thirty thousand visitors a year, 90 percent of whom are from the United States. Fortunately, the pressure exerted on this fragile ecosystem by tourism is now largely offset by a local conservation effort, though this has not always been the case. In 1976 Isla Espíritu Santo and Isla Partida came under the control of a communal landholding system known as an *ejido*. Despite their beauty, these arid islands provided few benefits to their owners, and in 1978 the entire area was designated a federally protected area, restricting activity and development. However, the *ejido* members continued to try to find ways to profit from their island parcels. In 1997 one member built tourist cabins on his property, but Mexican environmental official ordered the rental cabins demolished. In 2003 some $3.3 million was given to buy out the *ejido* to transfer the islands to the federal government for formalized protection and conservation. Today there's a balancing act and sometimes a struggle over these islands between the tourists and the economy that they support and the environmentalists looking to protect and preserve the fragile ecosystem that exists here.

GETTING THERE

Every year more tour operators appear offering adventures out to the sands of Isla Espíritu Santo, but the two companies that do most of the tour business in town are Baja Outdoor Activities (612-125-5636) and Mar Y Adventuras (612-123-0559). The types of tours that are offered vary widely, from four-hour *panga* trips around the islands to weeklong guided kayak adventures. Whether you choose to book your trip through an agency in town, through the front desk of your hotel, or when you get to the beach, be sure to ask plenty of questions so that you know exactly what you're getting. Most tours come with lunch, so find out what that lunch entails. If it doesn't sound appetizing, consider bringing your own. Also, if you are taking a *panga* over to the islands, make sure that it is equipped with life

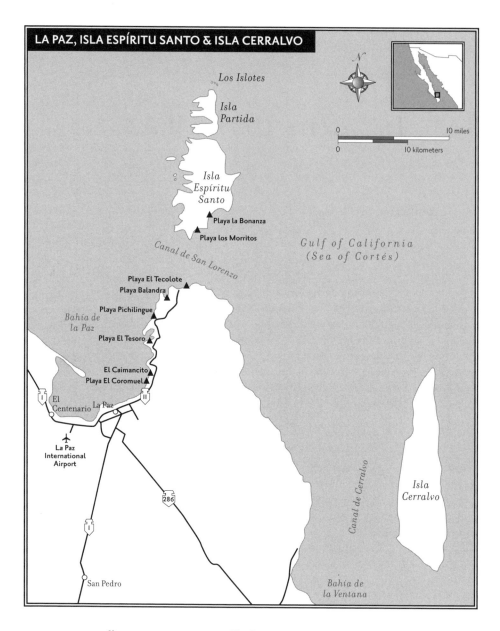

LA PAZ, ISLA ESPÍRITU SANTO & ISLA CERRALVO

Los Islotes

Isla Partida

Isla Espíritu Santo

Playa la Bonanza

Playa los Morritos

Canal de San Lorenzo

Gulf of California (Sea of Cortés)

Playa El Tecolote

Playa Balandra

Playa Pichilingue

Bahía de la Paz

Playa El Tesoro

El Caimancito

Playa El Coromuel

El Centenario

La Paz

La Paz International Airport

286

San Pedro

Canal de Cerralvo

Isla Cerralvo

Bahía de la Ventana

0 ——— 10 miles

0 ——— 10 kilometers

preservers—not all *pangas* operating out of La Paz carry them. Even if you don't plan on getting in the water, you never know when something unexpected will happen.

If you're planning on going on an unguided kayak trip to the islands, it's best to make the trip with someone who has done it before. The 4.5-mile crossing to Punta Lupona on the southern tip of Isla Espíritu Santo is fraught with tricky currents and potentially treacherous winds. Playa Tecolote is the best place to set off. Despite there being two freshwater wells on the islands—one at Caleta El Candelero toward Isla Espíritu Santo's northwestern side and one at El Cardoncito on Isla Partida's southwestern side—you should bring your own water. If it is absolutely necessary to drink well water, treat it first with water purification tablets or boil it for at least 10 minutes. This water is perfectly suitable for bathing. However, it's likely that you will need your own bucket and rope to get at it.

The two companies mentioned above both rent kayaks—but only to experienced paddlers. They also rent other necessary gear such as butane stoves and portable toilets, which are required for camping. Rise early to take advantage of the low morning winds, and bring as much of your own gear from home as possible. Things like snorkeling equipment are surprisingly expensive to buy or rent here. Campers and independent paddlers must also obtain a permit from SEMARNAT, located at Calle Ocampo 1045 (612-122-4414). The permit runs about $4.

A sea cave on the east coast of Isla Espíritu Santo

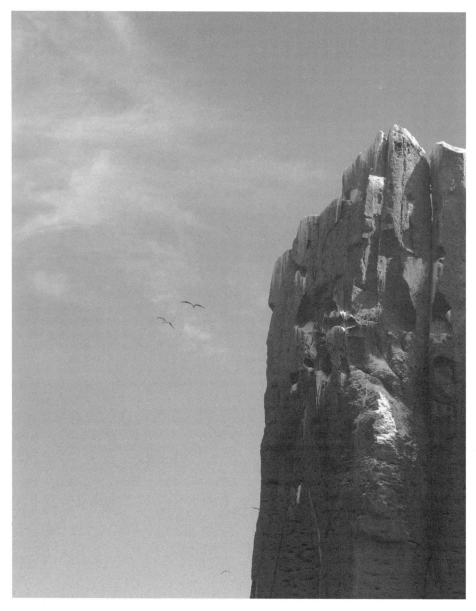

Sheer cliffs mostly comprise the east side of the gulf islands.

Consider, though, the distinct advantages of going with a tour company, whether this involves a complete guided trip or just a *panga* ride to the island. These companies can speed you safely to the islands' western sides, where kayaking is a relative breeze. They also know the best snorkeling spots and carry your gear for you. Most importantly, they can evacuate you back to La Paz if you become ill or confront some other unexpected circumstance.

The best time to kayak is from March to mid-April. This skirts the end of the whale-watching season when the air temperatures hang between 75 and 90 degrees and water temperatures are in the 60s. Also, the El Norte winds that have been known to pin kayakers down for days during the winter begin to die down during this period. The biggest drawback of going in March and April is that this is also the busiest time of the year.

Isla Espíritu Santo

This 14-mile-long island is one of the world's top kayaking destinations. Even for nonkayakers, a trip to this island is an imperative when visiting La Paz. By far the biggest island in the chain that lies off the coast of Playa Tecolote, Isla Espíritu Santo is notched with bays and sandy inlets along its western and southern sides. Many of these areas are adorned with white sand and rock reefs that provide great snorkeling. Among these spots are Punta Prieta at the upper north end of Bahía San Gabriel, Caleta El Candelero, and Punta Bonanza on the southeast side of the island.

All along they way, florid volcanic rock rises out of the sea in soaring cliffs. The entire western shore is protected from the prevailing winds, and thus paddling here is generally calm. The same can't be said for the exposed eastern shore of the island, which is defined by soaring cliffs, sea caves, and strange rock formations. Depending on the wind conditions, *panga* captains are sometimes reluctant to venture over to this side of the island.

Making your way inland, several good day hikes can be taken from virtually every campsite on the island. Follow the arroyos along the rocky bluffs, but tread carefully due to the abundance of loose rock underfoot. These trails will lead you to unbelievable vistas and hidden inland lagoons.

A fishing village at the southern tip of Isla Partida

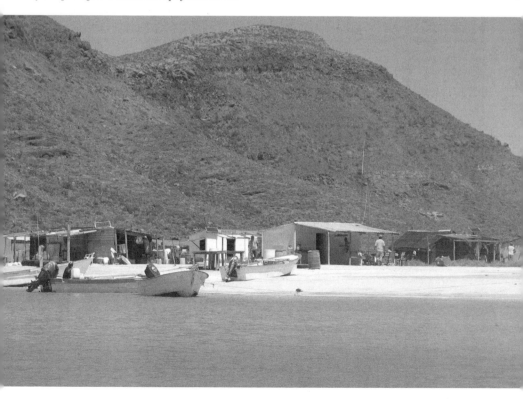

Isla Partida

The larger Isla Espíritu Santo is separated at high tide from its northern neighbor, Isla Partida, by a narrow channel that can become an isthmus at low tide. Indigenous fishermen have a small fishing camp here. Up the western side of the island, several coves cut out of the rock make for good anchorage. Toward the north you'll find the largest of these is the appropriately named Ensenada Grande, or "large cove." This is the best anchorage in this chain of islands, with clear blue water and creamy fine-grain sand. The cove cuts deep into the island, and its walls provide protection from southerly winds. The beach here is backed by steep arroyos that invite hikers to explore what else the island has to offer. If you follow the craggy landscape to the northern tip of the island, you'll come to El Embudo, a precipice that offers stunning vistas. The eastern side of this island features sheer walls made of alternating layers of black lava and ruddy volcanic ash. This vicinity is pounded by winds and lapping waves that have created several sea caves and other unique formations.

Los Islotes

Perhaps the highlight of any trip to these islands is the opportunity to snorkel with the community of sea lions that inhabit the tiny rocks at the north end of this island chain. These guano-covered rocks called Los Islotes are home to the largest colony of sea lions in the Sea of Cortés. The water around these rocks drops to a pile of boulders at a depth of about 16 feet and beyond the boulders it drops to about 65 feet, making it an ideal place for scuba diving. In late spring sea lion pups will swim with divers and snorkelers, as will the

A puffer fish caught off the coast of Isla Partida captures interest.

Manta rays breaching in the Sea of Cortez

females. However, always be wary of large, lone males that can be dangerous if you get too close.

Isla San José

If Isla Espíritu Santo and its environs are a little crowded for your taste, perhaps a jaunt out to the secluded Isla San José is what your itinerary needs. Located about 15 miles north of Espíritu Santo, this remote island provides fine camping beaches and a real opportunity to escape the crowds. A few tour companies in La Paz make the 90-minute *panga* ride out to this island, where snorkeling sites are teeming with tropical fish. During the early days of La Paz pearl fishing, this island became famous for its pearl deposits. Today it is little more than a refuge for pelicans and osprey, but there are a few human settlements on Isla San José and nearby islands. On the island of El Pardito (not to be confused with Isla Partida), between Isla San José and Isla San Francisco, a settlement of about 50 people is purportedly composed of the descendents of a single fisherman and his nine wives.

Isla Cerralvo

About 20 miles southeast of Isla Espíritu Santo lies Isla Cerralvo, a 16-mile-long rock that juts out of the sea. For the most part, a lack of good anchorage keeps people off the island. However, drawing sport fishermen to the coast of this island is the abundance of deep-water fish such as marlin, sailfish, and dorado, which are conducted to the area by deep-water channels that abut the island.

El Bajo Sea Mount

While it's not actually an island, El Bajo is a popular deep-sea destination. The Marilsa Sea Mount, also called El Bajo, is one of the best deep-sea diving locations in the Sea of Cortés. This is a group of three sea mounts rising up from the sea floor about 8 miles north-north-east of Los Islotes. The sea mounts top off at around 65 feet, and dives bottom out at 120 feet. This area is known for congregations of hammerhead sharks, though many other species of deep-sea fish also school and prowl in this locale, including marlin, Pacific manta, and whale sharks.

6

Loreto

On the surface, Loreto is a sleepy fishing village tucked between the indigo waters of the Sea of Cortés and the spectacular Sierra de la Giganta mountain range. This alone qualifies the town to be worth a visit. However, despite its rustic and unpretentious ambiance, this is a town that is rich in history.

History

Located 217 miles north of La Paz, this area was known as Conchó, or "red mangrove," by the Cochimi and Guavcura people who first lived on this land over ten thousand years ago. Jesuit priest Juan Maria Salvatierra established the first permanent settlement in 1697, making Loreto the oldest town in Baja California. As such, Loreto was also the first capital of the Californias until 1830, when the capital was moved to La Paz. This move allowed Loreto to retain the peaceful atmosphere that still exists today. Walking along the cobble-stone streets, you will see shaded courtyards set behind ancient wooden doors and cracked stucco walls. It is clear that the centuries have done little to change Loreto's charm and character.

The town's most conspicuous feature is the mission of Nuestro Señora de Loreto, located west of the main street (Salvatierra). This first mission of the Californias was established in 1752, though it has been rebuilt many times due to earthquakes and floods. From here, Father Junipero Serro set out on his 18th-century expedition that led to the establishment of 17 other California missions from the tip of Baja all the way north to San Francisco.

Despite its auspicious beginnings, Loreto has been little more than a dusty desert town through most of its history. When John Steinbeck came through more than 50 years ago while writing *The Log from the Sea of Cortez,* he found a town full of impoverished fishermen and a mission in ruins. In the late 1970s FONATUR, Mexico's tourism development agency, identified Loreto as one of the country's top four locations in terms of tourism potential—along with San José del Cabo, Ixtapa, and Cancún. While these other locations have since developed into major tourism centers loaded with major hotels and chain restaurants, Loreto remains a three-stoplight town—with only one that actually works. To be sure, there has been development in Loreto over the last 30 years. In fact, today tourism is Loreto's only industry. However, most of the local tourism development has been on a small scale with family-owned restaurants, ecotourism entrepreneurs, and small, independent hotels. Loreto has no movie theater, no malls, and local building codes prevent any structure from being taller than the mission. Unlike in many tourist towns where visitors are hermetically sealed in their resorts while locals live miles away, visitors to Loreto coexist with its residents.

The main thoroughfare of Loreto

An increase of tourism in recent years has meant an increase in expendable income among Loreto's residents. Consequently, cars have become somewhat of a status symbol despite the fact that the town is ideal for walking and bike riding. On weekend nights, locals flood the streets cruising up and down the *malecón* while laying on their horns well into the night. This makes Sunday mornings the ideal time for bike rides and strolls since most people sleep late. In fact, if you happen to be in Loreto on a Sunday, be aware that most businesses are either open until noon or closed altogether. The exceptions to this are the hotels, beer stores, and restaurants.

Although Loreto never developed into a tourist Mecca like Los Cabos and Cancún, it is clear why FONATUR targeted it 30 years ago. The area is blessed with temperatures that average in the 80s year-round and rich marine life. In fact, Loreto is unique in that it offers world-class sport fishing, diving, and snorkeling in a serene atmosphere relatively untouched by annoying beach vendors, beggars, and timeshare pitchmen. Loreto's charm lies in the fact that it is not just another Mexican resort conglomeration. Its fifteen thousand residents are laid-back and welcoming, its beaches free of monstrous hotel complexes and rowdy bars. You'll find a range of accommodations, from quaint boutique hotels and bed and breakfasts to an all-inclusive resort in nearby Nopoló. For the traveler looking to get away from the crowds in Los Cabos and wanting instead a less commercialized, quieter beach experience, you won't find many places better than Loreto.

GENERAL INFORMATION

Police
613-135-0035
Paseo Nicolas Tamaral and Heroes de
Independencía

Clinic/Medical Services
613-135-0039
68 Salvatierra and Juarez

Fire Department
613-135-1566

Post Office
613-135-0647
Deportiva between Juárez and Salvatierra

Tourist Office
613-135-0411
Francisco I. Madero one block west of Salvatierra in the Palacio Municipal (City Hall)
Open Monday through Friday 8 AM to 8 PM

Marina Park Office
613-135-0477
On the malecón next to the marina
Open Monday through Saturday 9 AM to 3 PM

Laundry: Lavendoría El Remojón
Salvatierra between Indepencía and Ayun-
tamiento
Open Monday through Saturday 8 AM to 3 PM

Bank: Bancomer
Francisco I. Madero one block west of
Salvatierra
Open Monday through Friday 9 AM to 3 PM

Supermarket: El Pescador
613-135-0060
Salvatierra and Independencia
Open daily 8 AM to 10 PM

Cyber Café: Internet Soledad
Salvatierra between Ayuntamiento and
Independencia
Open Monday through Friday 9 AM to 6 PM

Sporting Goods: Deportes Blazer
613-135-0911
Hidalgo #23
Open daily 9 AM to 10 PM

Pharmacies:

FARMACIA DE LAS CALIFORNIAS
613-135-0341
Salvatierra next to El Pescador Supermarket.
Open daily 8 AM to 10 PM

FARMACIA FLORES
613-135-0321
Salvatierra and Avenida Calusio
Open daily 8 AM to 10 PM

FARMACIA DEL ROSARIO
613-135-0670; Calle Independencia and
Calle Juarez
613-135-0719; Salvatierra across from
El Pescador Supermarket.
Both locations open daily 8 AM to 10 PM

GETTING THERE

With an international airport located just a few miles south of town, Loreto can be surprisingly easy to access. However, it's a small airport, which does present limitations. Direct
flights to Loreto from the United States only originate out of Los Angeles and San Diego.
AeroMexico does offer service from Phoenix with a stop in Hermosillo in between.

Loreto also lies on Baja's Mexico 1, the Carretera Transpeninsular (Transpeninsular
Highway), making it highly accessible by car, as well. Loreto is 721 miles south of Tijuana
and just 86 miles south of Mulegé. From San Diego, it takes about 17 to 20 hours of driving
time, though staying off the road at night is highly recommended. If you drive from the
border, take time to make a reasonable itinerary, and plan to stay at least one night in one of

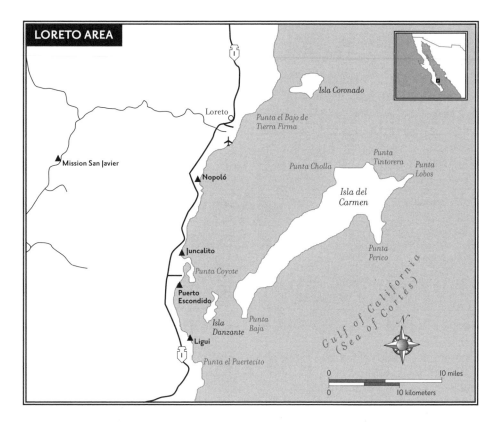

LORETO AREA

Isla Coronado

Loreto

Punta el Bajo de
Tierra Firma

Mission San Javier

Nopoló

Punta Cholla

Punta
Tintorera

Punta
Lobos

Isla del
Carmen

Juncalito

Punta Coyote

Punta
Perico

Puerto
Escondido

Isla
Danzante

Punta
Baja

Ligui

Punta el Puertecito

Gulf of California
(Sea of Cortés)

N

0   10 miles

0   10 kilometers

LORETO

To
Mulegé

N

0   0.25 mile

0   0.25 kilometer

Gulf of California
(Sea of Cortés)

Preparatoria

Mons. Modesto
Sanchez

Misioneros

José María Pino Suárez

Francisco I. Madero

Constituyentes
de 1974

Calle
Davis

Calle de la Playa

Marina

Independencia

Padre Kino

Paseo Juán Manuel Basaldua

Paseo Nicolas Tamaral

Ayuntamiento

Emiliano Zapata

Benito Juárez

Rosendo
Robles

Paseo Julian
de Mayorga

Paseo
Victoriano Arnes

Marquez de León

La Independencia

Paseo Pedro de Ugarte

Héroes de León

Benito Juárez

Av. Miguel Hidalgo

Ignacio
Zaragoza

Salvatierra

Ignacio Allende

Salvatierra

Francisco I. Madero

Nicolas
Bravo

Paseo
Francisco
Piccolo

Ebanstad

Baja California

Rio Loreto

To Nopoló

CAR RENTAL COMPANIES

Budget

LORETO AIRPORT, MAIN TERMINAL
613-135-0937; emergency: 613-104-3537
Open daily 7:30 AM to 7 PM

PASEO MIGUEL HIDALGO S/N BETWEEN LÓPEZ
MATEOS AND PÍPILA
613-135-1090
Open daily 8 AM to 7 PM

THE WHALES INN
613-133-0927
Boulevard Missión de Loreto, Nopoló

Europcar

LORETO AIRPORT
613-135-2260
Open daily 8 AM to 9 PM

LORETO DOWNTOWN
613-135-2306
Salvatierra at the corner of Independencia
Open daily 8 AM to 8 PM

Hertz

LORETO AIRPORT
613-135-2212; fax 613-135-0700
Open daily 8 AM to 10 PM

LORETO DOWNTOWN
613-135-0800
Calle Romanita between Hidalgo and Salvatierra
Open Monday through Friday 8 AM to 8 PM, Saturday 8 AM to 7 PM, and Sunday 8 AM to 6 PM

the many towns that dot the coast along the way. South of Mulegé, the road passes through some of the most scenic views in Baja as you skirt Bahía Concepción. The drive from the south is less scenic and at times much more treacherous. Loreto is 295 miles north of La Paz and begins with 50 miles of roads that wind intermittently through mountain passes. The road straightens as you drive through a desert of shrubbery and saguaro cactuses, then takes you through Ciudad Constitución and on to Ciudad Inserjentes, where the road becomes winding and hazardous once again. Drive this road during the day only, and take your time. If you have to stop for the night, Ciudad Constitución has many hotels to serve you. The fact that the locals drive this road at a much slower speed than the tourists should give you some clue as to how dangerous it can be.

If driving is not your thing, you will find hourly service to Loreto from La Paz for about $10. The bus station (613-135-1255) is on Salvatierra and Paseo Tamaral, about a 10-minute walk from the *malecón.* Its hours of operation are from 7 AM to midnight. The buses are usually not too crowded except on holidays. You can also make arrangements for bus travel at the main office of Autotransportes Baja California (ABC bus line) located at the corner of Salvatierra and Boulevard Juárez. Call for the latest scheduling and prices: 613-135-0767.

GETTING AROUND

With its narrow stone streets and manicured tree arches, Loreto is a town that lends itself to walking. In the city itself, hotels, restaurants, shops, and other services are all within a few blocks of each other. However, the better beaches are all outside of town.

If you'd rather bike it, several of the town's ubiquitous tour companies also rent bicycles. There is no municipal bus service in Loreto, but taxis are readily available, though they are not metered, so you should agree to a price before getting in. Knowing a little Spanish in

Loreto has retained the feel of its colonial past.

this situation is definitely an advantage. And you can always rent a boat to take you to the offshore islands, where you will find some of the best beaches.

If you want to strike out on your own, several car rental companies operate out of the Loreto airport as well as in town.

WEATHER

Loreto enjoys practically 360 days of sunshine a year. Winter weather is generally mild, with daytime highs averaging 70 to 85 degrees from November though June and evening lows dipping into the 50s only in January and February. Water temperatures also stay fairly warm through November, averaging in the 80s and dropping into the high 60s in January and February. In July and early August, daytime highs begin to creep into the 90s, and the air gets a bit humid. Evenings are warm, with temperatures remaining in the 80s. However, Loreto doesn't get truly uncomfortable until late August and September, when temperatures can get well above 100 degrees, and not even the sea provides respite from the heat, with water temperatures reaching an average of 90 degrees—the same as a warm bath. If there's a time of year to stay away from Loreto, September is it. Many smaller hotels and businesses (of which there are a lot) close down, and those who can spend the month on the Pacific side of the peninsula, where temperatures are relatively cooler.

Along the malecón in Loreto

Accommodations

One additional benefit to Loreto never having been developed as a tourist center is that hotel prices are substantially less expensive than in Los Cabos or even La Paz. The few luxury hotels that are here offer prices that would qualify them as moderate hotels in other places, while budget hotels would be an absolute steal if they were in the tourist cities to the south. As is the case elsewhere in Baja, you'll notice that many of the hotels here are run by expatriate American owners. These hosts can be a great resource for translation and travel advice.

Budget Hotels

IGUANA INN

Owners: Mike and Julie Ramos
613-135-1627
www.iguanainn.com
Corner Benito Juárez and Calle Davis Col

Centro
Credit Cards: None
Special Features: Kitchenettes

This bungalow hotel is hands down one of the best deals to be found in Loreto. With four colorful and spacious bungalows set around an attractive courtyard, the Iguana Inn is a pleasant place to relax after a long day of exploring Baja. Tables and chairs outside each room facilitate conversations with fellow travelers. But if you'd rather stay in, movies and books are freely available, too. The courtyard is complete with a Spanish-style fountain as well as a barbecue pit where you can grill up your day's catch. Each bungalow is equipped with a small refrigerator and a kitchenette. The on-site owners, Mike and Julie, offer casually personal service and pride themselves on keeping the bungalows renovated and clean. They are also extremely knowledgeable about the area and more than willing to offer advice and information. Their kayak kept in the driveway is available to take out for a spin at the marina, which is a short walk away. Rates: $48 to $59.

HACIENDA SUITES
Owners: Amador Family
800-224-3632 (Mexico) or 1-866-207-8732 (U.S.); fax 613-135-0202
www.haciendasuites.com
Salvatierra #152
Credit Cards: V, MC, AE
Special Features: Swimming pool, two bars, mini market, gift shop

This hotel has somewhat of a hacienda ambience, with the rooms built around a central courtyard that's dominated by a swimming pool. Arched entryways and *saltillo* tile give the courtyard a distinctly colonial feel to what otherwise might be reminiscent of a Best Western. The rooms are spacious and well kept, though the decor is definitely American budget hotel. It's located across the street from the bus terminal and several blocks from the beach, though the walk is manageable. This hotel does offer room service and a restaurant that serves a good breakfast as well as two bars and a well-maintained garden area. The staff is friendly and speaks English, and every Saturday night they put on a Mexican fiesta that features dances and music from around Mexico. Rates: $44.50 double occupancy.

HOTEL PLAZA LORETO
Manager: Ruth Martinez
613-135-0280; fax 613-135-0855
www.loreto.com/hotelplaza
Avenida Hidalgo #2
Credit Cards: None
Special Features: Laundry service, travel agent service

Located in the center of downtown Loreto, this hotel is just one block from the mission and three blocks from the waterfront. It's a simple hotel centered around a beautiful courtyard that's ideal for meeting up with other travelers; a shaded terrace on the second floor overlooks the mission across the street. The 24 rooms are clean, comfortably air-conditioned, and attractively decorated with traditional Mexican decor. However, the beds are on the hard-and-slightly-lumpy side. Because of the Hotel Plaza's central location on the city's main street, noise can be a nuisance at times. If possible, request one of the rooms with a view of the mission. Rates: $51 to $73.

MOTEL EL DORADO
Manager: Marcos Drew
613-135-1500 or 1-888-314-9023 (U.S.); fax 613-135-1700
www.moteleldorado.com
Corner Hidalgo and Pipila
Credit Cards: None
Special Features: Pool, restaurant, sports bar, laundry service, Internet service

This is one of Loreto's newer hotels, located one block west of the *malecón*. The hotel offers several services, including laundry and Internet. It also offers the convenience of arranging fishing trips at the front desk. The 11 rooms are simple but spacious and clean. They are centered around a sports bar called Pelicano Loco that's a great place to hang out, but it's only open from 1 PM to 8 PM because it borders a couple of residential properties. Rates: $50 double occupancy.

LAS TROJES BED & BREAKFAST
Manager: Agustin Salvat
613-135-0277; fax 613-135-1207
www.loreto.com/costa2.htm
Calle de la Playa, Loreto
Credit Cards: None
Special Features: Internet, airport pickup, Direct TV, outdoor hot tub

Located just off the beach and a quarter mile away from the center of town, Las Trojes is a nice find for travelers looking for something a little different. This hotel is made of actual Trojes, or ancient granaries, from the mountainous state of Michoacán. The hotel's proprietor, Agustin Salvat, had the structures shipped to Loreto a decade ago and assembled by Tarascan Indians from Michoacán. The result is one of Loreto's more interesting hotels. Each of its eight rooms has been uniquely designed with full bath, air-conditioning, and ceiling fans. They are clean, well arranged, and the rates are reasonable. Continental breakfast is included as is free use of bicycles. Group discounts and long-term rates are available, and children are always welcome. This hotel also offers airport pick-up on request. Rates: start at $50.

Midrange Hotels

BAJA OUTPOST
Owner: Leon Fichman
613-135-1134
1-888-649-5951 (U.S.)
www.bajaoutpost.com
Boulevard Adolfo Lopez Mateos
Credit Cards: None
Special Features: Diving tours

More than just a hotel, Baja Outpost is a certified full-service tour-guide operation. Although Baja Outpost offers many activities—including kayaking, horseback riding, and hiking—the specialty of the house is diving. The hotel has an excellent location close to the center of town and the beach. They offer seven good sized rooms and eight palapas. The rooms open up onto an attractive garden patio with several hammocks and an ocean view. A continental breakfast is included with the price of the room. Even if you don't stay here, Baja Outpost is a great resource for divers, offering complete equipment rentals and the capability to service up to 30 divers a day. Rates: start at $85 double occupancy.

COCO CABAÑAS
Owners: Steve and Barrett Scalapino
613-135-1729; fax 613-104-2264
www.cococabanasloreto.com
Calle Davis
Credit Cards: MC, V (through PayPal)
Special Features: Pool, barbecue area, kitchen, gated parking.

This hotel offers eight cabañas that open up onto a palm-landscaped central patio with a small swimming pool. Adjacent to the pool is a fish-cleaning station and barbecue that you can use to grill up your catch of the day. Six of the cabañas have a double bed and a twin bed; the other two have a double and a set of bunk beds. Each room is also equipped with a full kitchen, including a small refrigerator, a stove, and a microwave. A free video library is nice for kicking back after a long day of exploring Loreto and its environs. There is also a gated parking area on the grounds. This hotel has a great location: one block from the waterfront at the north end of the *malecón* and two blocks from downtown Loreto. The American expatriate owners are more than happy to offer advice or make arrangements to make your trip more enjoyable. Rates: $70 double occupancy.

LAS CABAÑAS DE LORETO
Owners: Jill and Rick Jackson
613-135-1105 or 707-933-0764 (U.S.)
www.lascabanasdeloreto.com
Calle José M. Moreles
U.S. mailing address: 1141 East Mac Arthur, Sonoma, CA 95476
Credit Cards: None
Special Features: Wi-Fi hotspot, outdoor barbecue area

Located on a gated property, this hotel is an easy walking distance from restaurants and shopping. It has four fully equipped cabañas, three of which have a queen-sized bed and a twin bed while the remaining cabaña—the Sailfish cabaña—has two queens. The cabañas are located behind the main house, known as Casa de Loreto, and face an inner courtyard. Additionally, the property's main house offers two master suites equipped with a single queen-sized bed in each. The main house also has an upper-deck patio with a view of the *malecón.* The property is also furnished with an outdoor kitchen for barbecues, several hammocks, a swimming pool, and a hot tub. For travelers who can't leave their laptops behind, the hotel is also set up as a Wi-Fi hotspot. This hotel offers laundry service for $4 a load plus off-street parking.Las Cabañas de Loreto is located one house off the *malecón,* just a five-minute walk from the public beach in front of the Hotel Oasis. Rates: start at $85 double occupancy.

EL SANTUARIO ECO-RETREAT CENTER

Owner: Bill Paff
613-104-4254 or 805-541-7921 (U.S.)
www.el-santuario.com
Ensenada Blanca, Km 86 Mexico 1
Credit Cards: None
Special Features: Variety of healing arts, eco-activities, guided tours

This eco-retreat center is located 25 miles south of Loreto on the bay of Ensenada Blanca. If you don't want to rent a car to get here, you can hire a taxi at the airport (the cost of the trip will vary depending on the number of people in your party). The property consists of six secluded bungalows, some situated on private white sand dunes while others face the beach. Simple living is the rule here since the rooms are designed to be environmentally sensitive and contain no electrical outlets, TVs, or phones, though there is a cell phone and Internet access in case of an emergency. Showers and toilet facilities are located outside each bungalow. The toilets are designed for composting, and the showers are solar heated, with the runoff distributed to nearby plants. Local materials were used to construct the bunga-

lows as well as the outdoor kitchen and dining area. A local Mexican cook prepares the meals with fresh seafood and locally grown fruits and vegetables. If you prefer, you're always welcome to prepare your own meals or learn from the cook. The resort also offers healing retreats and a variety of healing arts services, such as yoga classes, private massage, and acupuncture. Although only several people are likely to be staying at the retreat at any given time, El Santuario is equipped to host group gatherings, including the availability of a 30-foot diameter yurt, a tentlike structure ideal for music, dance, or group meditation. Or simply enjoy the natural surroundings with a horseback ride or guided hiking tour. Rates: $120 double occupancy.

HOTEL OASIS

Owner: Pascal Pellegrini
www.hoteloasis.com
613-135-0112 or 1-800-497-3923; fax 613-135-0795
Calle de la Playa at Zaragoza
Credit Cards: V, MC, AE
Special Features: Pool, bar, restaurant, tennis court

Established in 1960, the Hotel Oasis is one of Loreto's oldest hotels. It also has one of Loreto's best locations: right on the beach at the south end of the *malecón.* By Loreto standards it's a fairly large hotel, with 40 rooms, each with a hammock strung outside the entrance. Not all rooms have an ocean view, so you should request one when making reservations. Rooms are furnished with two double beds, with TVs and phones on request. The rooms are clean, though they do show their age. The restaurant opens at 5 AM to serve guests heading out early on all-day kayaking excursions and fishing trips. At night, the restaurant occasionally offers seafood, chicken, and steak buffets. The food is well done, though the choices are limited. The Oasis also has a small bar and a good-sized swimming pool that is advertised as being heated, though that hardly seems necessary. Rates: $115 to $144 double occupancy.

DESERT INN

613-135-0090 or 1-800-800-9632
(U.S./Canada); fax 613-135-0026
www.lapintahotels.com/loreto
Prolongación and Calle Davis
Credit Cards: MC, V, AE
Special Features: Restaurant, two bars, on-site parking, gift shop, laundry service.

Unlike most of Loreto's hotels, La Pinta is part of a chain of hotels along the Baja peninsula. Located on the beach just over a mile north of town, La Pinta is a two-story villa with 48 rooms facing the Sea of Cortés. All rooms have sliding-glass doors that open onto either a private balcony or a covered beach patio. Some rooms have fireplaces. An on-site restaurant—with a small bar—serves good Mexican food. The pool area is attractive and has a bar, as well. A game room and a gift shop are also on the grounds. With its beachside location, fishing boats pull right up in front of your hotel room to take you out for the day. Rates: $79 double occupancy.

SUKASA BUNGALOWS

Owners: Joyce Clagett and Beth Borntrager
613-135-0490
www.loreto.com/sukasa
Calle de la Playa
Credit Cards: MC, V

This small waterfront establishment offers simple, personalized service. The three air-conditioned bungalows are spacious and decorated in a colorful Mexican style—including tiled floors—that is sure to put you in the right mood as soon as you arrive. The two smaller bungalows have a king-sized bed, a living area with two twin-sized sofa beds, and a small kitchen equipped with plates and utensils as well as a refrig-

erator and microwave (no stove, though). The larger casita has all of these same amenities as well as a stove/oven in the kitchen. Bungalows are also equipped with small TVs—which only get three Spanish channels, so you're more likely to watch movies from Sukasa's video library. The bungalows open onto a tiled garden patio that is complete with a palapa and hammock—a great place to relax and talk about the day's adventures. Besides the bungalows, you can rent a two-story "main house" on a weekly basis. It is a one bedroom, two bath house with a king-sized bed and a large balcony. Also available is a yurt. This 14-foot-diameter waterproof and air-conditioned tent has a private bathroom and is furnished with a queen bed, a small refrigerator, and a coffeemaker. A unique vacation experience! Rates: $55 for the yurt, $75 for a small bungalow, and $85 for the casita.

Luxury Hotels

DANZANTE BAJA

Owners: Mike and Lauren Farley
408-354-0042 (U.S.); fax 408-354-3268
www.danzante.com
Km 89 Mexico 1
Credit Cards: MC, V
Special Features: Eco-resort, all-inclusive rate

Located 25 miles south of Loreto, this Mexican hacienda hotel sits on 10 seaside acres. This hotel was designed to harmonize with the natural surroundings and gets all of its power from solar energy. It is comprised of nine suites built on a rocky, volcanic hill facing the Sea of Cortés. The buildings are made of handmade adobe bricks with ceilings of cactus wood strips and handwoven palapa roofs. The property is landscaped with desert vegetation, including many colorful bougainvillea, cordon and pitahaya cacti, and tall mesquite trees. Each suite has French doors that open onto a quarried slate terrace—an ideal place to relax in your hammock and take in the panoramic view of the mountains and the sea. There are no TVs or phones in the rooms and limited cell phone access on the premises. If you are looking for nightlife, this is not the place for you. However, there is plenty to do in the ecologically friendly resort. Fronting the beach, the resort is ideal for kayaking and snorkeling, and there are several hiking trails nearby. Guests are also invited to join guided horseback trips into the backcountry or just ride along the beach. After your strenuous day, relax your sore muscles with a therapeutic message in your room. Meals are served family style and typically feature seasonal seafood and local fruits and vegetables. However, the staff is more than happy to help you set up your own beach barbecue, where you can cook your own fresh catch of the day under the stars. Rates: $398 double occupancy from November

through April 15, and $360 double occupancy from April 16 through October.

INN AT LORETO BAY
Manager: Maude Valdez
800-507-6979 (Mexico) or 1-866-850-0333 (U.S.)
www.innatloretobay.com
Boulevard Misión de Loreto, Nopoló
Credit cards: MC, V
Special Features: 155 rooms, handicapped accommodations, baby-sitting and concierge services

Formerly known as the Camino Real, the Inn at Loreto Bay is located in Nopoló, 5 miles south of Loreto. It's situated on its own cove in front of a beautiful and spacious white sand beach, which is a perfect playground for kids and adults alike. With a great view of the Isla del Carmen, the beach is one of the best in the area for swimming,

Inn at Loreto Bay

snorkeling, or just lounging around. Adjacent to the beach is an 18-hole, 72-par golf course that offers the same spectacular views of the Sea of Cortés and the Sierra de la Gingante mountains. The hotel has 155 rooms, each with a patio or balcony, and most having a view of the sea—though you should request this, just in case. The tiled bathrooms are spacious and have granite countertops. Each room is furnished with air-conditioning, a digital safe box, satellite TV, and a minibar as well as a king-sized bed or two double beds. The higher-end suites also have a private Jacuzzi on a large terrace. Facing the beach is a patio pool, which is beautiful but fairly small for the size of the hotel—however, with this beach, you probably won't even consider the pool. The restaurant and bar offer room service. Other services include baby-sitting, concierge, currency exchange, and laundry. Check the Web site for special packages, including an all-inclusive rate. If you'll be spending most of your time in the hotel, you should consider opting for the all-inclusive price since the food and drinks are expensive otherwise—although you can find much better meals and libations in Loreto for a fraction of the price. Rates: start at $125 for a standard room double occupancy.

LORETO PLAYA BED & BREAKFAST
Owners: Roberto and Paulette Lane
613-135-1129
www.loretoplaya.com
Calle de la Playa
Credit Cards: MC, V (through PayPal)
Special Features: Gourmet breakfast, discreet and personalized service, nonsmoking

Romance is the name of the game at this inn located right on the beach on the north side of town, about eight blocks from the central plaza. Owners Roberto and Paulette have designed this small, tastefully decorated B&B to cater to couples. The first suite has a sitting room with a TV/DVD, a refrigerator,

and a microwave. The separate bedroom is furnished with a king-sized canopy bed, and off the bedroom is a private terrace as well as a large bathroom with a tiled tub built for two. A similar suite on the second floor has the addition of a rooftop perch with an unobstructed view of the area and a hammock built for two. Adjacent to the main house is a smaller two-bedroom, two-bath beach house that sleeps up to six. A gourmet breakfast is included in the rates. Reservations are required. Rates: start at $145 double occupancy.

POSADA DE LAS FLORES LORETO
Owners: Guiseppe Marcelletti and Ursula Croci
613-135-1162, 619-378-0103 (U.S.), 555-208-2214 (other countries)
www.posadadelasflores.com
Francisco Madero just north of Salvatierra
Credit Cards: MC, V
Special Features: Rooftop garden pool, laundry service, continental breakfast

This boutique hotel, designed in the tradition of an 18th-century Mexican hacienda, is located right in the heart of Loreto. The downside of this is that the rooms can be noisy, depending on the kind of night they are having at Mike's Bar down the street. The 15 units—10 standard rooms and 5 junior suites—all have satellite TV and safety-deposit boxes. Most standard rooms have a

The Hotel Posada de las Flores in Loreto

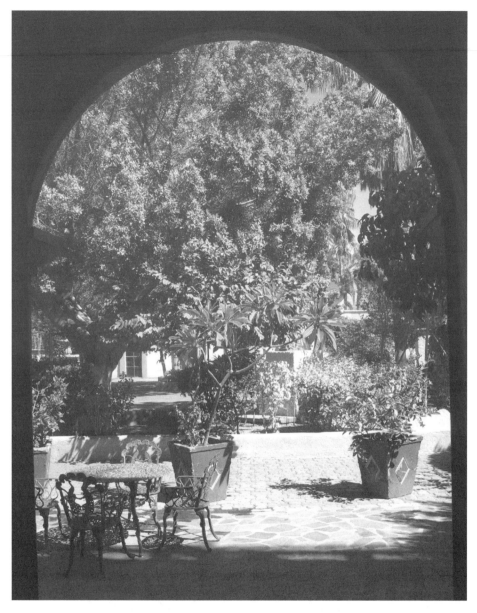

The view of the street from Hotel Posada de las Flores in Loreto

queen-sized bed, though three of them have two twins. These rooms are beautifully furnished but rather small. Junior suites have one king-sized bed. One unique feature of the hotel is a glass-bottom pool located in the rooftop garden, which is itself a perfect place to relax with a cocktail from the rooftop bar and enjoy the sunset. The inner courtyard area of the hotel is elegantly and colorfully decorated, though the canned music adds nothing to the ambiance. There are two restaurants on the premises. Vecchia Roma is an excellent Italian restaurant and has a good selection of wines. And a delicious continental breakfast, included in the price of the room, is offered from 8 AM until 10 AM. However, it's served at the Santa Lucía restaurant at the south end of the *malecón* about five blocks away. Another quirky detail about this hotel is that children under 12 are not allowed. Rates: start at $150 to $180 for a standard room double occupancy.

WHALES INN
Manager: Claudia Ramos Arellanos
613-133-0700
Boulevard Mision Loreto s/n, Nopoló
Credit Cards: MC, V
Special Features: Fitness center, meeting facilities, laundry service

This 236-room resort was formerly the Diamond Eden and the Solare Resort. It's located in Nopoló, across the street from the Loreto Tennis Center and next to an 18-hole golf course. The rooms are clean though not overly spacious. First-floor rooms are equipped with garden patios, while upper-floor rooms have private balconies. Not all rooms have a good view of the beach, so be sure to request this when making reservations. The facilities include two restaurants as well as a poolside snack shop. The hotel also has a fitness center and a hot tub that's reputed to be the largest in Baja, which is not necessarily a plus. Two beaches are adjacent to the property, one of which allows topless sunbathing. This resort allows families most of April (8–27), from July 5 through August 15, and from December 20 through January 3. The rest of the year it operates with an "adults only" policy, catering to those 18 and over. This is an all-inclusive resort, so food and drinks are included in the price of your room. Rates: start at $115.

RV Parks

EL MORO HOTEL AND RV PARK
Manager: Arstides Hernandez Solis
613-135-1162
www.loreto.com/elmoro
Rosendo Robles No. 8

This hotel/RV park is located only a hundred yards from the waterfront and near the center of Loreto. The facilities are a bit cramped, but you can't beat the location. The RV lots—which are either 6 by 11 meters or 9 by 11 meters—are all equipped with full hookups. The hotel offers eight rooms with private bathroom and showers. Rates: $15 per night for RVs with full hookups and $5 per night for tents.

TRIPUI HOTEL AND RV PARK
Manager: Eva Bustos
613-133-0814; fax 613-133-0828
P.O. Box 100, Puerto Escondido, 23880, Mexico
www.tripui.com
Special Features: Twenty-four-hour security guard

This large RV park/hotel—located in Puerto Escondido, 15 miles south of Loreto—contains 31 transient spaces and 133 yearly spaces to suit a variety of types of RVs. The property also has a launching ramp and boat storage, and supplies such as propane tanks can be purchased at the local store. The park is a half mile off Mexico 1, which makes it convenient without being too noisy. A swimming pool, gift shop, and a restaurant are also on the premises. The main office has Internet access for a fee. Recently added to the premises is a 16-room hotel, which has rooms furnished with a double bed and full bathrooms with tubs and showers. The hotel provides transportation to and from the Loreto airport. Rates: $18 per night for a site with full hookups and $10 per night for tents.

LOREMAR RV PARK
613-133-0711
Francisco Madero

This RV park is situated on a 5-acre site near the beach. Facilities include pool, lit tennis court, and flush toilets. Rates: $18 per night.

DINING

Loreto offers a variety of dining establishments. If you are the adventurous type, some of Loreto's best food can be had for less than $3 from such roadside vendors as Cesars Taco y Taco across the street from the Hotel Plaza Loreto or McLulu's, a taco stand on Salvatierra (open 10 AM through 7 PM).

If you are more in the mood to sit down and be waited on, you'll find tempting choices all over town. Breakfasts are normally inexpensive, with many restaurants posting their specials on a chalkboard out front. Choices include Mexican standards such as *pan dulce* (traditional sweet bread), *huevos rancheros* (ranch-style eggs), and *huevos a la Mexicana* (Mexican-style eggs). If you're craving something more familiar, you'll have no trouble finding pancakes, omelets, or other favorites from north of the border.

Most restaurants in town are open for lunch as well as dinner. And although lunch is generally casual, if you do choose to eat in town, consider resisting the temptation to eat lunch in your beach attire—shirtless or in your bikini. While the proprietor may not say anything, local patrons seem to frown on this.

Once the sun goes down, restaurants fill up. Choosing where to eat can be almost as much fun as eating. Many restaurants display sample entrées next to their menu. Keep in mind that few establishments take credit cards, with the exception of higher-priced restaurants and those located in hotels that accept credit cards for accommodations. Furthermore, some may have restrooms that are not up to the cleanliness standards expected by some travelers. But they are still regulated by the health department and serve only purified ice and water.

Mexican

CAFÉ OLÉ
613-135-0496
Madero #14, one block north of Salvatierra
Price: Inexpensive
Serving: B, L, D
Wheelchair Accessible: Yes

This unassuming eatery may be the most popular restaurant in town. Located under a palapa, along a cobblestone street right off the city square, it serves breakfast, lunch, and dinner and specializes in Mexican fare—though the hamburgers and fries aren't half bad. With several indoor tables as well as a few streetside ones, there's perhaps enough seating for 30 diners. Open Monday through Saturday 7 AM to 10 PM.

EL CANIPOLE
613-133-0282
Pino Suarez and Magdalena de Kino
Price: Moderate
Serving: B, L, D
Wheelchair Accessible: Yes

Food is treated as art at this eatery, which claims to be Loreto's oldest restaurant. The staff whips up the food after you order, including the salsa. This adds to the prep time, but it's well worth the wait. For a real treat, try the chicken mole. Located one block west of the municipal building, Open 8 AM to 11 PM Monday through Saturday and 2 PM to 8 PM Sunday.

LA CASCADA
Salvatierra and Zapata
Price: Moderate
Serving: B, L, D
Wheelchair Accessible: Yes

This restaurant features homemade Mexican cuisine and seafood. The portions are large, and the fresh guacamole and tortillas

Loreto's town courtyard

remind you why you came to Mexico. A large covered patio is a great place to relax and enjoy a margarita. Come for breakfast, lunch, or dinner. Open Friday through Wednesday from 8 AM to 10 PM.

LA PALAPA

613-135-0284
Madero and Hidalgo, next to La Terraza
Price: Inexpensive to Moderate
Serving: L, D
Wheelchair Accessible: Yes

An open-air grill facing the street will lure you into this casual restaurant, which serves Mexican food as well as seafood. Once inside, you'll be given a generous tray of chips and salsa while you wait for your order. The food is good, but a table can be hard to find on busy nights, and there is no host or hostess to take your name. You may have to pull up a seat at the bar and jockey for a table. Bring your catch of the day, and they'll even cook it up for you.

MACAW'S

Malecón and Morales
Price: Inexpensive
Serving: L, D
Wheelchair Accessible: Yes

Located across the street from the malecón, two blocks south of Salvatierra, this bar/restaurant features a great view of the Sea of Cortés. The food is good, too, particularly the guacamole, and the drinks are served stiff. Both indoor and outdoor seating are available. During football season, NFL games are shown on two small TVs all day Sunday and again for Monday Night Football. Overall, a good place to enjoy a drink and listen to music. Open daily 8 AM to 10 PM.

MEXICO LINDO Y QUE RICO

613-135-5004
Avenida Hidalgo and Colegio
Price: Inexpensive
Serving: B, L, D
Wheelchair Accessible: Yes

The name of this restaurant means "Beautiful Mexico and How Delicious." The staff here approaches their food with the same enthusiasm. The menu features Mexican classics such as huevos a la Mexicana and huevos rancheros for breakfast and chili rellenos and tortilla soup for lunch and dinner. The portions are large, and the food is on the spicy side, so have a beer and take it easy. Open Tuesday through Sunday 7 AM to 10 PM.

MITA GOURMET

613-135-2025
13 El Centro Historico
Price: Moderate to Expensive
Serving: D
Wheelchair Accessible: Yes

Located across the plaza from the municipal building, Mita Gourmet is a great place to go for Baja cuisine. Everything is prepared fresh, and the owners go out of their way to make sure you are taken care of. The menu has a variety of selections, though the seafood dishes are especially tasty. Open Wednesday through Monday 3 PM to 10 PM.

SANTA LUCIA

613-135-1332
Calle de la Playa and Fernando Jordan
Price: Moderate
Serving: B, L, D
Wheelchair Accessible: Yes

This pleasant little restaurant is located across the street from the *malecón*. Its heavy wooden tables and handcrafted chairs are housed within a high-ceilinged palapa with large windows facing the water. This makes it the perfect place to enjoy breakfast and watch the sun rise over the Sea of Cortés. For breakfast, they offer a variety of homemade sweet breads, freshly squeezed juices, yogurt, and pretty decent coffee. For lunch and dinner, they offer traditional Mexican fare as well as sandwiches on freshly baked bread along with a full bar. You can also order delicious boxed lunches to take on excursions: a sandwich, a drink, and a homemade fruit pastry.

TIO LUPE'S

613-135-1882
Salvatierra and Madero
Price: Inexpensive
Serving: B, L, D
Wheelchair Accessible: Yes

This is a classic Baja Mexican restaurant, complete with a full bar and plastic Corona chairs and tables. There are colorful murals on the wall and a palapa roof, just so you don't forget where you are. The food is good, though the building is a bit run down. Then again, you won't even come in here if you're looking for fancy digs. Open daily until 11 PM.

Steak and Seafood

CHILE WILLIE

613-135-0677
Lopez Mateos and Padre Kino at the north end of the Malecón
Price: Inexpensive to Moderate
Serving: B, L, D
Wheelchair Accessible: Yes

Located in a palapa on the beach just north of the *malecón,* this restaurant offers wonderful views of the Sea of Cortés as well as a competent steak and seafood menu. There is a full bar on site, as well, making it an ideal place to relax with friends old and new. MasterCard and Visa are accepted here, as are traveler's checks. Open daily from 11 AM to 10 PM. Also open for breakfast from October through April.

EL NIDO

613-135-0284
Salvatierra #154
Price: Moderate
Serving: L, D
Wheelchair Accessible: Yes

This restaurant is known for its Sonoran beef, seafood, and wine selection. It's also famous for its giant margaritas. The ranch-style atmosphere is complemented by gracious service. All dinners come with bean soup, salad, and a baked potato. Credit cards are not accepted here, though traveler's checks are OK. Reservations are recommended. Open daily 2 PM to 10:30 PM.

EL TASTE

613-135-1489
Benito Juarez and Zapata
Price: Moderate
Serving: L, D
Wheelchair Accessible: Yes

This steak-and-seafood restaurant, formerly known as Caesar's, offers meals in a distinctly Mexican atmosphere. Portions are often large enough to share, and the full bar makes some great drinks. It's located across the street from the gas station you pass on the way into town. Open daily 2 PM to 10 PM.

THE LOBSTER TRAP

613-135-0027
Located upstairs at the Quatros Altos
Price: Moderate to Expensive
Serving: L, D
Wheelchair Accessible: No

This upstairs establishment has the same owner as El Nido Steakhouse. Located two blocks west of the city square, it's a seafood restaurant that specializes in lobster dishes. The staff strives to create an inviting party atmosphere that's great for getting together with friends. Open daily 2 PM to 10:30 PM.

LA TERRAZA

613-135-0496
Madero and Hidalgo, upstairs from Café Olé
Price: Moderate to Expensive
Serving: L, D
Wheelchair Accessible: No

A variety of fare is offered here, from Mexican food like fajitas to north of the border fare like New York steak to more international cuisine like shish kabobs. Located upstairs from Café Olé, it's in a great location right in the center of town. Try to get a window seat, which overlooks Loreto's main street, and do some people watching while you eat. Bring your catch of the day, and they'll cook it up for you. Open Monday through Saturday 1 PM to 10 PM.

PLAYA BLANCA

613-135-1126
Corner Paseo Hidalgo and Madero
Price: Moderate
Serving: L, D
Wheelchair Accessible: No

This casual-dining establishment one block south of the central plaza offers a variety of Mexican and seafood dishes. Its upstairs location also offers great views.

Fast Food

ARMONDO'S PIZZA

613-135-0245
Benito Juarez at Tamaral
Price: Inexpensive
Serving: L, D
Wheelchair Accessible: No

This small restaurant—across the street from the El Pescador Supermarket—offers good pizza at an inexpensive price. In the evening they also offer hamburgers. Indoor as well as patio dining. Open Friday through Wednesday 11 AM to 10 PM.

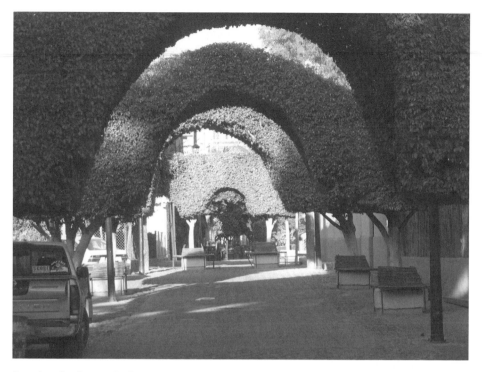

Loreto's sculpted tree arches lead you to the sea.

TIFFANY'S PIZZA PARLOR AND CAP-PUCCINO BAR

613-135-0004
Avenida Hidalgo and Piño Suarez
Price: Inexpensive
Serving: L, D
Wheelchair Accessible: Yes

This small, home-style restaurant offers a change of pace from chips and salsa. Besides good pizza, you'll find hamburgers, organic coffee from the Mexican state of Chiapas, and real espresso drinks. Open Wednesday through Monday 11:30 AM to 9 PM.

WINS RESTAURANT

613-135-1320
Salvatierra, east of El Pescador Supermarket
Price: Inexpensive
Serving: B, L, D
Wheelchair Accessible: No

Wins is the closest thing Loreto has to an American fast-food hamburger restaurant. It's hard to miss since you pass it on your way into town. Breakfast, lunch, and dinner are served here. Open daily 8 AM to 10 PM.

BARS AND NIGHTLIFE

To be perfectly honest, Loreto is not a place to come for lively nightlife. If that's your interest, head to Cabo San Lucas. Here there are really no clubs for dancing, and while several hotels and restaurants have bars, you can pretty much count on them closing early. When that happens, your choices are few and far between. Here are a couple:

JARROS & TARROS

Paseo Hidalgo

This billiards bar is located on Paseo Hidalgo next to Deportes Blazer. Open

Monday through Saturday from 6 PM to 2 AM, although it is known to close around midnight on some nights.

MIKE'S BAR
613-135-1126
Paseo Hidalgo

This is the one place in town that really parties into the night. It doubles as a sports bar and a place for live music. Open Monday through Saturday from 11 PM to 3 AM.

BEACHES

Loreto is surrounded by miles of sandy beaches ideal for snorkeling, kayaking, sportfishing, or just enjoying their beauty. Along the waterfront in town, large boulders create a breakwater for the city. The beaches in town, west of the marina and on the other side east of the *malecón,* are made up of coarse brown sand and are not as nice as other nearby beaches but are safe for swimming.

NOPOLÓ Nopoló is a community 5 miles south of Loreto. This area has been the focus of tourism development since the 1970s, but it has only recently gotten under way in earnest. Currently, developers are building several condominium complexes and a wellness community along the beach here. Despite this, the beach at Nopoló continues to be beautiful,

Nopoló Beach is beautiful, quiet, easily accessible, and great for snorkeling or just exploring.

The emerald water of Juncalito Beach plays host to myriad tropical fish.

quiet, and easily accessible. With the Isla del Carmen visible in the distance, this beach offers good snorkeling and fishing as well as rocky coves to explore while watching pelicans dive-bomb for their dinner. To get here, access Mexico 1 at 2 miles south of the airport, and take the exit for Nopoló. Follow the main road until it dead ends in a cul-de-sac at The Inn at Loreto Bay. Parking on the street is not a problem. To get to the beach, walk around the hotel, or, if you don't mind acting like a guest, walk directly through the hotel lobby.

EL JUNCALITO Located 14 miles south of Loreto off Mexico 1, this beach is set in a protected cove that is rich with tropical fish. It's popular among campers, and the gorgeous and isolated emerald waters and fine sand make it the perfect place for roughing it. You will have to keep an eye out to spot the inconspicuous sign on the east side of the highway marking the turnoff to this beach. El Juncalito is located about a mile north of the turnoff to Puerto Escondido. This leads you a half mile down a bumpy dirt road that comes out on the south end of the beach.

PUERTO ESCONDIDO Sailors know Puerto Escondido as the most well-protected anchorage in the Sea of Cortés, mainly due to the Sierra de la Giganta Mountains that come right down to the water. These rocky cliffs are perfect for exploring and offer wonderful views of the bay. Puerto Escondido, which means "hidden port," is actually made of two harbors, an outer harbor known as "The Waiting Room" and an inner, hidden harbor, that gives the town its name. Puerto Escondido was the planned site of a resort hotel. Construction was begun in the 1980s but was never finished. The ruins of this debacle remain and are themselves a point of interest. Puerto Escondido is located 15 miles south of Loreto just east of

Puerto Escondido offers wonderful views of the bay.

Mexico 1. On the south end of the harbor, there's a beach that's ideal for camping. If you need supplies, the Tripui Resort & RV Park (613-133-0818; www.tripui.com) is just down the road near the turnoff from Mexico 1.

PLAYA LIGUI This small beach lends itself to exploration with several beautiful inlets that are excellent for snorkeling and scuba diving. Desert brush surrounds the beach, and vultures and pelicans circle the rocky hills that rise up in the near distance, which add to the feeling of seclusion. This beach is 21 miles south of Loreto on Mexico 1. Follow the dirt road three quarters of a mile east of Mexico 1, and turn right once you reach the water; continue for less than a mile.

ISLA CORONADO The island of Coronado juts out of the sea with incredible rock formations on the eastern side where sea lions bask in the sun. The island is made up of huge volcanic pillars that create a rock wall that's 40 feet high in some places. Myriad sea life populates the island's waters, including moray eels, rock scallops, bumphead parrotfish, angelfish, and tigerfish, just to name a few. La Lobera, on the southeast side of the island, is popular with divers. On the west end of the island are several emerald coves with white sand beaches—wonderful spots to while away the day as you bask in the sun. You can get here by hiring a boat from one of Loreto's many tour companies. Keep in mind, some beaches are shallower and better for kids, some beaches are prone to be sullied by dead squid because of currents, and some beaches are more secluded than others. Specify what you are looking for to your boat captain so that he can select a spot that's just right for you.

ISLA DEL CARMEN At over 18 miles long, this is the largest island in the Loreto Bay National Park. It was once home to a large salt-mining company, the remnants of which are now a ghost town. The boat ride to Isla del Carmen is a bit longer than the one to Isla Coronado, but this island has many great diving spots. A 120-foot fishing boat that was wrecked in the island's Salina Bay has become home to a variety of marine life and schools of fish, making it an ideal opportunity for divers. Some tour companies offer overnight camping trips that include hiking and sea kayaking.

ISLA DANZANTES Danzantes is a small island lying south of Isla del Carmen. It's generally less traveled than the other, larger islands, and with its white sand beaches and rocky coves, Danzantes can seem like a paradise to those looking for an isolated experience. On the north side of the island is Faro Norte, an underwater series of coral-lined cliffs that drop to over 100 feet. On the south end of the island is Piedra Submarino, or "Submarine Rock," named for its resemblance to a submarine from a distance. This rock formation provides a habitat for colorful sea stars and murex snails.

RECREATION

What Loreto lacks in nightlife, it more than makes up for in recreational activities—there's enough to see and do in Loreto during the day to get you into bed early. The main reason to

Incredible rock formations, white sand beaches, and great diving locales can all be found on Isla Coronado.

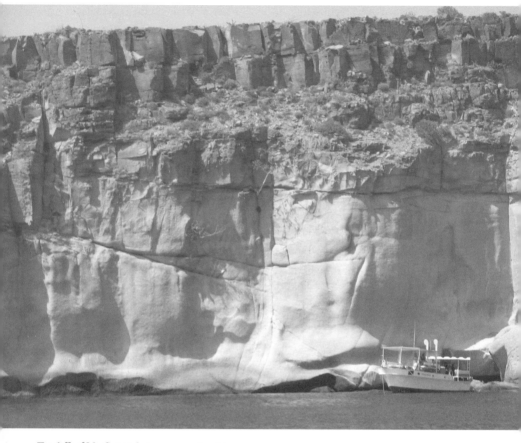

The cliffs of Isla Coronado tower over a tourist panga.

come to Loreto is the calm, clear water and the nearby islands. Fishing, sailing, kayaking, diving, and snorkeling are all outstanding here. The nearby desert mountains also present opportunities for outdoor adventures.

Fishing

Though the Sea of Cortés offers many fine fishing locations, Loreto stands out as one of the finest. The town is located far enough north into the Sea of Cortés that the choppy water of the Pacific is not a factor. This allows Loreto fishermen to go out in smaller craft than are possible farther south at the East Cape and Los Cabos. Loreto fishing fleets are usually comprised of 22-foot open skiffs called *pangas*. These boats are perfectly suited for light-tackle and stand-up fly fishing. Loreto's waters offer some of the best fishing in the world— especially if you are hoping to hook dorado or yellowtail. Loreto has been called Baja's dorado and yellowtail capital. Dorado, which is among the most sought-after species in Baja, usually arrive in the waters off Loreto in June, swimming in schools and feeding on baitfish and squid. Their numbers don't taper off until early August. Then, through September, the large bulls are left to swim alone off Loreto's coast. Dorados weighing 50 pounds or more are not uncommon during this time. As the dorados disappear, yellowtail move in and populate Loreto's waters from November through April. Other species of sport fish in these waters include the Pacific sailfish (April through October), marlin (May through October), and yellowfin tuna (July through October).

Hiking/Mountain Biking

You will find many excellent opportunities for hiking or biking in the rugged mountains of Sierra de la Giganta to the west as well as in the winding canyons south of Loreto. There are no formal trails but the locals know many wonderful spots. For most of the year, mountain paths will lead you by hidden freshwater pools that are scattered throughout the area. Unique flora and fauna as well as rare desert animals live along these sparsely traveled trails, providing birdwatchers and other nature lovers a great opportunity to view unusual species. There are trails suitable for novice hikers as well as the experienced. You can rent gear and arrange hikes though Las Parras Tours and Juncalito Eco Tours (see "Tour Companies").

Horseback Riding

Several local tour companies offer horse or mule excursions that take you along the beautiful backcountry leading to the San Javier Mission or other desert locales. Some of these trips are multiday affairs in which you eat and sleep at different ranches along the way. These outings last from three to five nights.

Loreto Bay offers abundant fishing opportunities.

Kayaking around Isla Coronado is a unique experience.

Kayaking

The calm waters off Loreto make kayaking the perfect way to explore. Several local tour companies offer a variety of kayaking adventures, ranging from two-hour tours to all-day excursions to Isla Coronado to overnight adventures to the Isla del Carmen all the way to 10-day kayaking expeditions to La Paz. Most long trips are not available during the hotter summer months. If you are just looking to take a kayak out for a couple of hours, check with your hotel. Many have kayaks that you can use for free.

Scuba Diving & Snorkeling

Loreto's offshore islands provide some of the best diving in the Sea of Cortés. Coronado, Carmen, and Danzantes as well as the islands farther south in the Loreto Bay National Marine Park—Monserrate and Catalan—provide dozens of dive sites for divers and snorkelers of all levels. Because the islands are volcanic formations, they have characteristics that make them a sort of playground for fish and humans alike. Their rocky shorelines, coral reefs, and huge underwater rock formations attract schools of tropical fish and other sea life such as giant mantas and 40-foot whale sharks. The majority of the dive sites are fairly shallow and ideal for the novice, but there are also spots for divers looking to explore deeper sites. Access to these sites is determined by the ever-changing sea current as well as other water conditions.

BAHIA SALINA Bahia Salina is—as the name suggests—near the old salt-mining operation on Isla del Carmen. The wreck of a 120-foot fishing boat sits in 35 feet of water, giving shelter to a variety of marine life. A great underwater photography opportunity.

PUNTA COYOTE Located outside of Escondido Bay, Punta Coyote features an underwater drop of approximately 120 feet. Colorful reef fish populate the crevices and fissures of the rock, while sea fans and other, fingerlike, gorgonians seem to reach out as you make your descent.

LOS CANDELLEROS Five miles south of Puerto Escondido, this chain of islets juts out of the water like massive fingers and offers sheer vertical facades dropping to depths of nearly 200 feet. Deep crevices in the rock face provide cover for dozens of species of fish.

LAS GALERAS Rocky outcroppings north of Isla Monserrate provide steep walls and large underwater boulders. This site is great for snorkeling. Just beyond it, the water drops to nearly 100 feet to an area filled with finger reefs.

LA LOBERA On the southeast side of Isla Coronado is La Lobera. Intricate sea fans and black coral cover a rock wall that descends to a depth of around 100 feet. Small crevices provide cover for moray eels and pargo.

LAS TIJERATAS Also located on the southeast side of Coronado, here a huge collection of boulders and giant pillars drop to around 75 feet. Myriad tropical fish and playful sea lions swim about as you dive.

Whale Watching

With three major whale-watching locations nearby—Laguna Ojo de Liebre, Laguna San Ignacio, and Magdalena Bay—Loreto is an ideal place to see gray whales and their calves frolic in the Sea of Cortés. No other Baja lagoon can claim to be home to more than a thousand gray whales as they gather to mate and give birth. Local tour companies offer a range of whale-watching options. If you're a casual traveler, you can hire a panga to take you out for a few hours. If you're the adventurous type, some tour companies offer a more close-up whale experience by kayak. For more serious whale explorers, multiday excursions are available.

Snorkelers at Nopoló Beach get up close and personal with pelicans.

Tour Companies

Loreto's tour companies offer a wide variety of services, making it important to discuss the particulars of your tour with the tour representative ahead of time so that you know exactly what to expect. Whale-watching trips are available from January through March. Many tour operators don't offer kayaking trips from August through October because of the hot weather, but these hot months are the peak months for underwater visibility, so it's the best time for snorkeling and diving.

ARTURO'S SPORT FISHING FLEET

613-135-0766
Fax: 613-135-0022
www.arturosport.com
Salvatierra

Arturo's offers service in the full range of Loreto's recreational activities. They run a fleet of 12 boats between 22 and 27 feet. Additionally, they have 27 wet suits of various sizes and 50 diving tanks. They also offer snorkeling trips to Isla Coronado and whale-watching excursions of seven to eight hours for groups of three or larger. Arturo's also offers guided tours of the nearby Mission of San Javier as well as hikes to the cave paintings near Mulegé.

THE BAJA BIG FISH COMPANY

613-104-0781
www.bajabigfish.com
Francisco Madero and Fernando Jordan

This tour company specializes in fishing expeditions. You can choose between the standard 20- to 22-foot *panga*, the 23- to 25-foot super *panga*, or the even larger deluxe *panga*, which carries up to four people. They also offer full vacation packages through several of Loreto's hotels. Check their Web site for more details.

THE BAJA OUTPOST

613-135-1134 or 1-888-649-5951 (U.S.)

www.bajaoutpost.com
Boulevard Adolfo Lopez Mateos

The Baja Outpost is the only diving operation in Loreto that is a member of CMAS, FMAS, NAUI, and PADI. They offer a variety of diving packages that include a stay at their small hotel running anywhere from two to nine days. Other types of tours are also available, including whale watching, mountain biking, and kayaking.

C&C TOURS

613-133-0151
Paseo Hidalgo

This tour company, run by Cecilia Haugen, a young geologist, takes guests on hikes through winding desert trails to see natural-spring water pools, citrus trees, and the ancient Mulegé cave paintings. They also offer tours of the San Javier Mission as well as a cheese-and-wine tour of Loreto.

CORMORANT DIVE CENTER

613-135-2140
www.loretours.com
Miguel Hidalgo and Misoneros

Cormorant offers dive tours to the islands of Coronado, Carmen, and Danzante. They also have a scuba-diving training program. If scuba is not your thing, they have snorkeling trips to Coronado and Carmen. Additionally, Cormorant offers whale-watching tours, ATV tours, mountain-bike tours, and guided tours of San Javier Mission and the Mulegé cave paintings.

DESERT & SEA EXPEDITIONS

613-135-1378
www.desertandsea.com
Paseo Hidalgo between Colegio and Piño Suárez

Desert & Sea specializes in eco-friendly tours of Loreto's environs. Five-hour tours of Isla Coronado include lunch and require a minimum of four people, while tours of the nearby rock art and the San Javier Mission last approximately six hours and include nature guides. Whale-watching trips lasting approximately eight hours are available January through March. These, too, require groups of four.

DOLPHIN DIVE CENTER

613-135-1914 or 626-447-5536 (U.S.); fax 626-447-8685 (U.S.)
www.dolphindivebaja.com
Avenida Juarez between Mateos and Davis

This tour company offers snorkeling trips to Isla Coronado and diving expeditions to Coronado, Carmen, and Danzantes. The PADI-dive operation also offers a variety of diving certifications. Additionally, Dolphin gives guided whale-watching trips and tours of the Mulegé cave paintings and San Javier Mission.

GUAYCURA ADVENTOURS

613-135-1378 or 613-104-3581 (cell)
www.guaycura.com

A full range of services is offered by this tour operator, including sportfishing, scuba-diving, whale-watching, and mission tours. Additionally, they offer horseback riding, beach camping, and Jet Skis.

JUNCALITO ECOTOURS

613-104-4030; fac 613-135-0240
www.loreto.com/josetorres/index.htm
Juncalito Beach

This is a small outfit offering complete services for sport fisherman, scuba divers, and explorers. Owner José Torres has a fleet of three *panga* boats equipped with live-bait tanks. Juncalito is also a good source for hiking information.

LAS PARRAS TOURS

613-135-1010; fax 613-135-0900
www.lasparrastours.com
Madero #16

A variety of services can be had with this tour company, including guided tours of the Mulegé cave paintings and San Javier Mission. They also offer kayak tours ranging from one hour to all day and mountain bike and horseback tours lasting four to five hours. Whale-watching tours last eight hours and include lunch. Las Parras also offers scuba-diving trips as well as day or night sailing tours.

PADDLING SOUTH

1-800-398-6200 (U.S.); fax 707-942-8017
www.tourbaja.com
U.S. Office: Calistoga, CA

Although headquartered in California, this tour company—along with principal owner Trudi Angell—is based in Loreto. They offer sailing, kayaking, and mountain biking adventures. They also offer multiday saddle tours through Loreto's mountain trails and to the Mulegé cave paintings. Check their Web site for trip dates and prices.

Other Attractions

MISIÓN NUESTRA SENORA DE LORETO
Salvatierra between Misioneros and Piño Suarez

Established in 1695 by a Jesuit priest named Juan Maria Salvatierra, this mission was the first permanent establishment on the Baja Peninsula. The settlement surrounding the mission quickly became the religious and administrative capital of the entire peninsula. The Spanish had been trying to colonize this region since the conquistador Hernán Cortés had attempted to establish a settlement at the Bay of Santa Cruz (present-day La Paz) 150 years

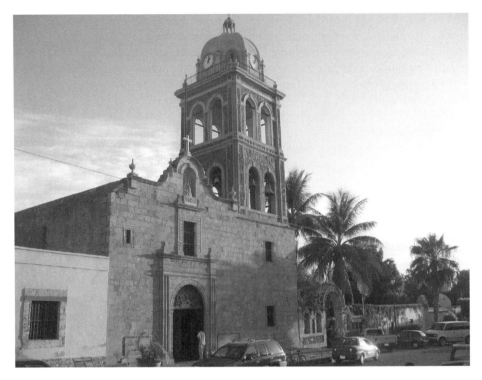

The original mission was established in 1695 and was the first permanent establishment on the Baja Peninsula.

earlier. As Cortés and other Europeans had done elsewhere in the New World, the Jesuits who settled at Nuestra Senora brought diseases that the native inhabitants had never been exposed to. In less than a century, much of the region's indigenous population had been decimated by smallpox, plague, typhus, and measles. Out of an initial estimated population of around 48,000, only around 8,000 Natives remained by 1776.

Over the years the mission has been threatened by several natural disasters such as tropical storms and earthquakes, which took their toll on the structure. In an effort to salvage the ediface, it has been under almost constant reconstruction since 1955. Unfortunately, many of these efforts have failed to preserve the original artistry of the building. One alteration was the addition of the bell tower along Calle Savatierra. However, the mission's baroque stone facade remains an impressive monument to the region's history. A statue of Our Lady of Loreto rests on a pedestal above a small choir window. Below that, modest pilasters support a frieze with the inscription: HEADQUARTERS AND MOTHER OF THE LOWER AND UPPER CALIFORNIA MISSIONS.

MUSEO DE LAS MISIONES
613-135-0441
Salvatierra #16
Open 9 AM to 6 PM Tuesday, Wednesday, Friday, Saturday, Sunday
Admission: $3

This museum highlights the history of the 18 Jesuit missions of southern Baja California. It also has a modest anthropological collection that showcases the indigenous history of the region.

BAY OF LORETO NATIONAL MARINE PARK

613-135-1429

www.loreto.com/marinepark/index.html

This national marine park was established by a presidential decree in 1996. The protected area covers 1,283 square miles, from Isla Coronado south to Isla Catalana. In 2005 the park was added to the United Nations list of protected World Heritage Sites. The park contains over eight hundred recognized species of marine life, many of them endangered. The goal of this park is the long-term protection of local fishery populations through the monitoring of fishing operations and the enforcement of park regulations. The marine park visitors' center features a marine conservation library and displays of the region's natural history and has become a meeting place for tourists, marine researchers, and students from around the world. Currently plans are in the works to add a sea and desert eco-center to promote the conservation of local flora and fauna in addition to local marine life.

CAMPO DE GOLF LORETO AND CHAMPIONSHIP TENNIS CENTER

613-133-0788 or 613-133-0554

www.gotoloreto.com/land-sport.html

Boulevard Misión San Ignacio s/n, Nopoló

This 18-hole golf course offers spectacular ocean and desert vistas. It has a par-72 rating, two beautiful artificial lakes with regulated water levels, numerous sand traps, and several desert plant species and a variety of palm trees that create obstacles to put your game to the test. Tee times are 7 AM to 5 PM Tuesday through Sunday. Reservations are recommended. Greens fees are $40 for 18 holes plus $40 for a cart and $25 for 9 holes plus $20 for a cart Adjacent to the golf course is Nopoló's Championship Tennis Center, which features eight professional lit tennis courts with stadium capacity of 250. Facilities also include a restaurant/bar, a pro shop with men's and women's locker rooms, as well as a nearby children's pool. The tennis courts run $7 an hour ($10 per hour for lit courts), and pool access is $5. The facility is open daily 7 AM to 11 PM.

SHOPPING

To be honest, if you come to Loreto for the shopping experience, you'll probably go away disappointed. The town has a handful of shops on Salvatierra and within a block of the mission, where you can find some nice things, but the selection is limited relative to elsewhere in Mexico. A few boutiques sell fine handcrafts, such as handwoven rugs, wrought-iron furniture, and silver jewelry. You'll also find a variety of sweatshirts, hats, beachwear, and T-shirts, as well as *artesenía*, a term for the myriad handmade arts and crafts found throughout Mexico. In Loreto you'll find genuine silver jewelry, paintings, fine textiles from the mainland, ceramic and wood sculptures, blown glass, and metal designs. Don't hesitate to ask questions about the art or bargain with the local vendors as this is a long-running and fun tradition in Mexico.

La Casa de la Abuela offers a variety of locally made clothing and handcrafts.

El Alacran (613-135-0029; Salvatierra 47) Provides a wide variety of goods, including traditional Mexican *artesenía* and Taxco silver as well as T-shirts and beachwear. Open Monday through Saturday 9:30 AM to 1 PM and 3 PM to 7 PM.

La Casa de la Abuela (613-135-3544; Salvatierra, in front of the Mission Museum) A variety of beachwear, Mexican *camisas*, leather goods, and handcrafts can be found in this shop. Prices are reasonable. Open Wednesday through Monday 9 AM to 10 PM.

Conchita's Curious (613-135-1054; Prolonación Misineros) This shop offers rustic and wrought-iron furniture, colorful Mexican art, and traditional clothing. Open daily 9 AM to 8 PM.

Maria Teresa Mendoza Villa (613-135-0684; Salvatierra 47) Located next to the Banomex, this small shop offers Mexican *artesenía* at reasonable prices. Open Monday through Saturday 9:30 AM to 7 PM.

Silver Desert Mexican Artwork in Silver (613-135-0684; Salvatierra #36, next to the bank) Offers jewelry made from Taxco silver as well as a variety of arts and crafts. Open daily 8 AM to 2 PM and 3 PM to 9 PM.

7

SIDE TRIPS FROM LORETO

Loreto's environs offer travelers some of the best of Baja California. If you like Loreto's small-town feel, you'll love Mulegé, the oasis town 86 miles to the north. This town is also located near the best examples of Cochimi petroglyphs, which lie in the mountains east of town. (Don't show up in Mulegé with an empty wallet, however. The nearest bank with an ATM is located 38 miles to the north in Santa Rosalía.) Along the way to Mulegé, you will pass Bahía Concepción and some of the most beautiful vistas in Baja. These beaches are great for enjoying the calm waters of the Sea of Cortés as well as for camping out. But they do lack amenities (which can be a good thing because it means fewer crowds), so come prepared.

For an amazing look back in time at Baja's colonial period, the San Javier Mission, 23 miles east of Loreto, is one of the peninsula's best preserved missions. Any of these excursions are great as a day trip out of Loreto or as a destination on its own with an overnight stay.

Mulegé

The village of Mulegé, 86 miles north of Loreto, is certainly one of the most charming towns in all of Baja. Mulegé is literally an oasis, one that has become a favorite destination for sportfishermen and travelers looking for rest and reflection. It sits in a valley along a freshwater stream that feeds the town's estuary before flowing into the sea. This stream—also called Mulegé—is what gives the town its lush landscape, with thousands of palm trees and twisted bougainvilleas filling this river valley that opens onto the Sea of Cortés. The town's close 7-mile proximity to the beautiful Bahía Concepción only adds to its draw. And if you're planning on beach camping, it's a good place to pick up provisions or get a hot meal.

Unlike most Mexican towns, the government offices and old church are not located on the main square but are instead found several blocks to the east, as is the old state penitentiary that now serves as the regional museum. The penitentiary building itself holds interest not simply because it's a century old (it was completed in 1907) but also because it was built without bars. The prison operated this way until the 1960s, when it was closed. Inmates were allowed to work outside the jail during the day as long as they returned in the evening. Escape attempts were uncommon, but on the occasion that one did happen, the other prisoners were among those who pursued the escapees to bring them back.

Desert flora east of Mulegé

HISTORY

Cochimi Indians were the first inhabitants of the area around Mulegé— their presence dates back fourteen thousand years—and they survived by fishing and gathering fruit and seeds. Their folklore maintained that they were the descendants of giants who created the now-famous cave paintings in the nearby hills. The Cochimi also practiced healing arts, for which they used special clay. These arts have been passed down and are still practiced by some of the Mulegé villagers today.

Soon after the Jesuit missionary Juan María Basaldúa arrived, he founded the Mission Santa Rosalia de Mulege in 1705. However, the existing structure which sits on the south side of the river from the main town dates from 1770. The mission was moved to this elevated location after a flood damaged the original structure. The dam below the mission was also built by the missionaries and Indians for the irrigation of crops. This mission is not as impressive as others in the area, although its elevated position provides nice views of the town and estuary. This building continues to function as the town's Catholic church, despite the fact that mission operations ceased in 1828.

GETTING THERE

Approaching the town from the south by car, you will cross the Rio Mulegé and make a right turn onto the town's main street, Avenida Gral Martínez, which turns into Calle Madero.

Mulegé also sits on the bus route that travels up and down the peninsula via Mexico 1, the Carretera Transpeninsular (Transpeninsular Highway). Arriving by bus, you'll be dropped off in front of the Doney Taco Shop at the entrance to town. From here, the walk is downhill east into town. If you'd rather hire a taxi, rides anywhere in town cost between $2 and $5. The nearest international airport is in Loreto, though a local airport with a 4,000-foot landing strip services regional and private charter planes. If you plan to arrive by plane, the airstrip's legal fight plan designation is El Gallito. Use frequency UNICOM 122.8. Be aware that fuel is generally not available here. For more information, call the Loreto Airport at 613-135-0565 daily between 7 AM and 7 PM.

GETTING AROUND

There is no local bus service, though the town is small enough to explore on foot, and this is definitely the best way to take in the feel of the place. Taxis can usually be found near where the long-distance buses drop off passengers as well as around the main plaza. For taxi dispatch, call 615-153-0420.

There are plenty of small grocery stores and other shops to buy provisions here as well as a few restaurants and several hotels. However, as mentioned previously, there is no bank or ATM in Mulegé and very few establishments accept plastic, so be sure to have your cash situation taken care of before you arrive. If you are desperate, the nearest ATM is 38 miles north in Santa Rosalia.

ACCOMMODATIONS

Although limited, accommodations in Mulegé are extremely affordable and fairly wide ranging. While most of the options are nothing too fancy, they are clean and comfortable. RV travelers, too, will have a lot to choose from when passing through this town.

CASA GRANADA

Owners: Lena and Kristian Peschmann
615-153-0688
www.casagranada.net
#1 Estero de Mulegé

This small four-room hotel provides attractive views of the Sea of Cortés and the Mulegé estuary. With a classic Colonial style and an almost tropical-island feel, the hotel is located a short walk from the airport; pilots and their passengers can arrive and be in their rooms within minutes. All rooms are located on the second floor and are therefore not wheelchair accessible. Rates: $75 double occupancy.

CLEMENTINE'S BED & BREAKFAST AND CASITAS

Owner: Cliff Taylor
615-153-0319
www.clementinesbaja.com
Km 131 Mexico 1, just south of Mulegé

This hotel offers four large Mexican-style rooms furnished with queen-sized beds. The rooms rent from between $55 and $70 (double occupancy), depending on the room you choose. Weekly rates are also available. Continental breakfast is included. The hotel also offers three fully furnished casitas—available on a weekly or monthly basis—complete with fully equipped kitchens, covered patios, and gas grills. Rates: $95 to $200, depending on the bungalow.

CUESTA REAL RV PARK AND HOTEL

Owners: Ken, Christina, and Jenice Wright
615-153-0321
www.bajaquest.com/cuestareal
Km 128 Mexico 1, just south of Mulegé

Located off the Carretera Transpeninsular on the south side of the Mulegé River, this facility features 10 large RV sites with full hookups as well as a small hotel with a dozen rooms. The property has an on-site restaurant/bar, a swimming pool on a shaded patio surrounded by palm trees, laundry facilities, and a gift shop. Rates: $8 per night for an RV site with full hookup.

HOTEL SERENIDAD

Manager: Diana Johnso
615-153-0530; fax 615-153-0311
www.serenidad.com
Km 130 Mexico 1, just south of Mulegé

One of Mulegé's oldest and most famous hotels, the Hotel Serenidad is also the location for the town's landing strip, making it a popular fly-in hotel since the 1960s. The hotel offers 50 rooms at $72 or $89 that accommodate two to three people. The grounds also offer small air-conditioned cottages at $128 that feature a bedroom with two double beds, a fireplace, and a living room. For true luxury, a three-bedroom, two-bath riverfront villa is available for anywhere between a five-day and a month-long stays; rates vary from $250 per day for stays of 5 to 7 days, $200 per day for 8 to 14 days at, or $175 per day for 15 to 30 days. The hotel grounds also offers 15 fully equipped RV sites for $15 a night for two travelers plus an additional $2.50 for each additional person. For recreation, this hotel has a boat ramp onto the Mulegé River plus a good-sized pool and a swim-up bar. The on-site restaurant serves good Mexican fare and is well know for its Saturday night pig roast.

LAS CASITAS

Owner: Javier Aguilar Zúñiga
615-153-3023
Calle Madero #50

Located right in the center of town, this is another of Mulegé's quaint hotels from the 1960s. The building is also famous for being the birthplace of the Mexican poet and composer Alan Gorosave. The hotel offers eight rustic but clean and colorful units situated around a central courtyard. The on-site restaurant-bar offers a buffet breakfast and traditional Mexican fare and seafood. Live music is also often featured, as are Friday night Mexican fiestas. Rates: start at $25.

OASIS RIO BAJA

Owner: Leon J. Nolet
615-153-0425
www.oasisriobaja.com
Km 134 Mexico 1

This large RV park situated along the Mulegé River is mostly occupied by permanent residents, though there are generally 5 to 10 spaces available for short-term rental.

POSADA DE LAS FLORES

Owners: Guiseppe Marcelletti and Ursula Croci
613-153-0188
www.posadadelasflores.com
Comicilio Conocida, Punta Chivato

Located 15 miles north of Mulegé up Mexico 1 and 7 miles east off the highway at tranquil Puna Chivato, this exclusive hotel is affili-ated with the hotel of the same name in downtown Loreto. Sitting on 7.5 acres of beachfront property several miles from the nearest town, the hotel offers 10 rooms and 10 junior suites at prices significantly higher than you will generally find this side of Cabo San Lucas. Rooms are furnished with either two twin beds or a single queen, while most of the junior suites feature king-sized beds. Rooms have terraces while suites have porches overlooking the sea. Meals are included with the price of the room, which is good because the on-site restaurant is the only one within miles. The property also features a swimming pool and a tennis court. This hotel has its own private airstrip (frequency 122.8) and offers gas services. To drive to Punta Chivata, take Mexico 1 north out of Mulegé 15 miles, and turn right onto the graded dirt road just south of Palo Verde. Look for the sign that says Punta Chivato. Rates: start at $250 to $280 for a standard room plus 13 percent tax.

DINING

LOS EQUIPALES

615-153-0330
Moctezuma, Mulegé

This second-story restaurant, located one block north of the town square, is perhaps the most expensive in Mulegé. But considering you can stuff yourself on shrimp and margaritas for about $11, that's not really saying much. The food here is very good and the service friendly. Open daily 8 AM to 11 PM.

BEACHES

There's a beach on the south side of the river just east of Mexico 1 that's very decent for relaxing, fishing, and snorkeling and it's never crowded. Instead, though, it's well worth checking out the beaches to the south, along the beautiful Bahía Concepción. These are without a doubt some of the most beautiful and serene beaches in all of Baja. Or check out the secluded beaches north of Mulegé, along Bahía Santa Inés.

PUNTA CHIVATO   Punto Chivato is one of Baja's best-kept secrets—one that's in the process of getting out. It's located 15 miles north up Mexico 1 from Mulegé and east another 7 miles along a graded dirt road. (A 4,000-foot airstrip is located here at the Posada de las Flores Hotel.) The beach is located at the end of a 7-mile peninsula that reaches out into the Sea of Cortés and is the only south-facing beach on the east coast of Baja California. The result is a more temperate area during the peak fishing months of summer as cool prevailing winds flow right onto the beach. The Posada de las Flores (a newly refurbished hotel formerly known as the Hotel Punta Chivato) is the only hotel in the area. However, over the last five years there has been an explosion of homes being built along the beach here by homeowners from north of the border. Still, plenty of wide-open beaches are left that are great for walking and snorkeling. Dolphins often swim in the water not too far from shore. Closer in, along the white sand beaches and rocky shoreline, you'll find roosterfish, grouper, and cabrilla. The farther north you go past the hotel, the more remote the beaches become.

OTHER ATTRACTIONS

CAVE PAINTINGS   Just west of Mulegé in the foothills of the Sierra de Guadalupe Mountains are the most significant grouping ancient petroglyphs in Baja California Sur. Although their origin is not completely certain, they are thought to have been made by the Cochimi Indians who inhabited this region for many thousands of years before the arrival of Europeans in the 17th century. The mural-like paintings, in hues of red, white, black, and yellow, are believed to depict ancient rituals involving hunters and several types of animals, including deer, lizards, and fish. These paintings, which have been declared World Heritage Sites, appear on cave walls and ceilings as well as on rock walls exposed to the elements.

The finest group of petroglyphs is located in caves near Rancho La Trinidad, 18 miles west of Mulegé. Getting to this site is an adventure in itself. While most of the trip can be accomplished by SUV or on horseback, it also involves a hike of about 4 miles as well as several short swims. Another popular site is called San Borjitas, located near Rancho Las Tinajas. This site is much more accessible thanks to a new road that brings you within a mile of the cave.

Several tour companies operating out of Loreto offer tours of the cave paintings. However, Salvador Castro Drew, one of the most experienced and reputable guides, is found right in Mulegé. Contact him at Mulegé Tours: 615-153-0232; www.mulegetours.com.

Bahía Concepción

Along Bahía Concepción lie some of the most beautiful beaches anywhere. With calm water and secluded settings, this strip of land along the Sea of Cortés can provide you with some extremely memorable experiences. So alluring is the draw of this place that some people choose to spend entire seasons and even years along its shores.

Winter is the best time to visit due to the summer heat, though if you show up in late summer, you may be convinced that you have actually stumbled upon some lost Mediterranean shore, given the numbers of Italians who hang out here in August.

An entrance fee associated with these beaches generally runs between $7 and $10. You pay this either as you enter the beach, or someone will come around to collect. These fees help to keep the beaches clean, so don't fret. Someone paid that fee before you so that you could enjoy a pristine beach. Besides, services at these beaches tend to be minimal, with most featuring pit toilets and maybe a cold shower. Do not drink the water in the showers—it's untreated! Be sure to bring plenty of your own water; it's probably a good idea to pack at least a lunch, as well. Once you find yourself on the shore here, it can be hard to bring yourself to leave. Indeed, you might consider lingering and camping on the beach, either in your own tent or in a provided palapa or casita.

BEACHES

PLAYA FRAMBES Located 8 miles south of Mulegé, this is site offers comforts that most beaches along Bahía Concepción don't. Look for the road sign, and follow the graded road to the beach. Though not the most isolated beach along this bay, it's still a serene place to while away the day. The calm waters here are ideal for kayaking, and you can launch a small boat over the sand. If you choose to camp here, palapas along the beach cost $7 a night and offer a majestic view of the sea. Restrooms and flush toilets are available as are hot showers. Casitas with private showers run $30 a night. These have solar power and two double beds.

LOS NARANJOS This beach 10 miles south of Mulegé from Km 119 off Mexico 1 is easy to access (by Bahía Concepción standards), but you should still enter with care since the road has some soft spots. This beautifully tranquil beach has crystal-clear water and views of the mountainous Punto Concepción Peninsula in the distance. Tent campers are welcome, or opt for one of the several palapa cabins set up along the water. Cabins run about $10, and campsites are $7. Restrooms with flush toilets and hot water are available for a small charge. A small restaurant here serves up good eats for cheap. Be sure to bring your own water, though, and be aware that there is no security.

PUNTA ARENA You'll find this pristine, wide beach just south of Los Naranjos. Take the same exit as Los Naranjos, but stay to the left, and, as with Los Naranjos, watch for soft spots in the road. This beach has several permanent residences, though plenty of open beach is left over for tents and RVs. Some 50 campsites and a few palapas run about $7 a night. Minimal restroom facilities are provided but no security.

PLAYA SANTISPAC This beach is located at Km 114 of Mexico 1 about 12 miles south of Mulegé. The entry fee is about $7. It's blessed with an easy entrance that provides you with a

Beach camping along Bahía Concepción

Relaxing offshore at Playa Escondida

nice panoramic view as you make your way down to the beach; just look for the road sign. The long, wide beach offers stunning vistas of offshore islands and the peninsula on the other side of the bay. It also has two small restaurants; an unusual convenience along Bahía Concepción. Playa Santispac is located in a protected cove, which is why many people spend the entire winter here. Arrive early if you want to get a good spot because this beach does tend to fill up.

POSADA CONCEPCIÓN This beach is largely taken up by a 10-site RV park. Located at Km 112 of Mexico 1, this beach is the perfect setting-off point with a kayak to explore the offshore islands that are in close proximity. Entrance here runs about $10. It has an outhouse and hot showers for a nominal fee, though it does tend to be crowded by the many year-round RV residents who have come to call this beach home. If you're looking for a choice spot on the water, forget it. The permanent residents have taken them all. The RV sites set back from the beach are set aside for overnight visitors. However, there are plenty of other spots along this beach to be had in which you don't have to take a back seat to anyone.

PLAYA ESCONDIDA This beautiful beach is nestled between two tall ridges along Km 111 off Mexico 1, which provide protection from the prevailing winds, making it an excellent place to camp in winter. The rough road in plus a lack of services make this beach much less congested than some of the others just to the north. It's a perfect place to while away the day kayaking or just relaxing in the warm, calm sea. The entrance fee runs about $6, and pit toilets are available.

PLAYA LOS COCOS Located about a mile south of Playa Escondida, this beach is far enough away from Mulegé to be free of the year-round RV set that you'll be able to get a campsite right on the beach and enjoy the tranquillity of your surroundings without having to worry about your neighbor two steps from your tent flap. It's a great place for camping out and enjoying the surroundings. The road in is a little rough, but the beach is suitable for launching small boats. Admission is about $6 and includes pit toilets.

PLAYA EL BURRO This crescent-shaped beach, about 16 miles south of Mulegé along Km 109 off Mexico 1, is situated in a protected cove and is suitable for launching boats. While certainly not the longest or widest beach along Bahía Concepción, it is undeniably beautiful. Pit toilets and several palapas are available, though tent campers are welcome. Arrive early to get the best spots because this beach does attract travelers. The entry fee is about $7.

BAHÍA EL COYOTE Some 17 miles south of Mulegé along Km 109 off Mexico 1, this beach sits in a cove with a rocky shoreline at the south side, which both protects it from prevailing winds and provides good opportunities for snorkeling. This is a good beach for campers and RVs, though you should drive slowly along the access road coming in. If you're lucky, you can get a spot at the more secluded south end of the beach under a palm tree. An outhouse and cold shower are available. Entrance fee is about $7.

SAN BUENAVENTURA This pristine beach backed by steep hills is located about 25 miles south of Mulegé along Km 94 off Mexico 1. It's home to the Hotel San Buenaventura (U.S.: 619-955-6278; www.hotelsanbuenaventura.com), the only beachfront resort along Bahía Concepción. This hotel offers 18 rooms and 2 suites that feature hammocks and large balconies as well as a bar, restaurant, and a mini market. Rates range from $69 for a standard

Playa El Burro is a perfect beach for camping and swimming.

room to $199 for a two-bedroom beachfront suite with kitchen, dining room, and private parking. For campers—both tent and RV—the hotel has a gated, secure campground in front of the hotel on the beach. Each camping space is furnished with a palapa for shade, and flush toilets are available for use in the hotel. There is also a concrete ramp along the beach for launching boats. Parking is $10, showers and trash disposal runs $20, and electricity ramps the price up to $30.

EL REQUESÓN Located 26 miles south of Mulegé, this beach is just about the most beautiful spot along Bahía Concepción—and that's really saying something. It features two beautiful bays that bump up against each other and are separated by a narrow isthmus—submerged during high tide—that connects to a small island just offshore. The island provides additional exploration opportunities, though this place hardly needs it. The northern bay provides great opportunities for snorkeling and clamming while the southern bay is shallower and perfect for wading and relaxing. Several plalapas are set up along the beach, and tent campers are also welcome. Pit toilets are set back near the cliffs that rise up from the beach, but these toilets are not well maintained and are actually downright nasty. Plus the road in is rather rough, though it is short. Access to this beach runs around $10.

PLAYA LA PERLA This beach is along Km 91 off Mexico 1, just south of Playa Requeson. It has good access for RVs and offers about 10 palapas located along the shoreline. The camping area at the north side of the beach provides beautiful vistas of the Sea of Cortés. Minimal security is provided by the resident manager. Entry fee runs around $7.

The beautiful Playa El Requesón is just about the most beautiful spot along Bahía Concepción.

PLAYA ARMENTA Located 28 miles south of Mulegé along Km 90 off Mexico 1, this beach is situated in a wide cove with a rock reef that wraps around the south end. This provides protection from prevailing winds as well as good snorkeling. Pit toilets are available here as well as a few small palapas, making this beach good for tent camping. The access road is passable for RVs—just take it slow and realize that the fit is going to be tight in some places. Entry fee runs about $7.

Misión San Javier

Located 23 miles west of Loreto in the Sierra de Gigante Mountains, one of Baja California's most historically important missions sits in an isolated canyon high above the Sea of Cortés. This is Misión San Francisco Javier de Viggé Biaundó, commonly referred to as Mission San Javier. Considered one of the most beautiful and well-preserved missions in all of the Californias, San Javier is constructed of volcanic stone blocks and took more than 14 years to build. Atop the volcanic gray facade are domes and bell towers containing two bells, one dating from 1761 and another that arrived in 1803. Inside the mission, the unique baroque appearance is well preserved. The original golden alter is intact, with an 18th-century crucifix as well as several paintings, all transported here from Mexico City first by ship and then overland in a caravan of burros and wooden crates. There are also gilded 18th-century altars featuring statues of San Francisco Javier and Our Lady of Guadalupe, beautifully lit through stained-glass windows framed in wood, and 18th-century priestly vestments are displayed in a glass cabinet. This mission is often referred to as the jewel of the Baja California mission churches.

History

In May 1699 Jesuit missionary Father Francisco María Piccolo arrived in this area, which had a freshwater spring that the native Cochimí referred to as Viggé Biaundó. Father Piccolo soon began construction of a chapel at the site, about 5 miles north of the present mission location. However, in 1701 the mission was abandoned due to an ongoing Indian revolt.

In 1702 a Honduran missionary, Father Juan de Ugarte, arrived in the area and established the mission at its present site. He proceeded to construct dams and aqueducts to preserve the little available water. Ugarte also introduced cattle breeding to the local Cochimí as well as small-scale agriculture and the establishment of the first pack animal road to Loreto. Ugarte went on to succeed Juan María de Salvatierra as head of Baja California's missions, through which he helped to establish a mission at La Paz and the completion of El Triunfo de la Cruz, a ship that he sailed to the head of the Sea of Cortés to determine if Baja California was indeed an island. He returned to the mission that he had founded at San Javier and died there in 1730.

Between 1744 and 1758, another Jesuit missionary, Father Miguel del Barco, oversaw the construction of the mission building that stands today. The construction was an incredible feat, fraught with the hardships of transporting materials to an isolated location and complications wrought by a shortage of such specialized craftsmen as bricklayers and carpenters. There were long periods in which del Barco had to suspend construction due to labor and equipment problems.

Throughout this time period, the local Cochimí population suffered the ravages of European diseases. Despite the new agricultural and engineering techniques that they had learned from the missionaries, their population continued to dwindle, and by 1817 the mission had been deserted. Today it has been restored and declared a historic monument by Mexico's Instituto Nacional de Antropología e Historia (National Institution of Anthropology and History), or INAH. Walking along the grounds, one cannot help but be amazed by the mission's mere existence in such an isolated place, let alone by its beauty.

GETTING THERE

At Km 118 on Mexico 1, the Carretera Transpeninsular, about 4 miles south of Loreto, turn onto the dirt road heading east. This exit is clearly marked. This 23-mile stretch leads you along palm groves, remote ranches, and along the steep cliffs of the Sierra de la Gigante. There are also some marked trails that lead to some lesser-known Cochimí cave paintings. This road can be a little rough, but it's passable for most vehicles. Just take it easy. However, if it has been raining, you might want to consider taking the trip at another time.

San Javier is a small community of about 50 full-time residents. If the mission is locked, don't be afraid to inquire about gaining entrance from one of these folks. Also, as a courtesy be sure to slip a few pesos into the contribution box. This money goes to support the maintenance of the mission.

Road maps show another dirt road heading east out of San Javier and hooking up with Mexico 1 north of Ciudad Insergentes. This looks like a nice shortcut for anyone heading to La Paz or environs farther south on the peninsula, but don't even attempt to take this road unless you have a heavy-duty 4WD vehicle. And even then, road conditions will force you to drive so slowly that it's not even worth it. Better just to head west to Loreto, and take Mexico 1 from there.

ACCOMMODATIONS

CASA DE ANA
Owner: Ana Santana
613-135-1552 or 1-800-497-3923
www.casadeanaloreto.com/index.htm

The only accommodations in San Javier, situated in renovated 18th-century missionary housing, consist of five rustic adobe cabins. Bathrooms and hot water are available, though electricity is obtainable only from dusk until 10:30 PM. Bungalows rent for $35 for a room with two twin beds.

DINING

LA PALAPA
Just as San Javier has but one place to stay, it has but one restaurant. Located near the mission, the owner, Señora Santana, cooks delicious traditional Mexican dishes on a wood-burning stove. There is no menu. You eat what La Señora has cooked for her family that day—after all, it is her home. And you pay what you think the meal is worth.

Appendix: Events

January

Run Cabo Half Marathon

The run starts on Lázaro Cárdenas, the main strip of Cabo San Lucas, and takes runners into the desert and along the coast on the Carretera Transpeninsular before returning them to downtown Cabo. Entry fee is $44 for the half marathon and $22 for the 5K. For more information: www.runcabo.com/data/caboruninfo.html.

February

Cabo San Lucas Candlemas

This traditional event in marks the end of winter, taking place in early February when the holiday season officially ends. Celebrated across Mexico, Candlemas blends European and indigenous traditions. Call (866) LOS-CABOS for more information.

Todos Santos Art Festival

This weeklong festival showcases local artists, musicians, and craftspeople. Shows include Spanish guitar, classical music, films, and folk dancing as well as lectures and conferences on sea turtle conservation. For more information go to: www.todossantos-baja.com/todos-santos/art/art-festival.htm.

Carnival La Paz

This traditional celebration takes place over the six days leading up to Ash Wednesday and is probably the most notable annual celebration in La Paz. Unlike Mardi Gras, this is treated largely as a family event, with children participating in the parades and family picnics lining the streets.

May

Foundation Fair

This celebration, which takes place in the city of La Paz during the first week of May, has a wealth of events, including concerts, an off-road race, and a kayak festival.

June

"Coyote 300" Off-Road Race

An annual car and motorcycle race that takes place along the desert trails outside of La Paz.

July

Loreto Dorado Tournament

This three-day tournament held early in the month usually hosts between 70 and 100 anglers. The family-oriented tournament gives special recognition to all anglers under 16. It ends with an awards banquet, with honors for Big Fish and a special "just for fun" award called the President's Trophy. Tournament Reservations can be made by calling HQVDM at 1-800-474-2252, or visit: www.vagabundos.com/loreto_2007.htm.

Surf'n Panga Roosterfish Klassic

This annual Roosterfish tournament is held in Cabo San Lucas during early July. It features daily prizes for the largest fish, with various species categories.

September

Loreto 400 Off–Road Race

Loreto offers a great desert setting for this off-road race that features professional and amateur drivers.

October

Los Cabos Billfish Tournament

This three-day team event is held around mid-October. The entry fee of $4,000 covers up to six anglers, and a percentage of the total pot goes to the top three winners of the tournament. Daily cash prizes are also given out for the largest fish in a number of species categories. For further information go to: www.loscabosbillfishtournament.com.

Festival Fundador

The main festival of the town of Todos Santos, it takes place during the week of October 10 to 14. It celebrates the founding of the town in 1723, thus the name Festival Fundador, or Founder's Festival. During this celebration, the plaza fills with vendors and performers. Keep in mind, however, that many of the shops that the town is famous for close during this time.

Bisbee's Los Cabos Open Golf Championship

This two-player "scramble" golf tournament in San José del Cabo offers trophies for several divisions. A portion of the profits goes to Amigos de Los Niños (Friends of the Children), a nonprofit organization in Los Cabos. For more information go to: www.golfinmexico.net /bisbee.

Bisbee's Black & Blue Tournament

Held in San José del Cabo for more than 25 years Bisbee's Black & Blue Tournament has been producing record-breaking tournament game fish with a multimillion dollar prize purse to go with it. For more information go to: www.bisbees.com.

NOVEMBER

Tuna Jackpot

This four-day tuna tournament is held in Cabo San Lucas during early November. Participants earn daily cash prizes, and a percentage of the entry fees goes to the overall winner. The 2006 tournament champion brought home the prize with a 318-pound yellowfin tuna. For further information go to: www.loscabostunajackpot.com.

DECEMBER

Patron Saints Festival

This festival takes place at the Mission San Javier, 23 miles east of Loreto. Many of Loreto's citizens make pilgrimages to the mission at this time.

Index